This book is a pleasure to read, not least because it pricks so many pretensions. While it deals with an important subject, it manages to sustain a breezy style that draws you in. The subtitle tells you the stance of the authors: the emerging church movement, which taught an entire generation to rebel, is now old enough to find growing numbers of people learning to rebel against the rebellion.

> ~ D. A. Carson
> Trinity Evangelical Divinity School

Why We're Not Emergent crashes into the emerging conversation in a voice that hears "them" and talks back! This is a book we've been waiting for. With careful observation, faithful handling of Scripture, and an eye for the ironic and absurd, DeYoung and Kluck have given us a feel for what attracts some to emerging churches and thoughts about why that's sometimes a very bad thing. Buy and read this book. You'll enjoy it. And it could help you and the people you'll tell about it.

> ~ Mark Dever
> Pastor, Capitol Hill Baptist Church
> Washington, D.C.

Fifteen years ago in *No Place for Truth*, David Wells reminded us all that in our time, those who seem most relevant are in fact most irrelevant, and those who seem most irrelevant are in fact most relevant. That, as Gandalf would say, "is a very encouraging thought." Indeed, as I encounter what has been called the "young, Reformed awakening," for every young Christian who is convinced that in order to engage the culture the church must embrace the emergent paradigm of truth and church, there are nineteen who understand (because they really care about what the Bible says) that faithfulness is relevance. DeYoung and Kluck tell you why.

> ~ Ligon Duncan
> Senior Minister, First Presbyterian Church, Jackson, Mississippi

Two thoughtful young guys with different styles, Kevin DeYoung (the pastor-theologian) and Ted Kluck (the journalist), have teamed up to write *Why We're Not Emergent*. The result is a fair-minded, biblically grounded, insightful book. It's clear that DeYoung and Kluck are not motivated by the desire to criticize, but rather by their love of the church as the body of Christ. This is now the first book I'd give someone who asks the question, "What is the emerging church?" Highly recommended!

> ~ Justin Taylor
> Project Director, ESV Study Bible;
> blogger (Between Two Worlds)

WHY
WE'RE NOT
EMERGENT

(BY TWO GUYS WHO SHOULD BE)

KEVIN DEYOUNG
TED KLUCK

MOODY PUBLISHERS

CHICAGO

All Scripture quotations are taken from *The Holy Bible, English Standard Version.* Copyright © 2000, 2001 by Crossway Bibles, a division of Good News Publishers. Used by permission. All rights reserved.

Scripture quotations marked NIV are taken from the *Holy Bible, New International Version®.* NIV®. Copyright © 1973, 1978, 1984 by International Bible Society. Used by permission of Zondervan. All rights reserved.

Editor: Jim Vincent
Interior Design: Smartt Guys
Cover Design: David Carlson, Gearbox (studiogearbox.com)
Cover Photography: Fancy Photography and Digital Vision

ISBN-10: 0-8024-5834-3
ISBN-13: 978-0-8024-5834-6

Library of Congress Cataloging-in-Publication Data

DeYoung, Kevin.
 Why we're not emergent : by two guys who should be / Kevin DeYoung and Ted Kluck.
     p. cm.
 Includes bibliographical references.
 ISBN 978-0-8024-5834-6
 1. Christianity--21st century. 2. Emerging church movement. 3. Postmodernism--Religious aspects--Christianity. I. Kluck, Ted. II. Title.
 BR121.3.D49 2008
 270.8'3--dc22

                              2007042221

We hope you enjoy this book from Moody Publishers. Our goal is to provide high-quality, thought-provoking books and products that connect truth to your real needs and challenges. For more information on other books and products written and produced from a biblical perspective, go to www.moodypublishers.com or write to:

Moody Publishers
820 N. LaSalle Boulevard
Chicago, IL 60610

1 3 5 7 9 10 8 6 4 2

Printed in the United States of America

To Mom and Dad, Lee and Sheri DeYoung, with love.
I am proud to be your son.

For my parents, Ted and Karen Kluck.

CONTENTS

FOREWORD

I AM LOOKING OUT my hotel window on the ancient city of Budapest. Across the street is the Reformed quarter, the section of the city that attracted Reformed churches and people in the nineteenth century when Budapest was becoming industrialized and was flourishing. Not far away is Calvin Square, and on the street that I walked today I even saw a Calvin Café.

As I look upon those streets lined with acacia and sycamore trees and many old, stately buildings, I ponder a remarkable juxtaposition of two aspects of Hungary's history. On the one hand, here are buildings that, in their grace and solemnity, speak of another age and time. On the other hand, nothing of Budapest's more recent history under the Communists now remains. I have no doubt that its oppression left its marks on the human spirit, but today a visitor to Budapest, such as myself, sees nothing at all of this painful episode.

I am in Budapest this time for some meetings. We will be discussing the changeless truth of the Christian gospel in the midst of the ever-changing cultures in our world. And as I gaze out my hotel window I am struck by some of the parallels between what I am seeing and what we will be discussing. Are not these biblical truths a bit like the building that I am seeing, which have endured through the centuries and survived so many cultural epochs, wars, and conquests? As it turned out, the Communists' attempts at social engineering in the second half of the twentieth century, though unusually damaging, were also like any other cultural movement that arises, has its time in the sun, and then disappears. Is this not where we are today with the changeless truth of biblical Christianity in the midst of constantly changing cultures?

The analogy is not perfect, I know, and this suggestion of doctrines being like buildings does, I also know, rub postmoderns the wrong way. They think, as this book explains, that this kind of talk owes much more to the Enlightenment than to the Bible, that it betrays a kind of cultural captivity to what is modern. The idea of truth as something that can be known and that does not change seems altogether too objective, too rationalistic, too distancing, too remote, too unrelational, and too . . . well, too perfect for our ragged, disillusioned time when it is much more important to be honest about ourselves than to be parading abstract truths. This particular idea of truth, then, is one that we should be abandoning, not embracing.

This objection, though, is what gets us to the heart of the central issue of our time and one which this book skillfully and winsomely engages. I can only put this in my own language, plodding and obscure though I am. Mercifully, readers have these two authors to follow. They not only explore this issue in their own ways, but they do so with a lot of insight.

Kevin DeYoung and Ted Kluck are writing, as it were, from street level, as life is lived day by day in the world and weekend by weekend in the church. They have done a fine job of opening up the issues that are so important for the life and good of the church.

For each of us, it is difficult to step back from our own place in this world and see ourselves objectively. That seems an impossibility to postmoderns, who think we can never escape our own subjectivity in this way—nor do they even wish to. It is right here that we again engage the central issue of our time. If our own subjectivity is quarantined against scrutiny, how then will we ever develop a judicious sense of the relation between Christ and culture? And in the absence of this careful evaluation, do we not always slip into a Christ-or-culture position? Is this not where so many emergents are heading with the result that Christ is increasingly like (postmodern) culture?

The truth is that without the ability to be self-critical, we are likely to bring a mind-set with us into Christian faith that reflects our postmodern culture. Such a mind-set inclines us to live within the realm of the private and be cynical of everything else, to trust our own subjective impulses and distrust every-one else's, to think that truth was a fabrication of the Enlightenment and that tolerance of other viewpoints ranks at the top of the virtues.

Today we treasure relationships because we have so few that endure, we want to be heard because so few ever listen to us, we want to connect because we are so lonely, and we think that we are superior to every preceding genera-tion (which is still one place where the Enlightenment idea of progress has not yet been vanquished). These and many other such attitudes we are likely to bring into the church. They make up the place where we stand and from where we will evaluate any church.

What, then, is going to happen when the engagement of this internalized culture happens as the Word of God is preached? What should the Christian faith look like in this (postmodern) context? And how should we think about the emergents who have sought to incarnate Christian faith in this context?

Those are the questions addressed in this book. Let us now turn to the authors for their analysis and answers.

David F. Wells

Author of *Above All Earthly Pow'rs*:
Christ in a Postmodern World

There are two ways of getting home; and one of them is to stay there.

—G.K. CHESTERTON, *The Everlasting Man*

STILL SUBMERGENT AFTER ALL THESE YEARS

I WAS BORN IN 1977. I am a pastor. And I am not emergent.

I grew up in a suburb of Grand Rapids, Michigan, in a community with strong Dutch Reformed roots. I was nurtured in a Christian home by loving, God-fearing parents who work in missionary radio. Along with my parents and three siblings, I went to a medium-size Reformed church that was more broadly evangelical than Reformed. Rain or shine, in sickness and in health, for better or for worse, I went to church twice every Sunday, attended youth group Sunday evenings, and participated in midweek programs most every Wednesday night. In other words, I grew up in an evangelical home, in an evangelical church, in an evangelical part of the country.

For many, this upbringing explains why I am a conservative, Reformed pastor. But for others, it might seem strange that I have aligned myself so closely with historic evangelical orthodoxy in general and Reformed confessional theology more specifically. In many ways, I am a great candidate for the emerging church.

For starters, I am a part of generation X (or Y, or busters, or millennials; I can never keep the labels straight). I should resonate with 80s chic, dialogical preaching, and techno-savvy churches. With all the television and movies I've seen, I should be less linear, and more attuned to stories and images. At the very least, I should be in some quarter-life crisis of faith. I should be wondering how all that I've known as Christianity can survive in this postmodern matrix. I should be questioning church as we know it and reimagining church for my generation.

After all, I grew up in the evangelical ghetto of conservative West Michigan. I should be joining many of my peers in decrying the evangelical "bubble" and its closed-minded, doctrinally rigid accounting of the Christian faith. After having my evangelical faith deconstructed by many of the faculty at the middle-of-the-road denominational college I attended, I should have tried to make peace with my conservative upbringing and the more liberal Christianity of my professors by veering off into the emergent world of mystery, journey, and uncertainty—the perfect porridge of not quite fundamentalist, not quite liberal. I should have (after enjoying all the benefits of safety, provision, and love) rebelled against my family upbringing, finding it, in hindsight, stilted, stoic, and staid. I should have, like so many of those in the emerging church, chaffed against my evangelical past and charted a more emerging future.

But I haven't.

Presently, I pastor a medium-size church in East Lansing, Michigan, across the street from Michigan State University (about 45,000 students). I preach long, doctrinal, expositional sermons that proclaim the uniqueness of Jesus Christ, the reality of hell, the demands of obedience, the call to evangelism, the duty of mercy ministry, and the glorious truths of unconditional election and particular redemption (though not everyone in the church finds these last two truths as glorious as I do).

The church I serve has MSU undergraduates, grad students, international students and scholars, MSU employees, faculty, and department heads. There are non-MSU folks as well, but I'm amazed at how many are connected to the university in some way. Their presence at the church is no great commendation of my ministry. I've been at the church only a few years. Many of them were here long before I arrived. I mention the setting and makeup of the church simply to make clear that I am not the pastor of an ethnically, culturally, or theologically homogenous church. True, East Lansing is still the Midwest. It's not quite San Francisco or New York. But being a university town gives the city a much more diverse, academic, and liberal bent than, say, the town I grew up in seventy-five miles west of here.

My ministry in East Lansing has, up to this point, been short, unremarkable, and hopefully, faithful. A number of people have joined our church. Some have left. We've started some new ministries and stopped some others. There have been a few controversies and a few successes. Unbelievers have been converted and believers built up in the faith. We're plodding visionaries trying to learn the Bible, love one another, share the gospel, and worship God in spirit and truth.

The point is that at thirty years old I am no great success story as a pastor and no brooding melancholic either. I love preaching and love my church. I hope my congregation loves good preaching and loves one another.

Why begin with autobiography? Not because I have some great story to tell. Most of the rest of this book (my part at least) will be light on story and heavy on more academic reflection. I share a few pages about myself only to demonstrate that you can be young, passionate about Jesus Christ, surrounded by diversity, engaged in a postmodern world, and reared in evangelicalism and not be an emergent Christian. In fact, I want to argue that it would be better if you weren't.

WHAT AND WHO ARE WE WRITING ABOUT?

In discussing this new movement, we will be using the terms *emerging* and *emergent* interchangeably. Strictly speaking, our criticism is not with those who try to engage the emerging culture, but rather with the emergent church. Some have made a distinction between the two words, *emerging* categorizing those who are trying to contextualize the gospel for postmoderns, and *emergent* referring to the organization now headed up by Tony Jones and associated especially with Doug Pagitt and Brian McLaren. For example, Mark Driscoll, of Mars Hill Church in Seattle, who has distanced himself from the emergent church while still trying to engage postmoderns, argues that "the emergent church is part of the Emerging Church Movement but does not embrace the dominant ideology of the movement. Rather, the emergent church is the latest version of liberalism. The only difference is that the old liberalism accommodated modernity and the new liberalism accommodates postmodernity."[1] Driscoll may not be alone in making the distinction between emergent and emerging, but to carry the distinction through an entire book would be too burdensome for most readers.

When we talk about the emerging church, we are not simply referring to what is new, postmodern, culturally with-it, or generationally up and coming. Neither are we referring solely to the official Emergent organization. Some of the authors we quote are a part of Emergent Village, some aren't. We are talking about a movement led and inspired by a cadre of authors and pastors, who express many of the same concerns with the evangelical church, hit on many of the same themes, and often speak as the most influential voices in the emergent conversation. We don't want to get hung up on labels, let alone poison anything and everything that has been called emerging or emergent. But for the purposes of this book, the two words—emerging and emergent—mean the same thing.

As I've worked on this project, the number one question I've gotten from friends and family is, "So what is the emerging church anyway?" Defining the emerging church is like nailing Jell-O to the wall. The "what" and "who" of the movement are almost impossible to define. This is due, in part, because the movement is new (at least in name and style if not always in substance). New movements are always more amorphous and less codified.

But the Jell-O-like nature of the emerging church is also intentional. It is, after all, a "conversation." Emergent authors, bloggers, and pastors do not see themselves as leaders or authoritative theologians, but as talkers. This is one of the most admirable and frustrating parts about the emerging church. It's admirable because emerging Christians admit that their ideas are only exploration and experimentation and not definitive in any way. That's refreshingly honest and self-effacing. It's frustrating because the "we're just in conversation" mantra can become a shtick whereby emergent leaders are easy to listen to and impossible to pin down.

It's one thing for a high school student to be in process with his theology. It's another thing for adults to write books and speak around the world about their musings and misgivings. I agree there must be space for Christians to ask hard questions and explore the tensions in our faith, but I seriously question that this space should be hugely public where hundreds of thousands of men and women are eagerly awaiting the next book or blog or podcast arising from your faith journey. No matter what new label you put on it, once you start selling thousands of books, speaking all over the country and world, and being looked to for spiritual and ecclesiastical direction, you're no longer just a conversation partner. You are a leader and teacher. And this is serious business, for as James says, "Not many of you should become teachers, my brothers, for you know that we who teach will be judged with greater strictness" (3:1).

Back to the question at hand—attempting an explanation of the emergent church. To some "emergent" means nothing more than a new style and approach to worship ("couches, candles, and coffee"). To others it signals an appreciation for postmodernism. To yet others it means a return to a more ancient, primitive, and pristine form of Christianity. At a popular level, "the term *emerging church* has been applied to high-profile, youth-oriented con-gregations that have gained attention on account of their rapid numerical growth; their ability to attract (or retain) twentysomethings; their contemporary worship, which draws from popular music styles; and their ability to promote themselves to the Christian subculture through websites and by word of mouth."[2] Or, as Andy Crouch puts it in *Christianity Today*, emerging churches are "frequently urban, disproportionately young, overwhelmingly white, and very new."[3]

One of its critics has described the emerging church as a protest move-ment—a protest against traditional evangelicalism, a protest against modern-ism, and a protest against seeker-sensitive megachurches.[4] Others, sympathetic to the movement, have used the acronym EPIC: experiential, participatory, image driven, and connected.

Some definitions are so broad as to be of little help. What Christian does not want to "(1) identify with the life of Jesus, (2) transform the secular realm, and (3) live highly communal lives" and as a result "(4) welcome strangers, (5) serve with generosity, (6) participate as producers, (7) create as created beings, (8) lead as a body, and (9) take part in spiritual activities"?[5] Other definitions work with dichotomies, contrasting modern ministry with post-modern as the movement from rationalism to embodiment, power to servant-hood, information to formation, constraint to expression, parties to prayer, and theory to action.[6]

With such varied definitions, we have chosen to focus on the "what" of the emerging church by focusing on the "who." Admittedly, this requires more Jell-O nailing. As any emergent Christian will tell you, no one speaks for the movement and no one speaks for anyone else. Again, very convenient and very frustrating. At a certain level, the emerging church becomes whatever anyone who calls themselves "emergent" happens to think at the moment.

In an article from theooze.com on June 2, 2005, entitled "Response to Recent Criticisms," Tony Jones, Doug Pagitt, Spencer Burke, Brian McLaren,

Dan Kimball, Andrew Jones, and Chris Seay argue, "Contrary to what some have said, there is no single theologian or spokesperson for the emergent conversation. We each speak for ourselves and are not official representatives of anyone else, nor do we necessarily endorse everything said or written by one another."[7] Fine. But if seven men get together to respond to their critics in one article, they should at least admit they not only share much common ground, but they are also some of the lead influencers (if we can't say spokespersons) in the conversation. Call it a friendship, or a network, or a web of relationships, but when people endorse one another's book and speak at the same conferences and write on the same blogs, there is something of a discernible movement afoot.

Let this be crystal clear: We fully understand that *emergent* means a hundred different things to a hundred different people. So if what you read in these pages is not what you mean by emergent, so be it. We might encourage you to reconsider your labels, but if what we describe as emergent is not what you are as emergent, then by all means, be emergent. But if the emerging church exists as a real and identifiable movement ("conversation" if you like), then its spirit is surely captured in authors like Brian McLaren, Doug Pagitt, Peter Rollins, Spencer Burke, David Tomlinson, Leonard Sweet, Rob Bell, and Tony Jones.

Here we need to add three caveats. First, we don't think of our emergent sparring partners as "the bad guys." No doubt many people reading this book have been helped by these men, either in person or by their writings. Living in the town where Rob Bell grew up and Bell living in the town where I grew up, I have heard many people, including some of my friends, rave about all they've learned from Bell's teaching. I've heard him many times; he is a good teacher. And probably a good portion of what he teaches is perfectly fine. The same is probably true with most of the emergent authors we quote. We want to point out some serious concerns about their thinking (especially as expressed in their writing), but we don't want to demean everything they say nor criticize anyone who has ever been blessed by their ministries.

Second, we realize that not everyone we critique in this book would gladly wear the emergent label. We talk in a few places about men like Donald Miller and Erwin McManus. Their theology is certainly not identical to that of a Doug Pagitt or a Brian McLaren. We understand they may run in different circles, but we hear some of the same concerns and language being used. As we critique the emerging church we are not trying to critique a word or a label. We are trying to interact with a number of popular, mostly young, authors and pastors who advocate "doing church differently" in many of the same ways. Rob Bell is another example, one we quote frequently. Bell would probably not call himself or his church "emergent." But his writing hits the same themes and quite often reaches the same conclusions as those under the emergent umbrella. Bell has also acknowledged the formative influence McLaren has had in shaping his ministry over the past several years.

The third caveat is closely related to the second. We realize that none of the men listed above (or quoted in the book) is an official spokesman and none can be held responsible for what the others say. We recognize this diversity of opinions, but we couldn't call the book *Why We Don't Agree with Brian McLaren, Leonard Sweet, Rob Bell, and Doug Pagitt, Who May or May Not Agree with Each Other and Who May or May Not Speak for You as an Emergent Christian*. We think there are enough common themes, protests, and shared ideas in these authors, to name but a few, to engage them under the broader banner of the emerging church.

ARE YOU EMERGENT?

After reading nearly five thousand pages of emerging-church literature, I have no doubt that the emerging church, while loosely defined and far from uniform, can be described and critiqued as a diverse, but recognizable, movement. You might be an emergent Christian: if you listen to U2, Moby, and Johnny Cash's *Hurt* (sometimes in church), use sermon illustrations from *The Sopranos*, drink lattes in the afternoon and Guinness in the evenings, and always use a Mac; if your reading list consists primarily of Stanley Hauerwas,

Henri Nouwen, N. T. Wright, Stan Grenz, Dallas Willard, Brennan Manning, Jim Wallis, Frederick Buechner, David Bosch, John Howard Yoder, Wendell Berry, Nancy Murphy, John Franke, Walter Winks and Lesslie Newbigin (not to mention McLaren, Pagitt, Bell, etc.) and your sparring partners include D. A. Carson, John Calvin, Martyn Lloyd-Jones, and Wayne Grudem; if your idea of quintessential Christian discipleship is Mother Teresa, Martin Luther King Jr., Nelson Mandela, or Desmond Tutu; if you don't like George W. Bush or institutions or big business or capitalism or *Left Behind* Christianity; if your political concerns are poverty, AIDS, imperialism, war-mongering, CEO salaries, consumerism, global warming, racism, and oppression and not so much abortion and gay marriage; if you are into bohemian, goth, rave, or indie; if you talk about the myth of redemptive violence and the myth of certainty; if you lie awake at night having nightmares about all the ways modernism has ruined your life; if you love the Bible as a beautiful, inspiring collection of works that lead us into the mystery of God but is not inerrant; if you search for truth but aren't sure it can be found; if you've ever been to a church with prayer labyrinths, candles, Play-Doh, chalk-drawings, couches, or beanbags (your youth group doesn't count); if you loathe words like *linear, propositional, rational, machine*, and *hierarchy* and use words like *ancient-future, jazz, mosaic, matrix, missional, vintage*, and *dance*; if you grew up in a very conservative Christian home that in retrospect seems legalistic, naïve, and rigid; if you support women in all levels of ministry, prioritize urban over suburban, and like your theology narrative instead of systematic; if you disbelieve in any sacred-secular divide; if you want to be the church and not just go to church; if you long for a community that is relational, tribal, and primal like a river or a garden; if you believe doctrine gets in the way of an interactive relationship with Jesus; if you believe who goes to hell is no one's business and no one may be there anyway; if you believe salvation has a little to do with atoning for guilt and a lot to do with bringing the whole creation back into shalom with its Maker; if you believe following Jesus is not believing the right things but living the right way; if it really bugs you when people talk about going to heaven instead of heaven coming to us; if you disdain monological, didactic preaching; if you use the word "story" in all your propositions about postmodernism—if all or most of this tortuously long sentence describes you, then you might be an emergent Christian.

THE *HOW* OF THIS BOOK

Enough about "what" and "who." Let me make a few general comments about the "how" of this book. First, we write this book as Christians writing about Christians. Therefore, we want to critique as Christians. Hopefully, our writing is of the "faithful are the wounds of a friend" variety and not the slanderous, mean-spirited kind. Our disagreements are strong and stated strongly but, we trust, not bitter and cantankerous. Emergent writers are often provocative and passionate, and so are we. We take this to be a good thing, on both sides. Why not, especially in this soft, limp-noodle age, believe in what you write and write like you believe it? But passion and provocation are not an excuse to be un-Christian. We love Jesus and love the church. We believe emergent Christians love the same. The shape and substance of that love is what we disagree on.[8]

Second, though our approach is critical, don't assume we dislike all things emergent. The long sentence above describes Ted and me in some ways too. But because this book is *Why We Are Not Emergent* and not *An Evaluation of the Emerging Church*, we will not take much time to list what we appreciate about the movement, though we could. We too are wary of marketing gimmicks, how-to sermons, watered-down megachurches, and the effects of modernism. We fully recognize that the Bible has been abused and no one understands it exhaustively. We agree that there is more to Christianity than doctrinal ortho-doxy. We welcome the emergent critique of reductionistic methods of "becom-ing Christian" (sign a card, raise your hand, say a prayer, etc.). We are glad for the emergent correction reminding us that heaven is not a cloud up above for disembodied souls in the sky, but the re-creation of the entire cosmos. We fur-ther agree that we ought to be concerned about bringing heaven to earth, not just getting ourselves to heaven. In short, we affirm a number of the emergent diagnoses. It's their prescribed remedies that trouble us most.

All that to say we are taking Bell's advice given on the back of *Velvet Elvis* and applying it to the entire emerging church: "Test it. Probe it. Don't swallow it uncritically. Think about it. Wrestle with it." We write this book because the more we learn about the emerging church, the harder it is to swallow.

Third, for the most part we don't deal with the more academic side of postmodernism. From time to time, we engage authors like Grenz and Raschke, but most of our dealings are with the popularizers, practitioners, and pastors of the emerging movement. Emergent leaders have often cried foul when their books have been held up to academic scrutiny. "We are not professional scholars," they say, and neither are we. So it's a fair fight—more fair than fight, we hope.

Fourth, as was said earlier, what we critique may not be what some self-described emerging Christians believe. The conversation is diverse.[9] Dan Kimball is much more theologically responsible than Spencer Burke. Scot McKnight, who has aligned himself with the emerging church, is one of the few in the movement to gently critique the movement, for which we are thankful (though McKnight's books are not by and large the ones being read by college students and young emergent pastors). We have tried to read widely of the literature, but we haven't read everything in print, not to mention the books that have come since our writing began and whatever also might be on the blogosphere.

Similarly, it is possible that some authors in emerging circles, if push came to shove, would sound much more orthodox and evangelical than they come across in print. But the printed, public word is what we have, so we are responding with a printed, public word (as opposed to individually calling up every emergent leader to ask him, "Is this what you really mean?"). We have not knowingly misrepresented anyone's beliefs. But if we've missed something, or someone has changed his mind, or some blog out there has what these guys really believe, we will be happy to be corrected. In fact, if our book

makes emerging folks indignant enough to stand up and tell us more defini-
tively what they believe, we will consider this book a success.

We're not joking. We would love nothing more than for those in the emerging church to write up a statement explaining exactly what they believe on
controversial issues like hell, the atonement, and the uniqueness of Christ.
One of the hazards of being part of a movement whose only statement of faith
says that you don't believe in statements of faith is that you are bound to be
misread and lumped together with some ideas you don't like.

Once again, we have not knowingly misread the authors we critique. In fact,
we have tried to avoid unfairly ascribing the more extreme views to everyone
in the conversation. But when your movement avoids definition and doctrinal
boundaries as one of its defining characteristics, it should not be surprising
when people start to wonder aloud what you really believe.

Fifth, Ted and I write differently. This will be obvious. We approach our
subjects by different means and write with different styles. But we are happy to
write this book together because, for all our differences, we share the same heart
for truth, love for the Bible, and concern over the emerging church. Because our
approaches are hugely dissimilar, however, we thought it best to write separate
chapters rather than work (futilely) to make our writing sound like one voice.
We trust that any overlap in our chapters will not be too redundant and any
slight differences between ourselves will be clear.

Finally, we write for the church—for our church, for our friends in other
churches, and for our brothers and sisters in emerging churches. It's a privilege
to write, and an even greater privilege to be read. So thank you. We pray that
in some measure, small or large, as we speak the truth in love, we could all
grow up in every way into Him who is the head of the body, into Jesus Christ
(Ephesians 4:15).

Kevin DeYoung

MAYBE—THE NEW YES

IT'S 6:35 P.M. and I'm in a committee meeting. Do emergent churches have committee meetings? I am the "young guy" presence on the committee, brought in, no doubt, because I "understand these people." At any rate, this particular group is brainstorming ways to promote an upcoming talk by D. A. Carson. We're all staring intently at a group of response cards that will be handed out at the end of his talk. The cards include the usual stuff, like "Did you like the talk? Would you like a follow-up call? Check 'yes,' 'no,' or 'maybe.'" Somebody suggests that we remove "maybe." I suggest, since this is a talk on postmodernism, that we should remove everything except "maybe."

The joke doesn't get the laugh I'm looking for. Cue drums and cymbals.

I don't really like Christian books. When I think of the words *Christian book*, I think of sappy self-help stuff that middle-aged women gush about and then forget in a matter of weeks. I think of untouchable writers with initials (D. A.,

J. I., R. C.), or writers with dollar signs in their eyes penning long series that could and should be much shorter. I pretty much never wanted to write one, but here I am.

As I write this introduction I am halfway through playing a season of professional indoor football, as research for my second book. This assignment has me living the life of the professional athlete—long bus rides, practices, games, and forays in and out of bars all over the Midwest. I am "interfacing with the world" and "engaging a diverse culture" on a daily basis. It's grim. And these aren't the kind of bars where you have thinky discussions about books and religion; they're the kind of places you go to get bombed. To forget.

Let's establish a few things. I am thirty-one years old, married for ten years. I am not cool. I write for a living, but I don't lie around in my boxers until noon sipping Chianti out of the bottle, waiting to feel creative. I am not on a "journey," and my testimony is of the bland, "raised in a Christian home" variety. My first book was about heavyweight boxer Mike Tyson, and my second was about football—again, not especially cool. I have never witnessed to anyone in a bar. I have never been so disillusioned with church that I made mix tapes and took a Cameron Crowe-esque car trip to find myself. This won't be that kind of book.

As for the emergent church, I look the part. For writers there is no dress code per se, so I get around in jeans and a T-shirt most days. I have the requisite smart-guy dark-framed glasses (that will probably be dated by the time this hits the shelf). My wife keeps me in cool shoes, which is just one of the reasons I really appreciate her. As a result, people try to engage me in discussions about music and probably leave wildly disappointed. (My tastes run from 80s hair metal to rap—pretty Philistine stuff). People have also, lately, tried to recruit us into the emergent church. The meetings go something like this: We are verbally probed, to see if we have problems with our current church situation. Couldn't church be done differently? (It could.) Shouldn't we be engaging the culture at large? (We should.)

And then I sheepishly confess what I have to confess: I really like church.

My church, like many orthodox American Protestant churches, is pretty bland at first glance. It is a cinder-block bunker situated across the street from a university and up the road from about a hundred other churches. It has the requisite plastic chairs, lame carpet, and bad coffee. In five years I've never had a good cup of coffee there. But I love it. I love the people. And I love the teaching—it's challenging and theologically significant. It's spiritual meat in a world of beer, milk, and philosophical cookies. It's a bubble that I am proud to be a part of, and I am being challenged there in ways that I never thought possible.

I have friends whom I love dearly who are making bad choices in the name of "experience"; expressing a counterfeit freedom gleaned from pages of well-meaning spiritual-journey books outlining their authors' mistakes in all their sexy, glamorous glory. This book is for them. I believe that there is forgiveness for all of our sins, no matter how grievous the mistake, but I also know, from experience, that those sins create a chasm between us and our Lord.

But we're not really writing this book to change people's minds because, let's face it, that rarely happens. The book will (hopefully) be read, will (probably) be blogged about, and will then probably be raked over the coals for being any combination of mean-spirited, short-sighted, too thinky and academic (Kevin's chapters), or not thinky and academic enough (my chapters). But above all, this is our attempt at joining the "conversation," because we're concerned about a church that we love. Kevin's chapters are longer and more propositional. Mine are shorter, and more "experiential," because I'm not a seminary-trained theologian, rather, just a guy in the pew (or in our case, the plastic chair). We had fun with these differences, and they are intentional. If my chapters do nothing more than get you to keep reading Kevin's, then I will consider it a job well done. And if, like some evangelicals, you're too "frugal" to pay full price for the book and prefer to read it at the bookstore, read Kevin's chapters first. They'll be good for your soul.

And do know that while we do poke some fun at the emergent church and its cultural tics (okay, we poke a lot of fun at this), we wish to do so lovingly.

We strove to represent these guys accurately, and hope that if we were to run into each other at a conference, a coffee shop named *Ecclesia*, or a pub, we could truly enjoy each other's fellowship, cognizant of the fact that we will be together in the kingdom.

As an author, specifically in sports, I live in a world of "maybe." This book is my attempt at writing something of worth. Sports are great, but sports—like my hip glasses, my used Volvo, my music collection, my trends—will burn eventually. As a Christian man, specifically a husband and father, I need truth. I need to worship a God who makes demands on my character, with consequences. I need to know that Christianity is about more than me just "reaching my untapped potential" or "finding the God inside me." I need to know that I worship a Christ who died, bodily, and rose from the dead. Literally. I need to know that decisions can (and should) be made based on Scripture and not just experience. These are things that give me peace in a world of maybe.

Ted Kluck

Notes

1. Mark Driscoll, *Confessions of a Reformission Rev.: Hard Lessons from an Emerging Missional Church* (Zondervan: Grand Rapids, 2006), 21.
2. Eddie Gibbs and Ryan K. Bolger, *Emerging Churches: Creating Christian Community in Postmodern Cultures* (Grand Rapids: Baker, 2005), 41.
3. Andy Crouch, "The Emergent Mystique," *Christianity Today*, November 2004, 37.
4. D. A. Carson, *Becoming Conversant with the Emerging Church* (Grand Rapids: Zondervan, 2005), 11–44.
5. Gibbs and Bolger, *Emerging Churches*, 45.
6. Robert E. Webber, *The Younger Evangelicals* (Grand Rapids: Baker, 2002).
7. http://www.theooze.com/articles/print.cfm?id=1151
8. Despite all the talk of conversation and dialogue, some of the emergent books are prefaced in such a way that makes honest, constructive criticism very difficult. For example, McLaren writes in the forward to *Heretic's Guide to Eternity* by Spencer Burke and Barry Taylor (San Francisco: Jossey-Bass, 2006), "It's easy for inquisition-launchers to go on a fault-finding mission; they have lots of practice and they're really good at it. What's more challenging, and, regarding this book, much more worthwhile, is to instead go on a truth-finding mission. And yes, even in a book with 'heretic' in the title, I believe any honest reader can find much truth worth seeking. Perhaps even those who have become legally inebriated on the hops and malt of fault-finding, those who are inquisition-aholics but think they can quit anytime . . . perhaps

even they might get a brief glimpse in the mirror in these pages, a glimpse that will do them good" (ix–x). Bating your opponents as fault-finders and inquisition-aholics is not the best way to invite an open and honest conversation. It's grossly unfair to begin a book by prejudging those who might disagree as "legally inebriated on the hops and malt of fault-finding." It's like beginning this book by saying, "There are many leaders out there who hate the truth. They have no taste for it and no appetite for it. They will not be able to stomach this book. But perhaps with a little practice they will develop the taste buds for truth and be able to savor something in this book. Bon apetite!" Perhaps emergent folks will dislike this book because they love the truth and think we've missed it. And perhaps non-emergent folks are critical of McLaren, Burke, Pagitt, and others not because we are heresy-hunters, but because we want to correct our opponents with gentleness, in order that God may lead them to repentance and a knowledge of the truth (2 Timothy 2:25).

9. See Robert Webber, ed., *Listening to the Beliefs of the Emerging Churches: Five Perspectives* (Grand Rapids: Zondervan, 2007). The five perspectives move from right to left on the theological spectrum. Mark Driscoll is a conservative, Reformed biblicist (his chapter has more than 700 scripture references) who can be called emerging only in the sense that he is reaching emerging generations. John Burke is a warm-hearted evangelical who does not "fully fit into the emerging camp," but is softer around the edges than Driscoll (p.51). Dan Kimball is next along the spectrum. Kimball is the right-winger (theologically) of the emergent church, holding to Nicene orthodoxy (and believing in orthodoxy!), but clearly sympathetic with much of the movement. Doug Pagitt is more progressive than Kimball and sounds akin to old-school theological liberalism. Karen Ward is not the influencer that Pagitt is in the movement, but is aligned with the "heart" of the emergent movement.

The Way is not a method or a map. The Way is an experience.

    —LEONARD SWEET, *SoulTsunami*

I see myself now at the end of my journey, my toilsome days are ended. I am going now to see that head that was crowned with thorns, and that face that was spit upon, for me.

    —MR. STAND-FAST *in Pilgrim's Progress*

JOURNEY:
ARE THE PILGRIMS STILL MAKING PROGRESS?

HE WAS SHORT, stocky, bearded, and twice my age. I can't remember for sure, but I think his name was Chuck. What I do know for sure is that he was one of the best musicians in our little Presbyterian church. Chuck was a former club owner and a talented guitarist, knowledgeable in folk music and the folk music scene.

He would occasionally play the guitar in church, usually for the weekly "special music." Somehow the powers that be discovered that I played the guitar too (though not nearly so well). And so it came to pass that I took my turn and provided the offertory music. I played my Takamine and sang a rendition of Psalm 23. Unremarkable, but not embarrassing, which was about the best I had hoped for.

After the service, Chuck came up to me to talk about guitars and singing and, of course, folk music. I was way out of my league. I taught myself to play the guitar in college so I could lead simple praise and worship music for our college ministry group. My skills are pretty ordinary—good enough for a church offertory and that's about it. This man, however, clearly knew his stuff. He talked to me like I was the expert in music that he was. I nodded politely and, out of genuine curiosity, asked him about his past life in the folk music scene. After telling a few tales of people he had hosted (the Indigo Girls come to mind), he told me something I'll never forget—something that captures the postmodern ethos. He said, "In the music scene it's really cool to search for God. It's not very cool to find Him."

That line has stuck with me ever since as an apt summary not just for the world of entertainment, but for spirituality in the West. The destination matters little. The journey is the thing.

For emerging Christians, the journey of the Christian life is less about our pilgrimage through this fallen world that is not our home, and more about the wild, uncensored adventure of mystery and paradox. We are not tour guides who know where we are going and stick to the course. We are more like travelers. Spencer Burke of theooze.com writes:

> Tour guides don't feel free to deviate from the "route" other Christians have set. What's more, they're apt to impose that same kind of rigid structure on others. Becoming a traveler, however, enables you to be true to yourself . . . . As a traveler, I am free to love and to be loved. I'm not worried about taking a wrong step or losing my position. I'm just one more person on the journey—a beloved child of God.[1]

The old notion of spiritual pilgrimage used the idea of journey to symbolize our longing for heaven and our place as strangers in the kingdom of this world. As sojourners and exiles, Christians were called to abstain from the lusts of the flesh, "which war against [our] soul," and to "live such good lives among the pagans that". . . they "see [our] good deeds and glorify God on the day he visits us" (1 Peter 2:11–12 NIV). We were supposed to be living in faith, looking forward to a better country, that is, a heavenly one (Heb. 11:16). The journey of the Christian life was the way of the pilgrim fighting against fears and doubts, trying not to be squeezed into this world's mold, trusting that God has something better for us, even if we had not yet received what was promised (see Heb. 11:39–40).

In much of emergent thought, however, the destination is a secondary matter, as is any concern about being on the right path. "Evangelism," therefore, "should be seen as an opportunity to 'fund' people's spiritual journeys, drawing on the highly relevant resources of 'little pieces' of truth contained in the Christian narrative."[2] Similarly, Peter Rollins argues that instead of thinking in terms of destination (we became Christians, joined a church, are saved), we should think in terms of journey (we are becoming Christians, becoming church, becoming saved). Hence, we "need to be evangelized as much, if not more than those around us."[3]

The postmodern Way, as Leonard Sweet puts it so candidly, is an experience. The journey is more wandering than directional, more action than belief, more ambiguous than defined. To explain and define the journey of faith would be to cheapen it. The Christian faith is not a math problem to be solved, we are told. After all, to quote Rob Bell and to ignore the early Christian apologists, "you rarely defend the things you love."[4]

MOVING INWARD ON THE JOURNEY

In David Wells's newest book, he compares the notion of journey in *Pilgrim's Progress* with the contemporary idea. Christian, he notes, stumbled frequently on his pilgrimage. But by God's grace he always got back on the path, moved in the right direction, learned what others failed to grasp, and continued on the way. Wells writes:

This is really the difference between Bunyan's notion of spiritual pilgrimage and the postmodern idea of spiritual journey. . . . The point of spirituality is in the *experience* of the journeying, not in the *purpose* of reaching the destination. For Bunyan, the pilgrimage is about the certain knowledge that Christians have of "the better country" to which they travel and of the way in which they must conduct themselves on the journey in preparation for the One to whom they are traveling.[5]

Because the journey is an experience more than a destination, the Christian life requires less doctrinal reflection and more personal introspection. The postmodern infatuation with journey feeds on and into a preoccupation with our own stories. If my grandparents' generation could be a little stoic and not terribly reflective, my generation is introspective at a level somewhere between self-absorption and narcissism. We are so in-tuned with our dysfunctions, hurts, and idiosyncrasies that it often prevents us from growing up, because maturity is tantamount to hypocrisy in a world that prizes brokenness more than health.

I'm not advocating stuffing all our feelings, but we must learn that self-expression and being true to ourselves are not the surest guides to Christlikeness. Sincerity is a Christian virtue, as is honesty about our struggles. But my generation needs to realize that Christianity is more than chic fragility, endless self-revelation, and the coolness that comes with authenticity.

We live in a blogging culture, which suggests that just because we have an opinion on something it must be worthwhile and just because we are in touch with our spiritual journey it must be worth sharing. I know that Doug Pagitt's book *Reimagining Spiritual Formation* contains journal entries from Solomon's Porch to give the book a community feel, but how important is it really to know that Erin is a Taurus, but more like a Scorpio, and that Dustin likes Frosted Mini-Wheats, rollerblading, and making out with supermodels, and that he'd like to have a monkey named Scratch that makes leather wallets and flings poo at children?[6] I guess those revelations are funny, but they're also a funny way to begin a book about spiritual formation. In the postmodern world of spiritual journey, authenticity and sincerity have become the currency of authority, and dysfunction, inconsistency, and idiosyncrasy are worn as badges of honor.

But talking about monkey poo is not the real problem in postmodern spirituality. Talking about primate excretion is sort of odd, but in the grand scheme of things it's fairly harmless. There are, however, more serious problems lurking along the emergent journey.

IS GOD KNOWABLE?

The first problem with the emergent view of journey is that it undermines the knowability of God. Theologians have long held to God's knowability along with His immensity. That is, Christian theologians of every stripe have understood that we can't understand everything about God. God's knowledge of Himself is called archetypal; our knowledge of Him is called ectypal. God knows Himself exhaustively; we see through a glass dimly. God is infinite; our knowledge of Him is finite. All that to say, no Christian that I have ever known or read has ever claimed to have God figured out. And emerging Christians certainly won't be the first.

But emergent leaders are allowing the immensity of God to swallow up His knowability. In good postmodern fashion, they are questioning whether we can have any real, accurate knowledge about God in the first place. Brian McLaren, in noting his agreement with Tony Campolo, argues that in one sense all theologies are heresies because we can't truly speak of God using our human formulation. What is needed is "not absolute and arrogant certainty about our theologies, but a proper and humble confidence in God."[7]

Fair enough. Who wants to be arrogantly certain about anything? But McLaren posits a false antithesis, suggesting that we can know God personally but can't confidently know things about Him. The former kind of knowing is "personal knowledge." The latter is "abstract, rational, impersonal certitude."[8]

But what does it really mean to know God personally but not know anything rationally about Him? I can't love my wife without knowing facts about her, otherwise my love for her is just love of love, or worse, love for the sake of being loved. Unless I love her for the facts of who she is, what she has done, and what she does, I am loving a shapeless, formless void. No matter how much I rightly stress the importance of relationship with my wife beyond mere knowledge about her, I must have knowledge about her in order to have a relationship. After all, if I don't know any of the "abstract" and "impersonal" facts about my wife (like her hairstyle, eye color, height, etc.), how can I have a personal relationship with her? I won't even be able to pick her out in a crowd!

> **None of us ever infinitely understands God in a neat package of affirmations, but we can know Him truly, both personally and propositionally.**

It matters little how glowingly I speak about our relationship; if I cannot make clear, certain, unequivocal statements about my wife, how good is our relationship really? Prattling on about the wonders of personal relationship while refusing to make definitive statements about the one we love in the relationship is not the kind of talk that honors one's wife, or God for that matter.

I'm sure that emerging Christians would affirm that they know things about God. But their idea of knowledge is so provisional and lacking so much confidence (because the only other kind of knowledge in their minds is cold, linear, and infallible) that it's hard to imagine actually and accurately knowing God except as we experience Him. As Donald Miller says at one point in his wildly popular *Blue Like Jazz*, "I don't believe I will ever walk away from God for intellectual reason. Who knows anything anyway?"[9]

The emergent agnosticism about truly knowing and understanding anything about God seems to be pious humility. It seems to honor God's immensity, but it actually undercuts His sovereign power. Postmoderns harbor such distrust for language and disbelieve God's ability to communicate truth to human minds that they effectively engage in what Carson calls "the gagging of God."[10] For example, Tomlinson writes, "To say Scripture is the word of God is to employ a metaphor. God cannot be thought of as literally speaking words, since they are an entirely human phenomenon that could never prove adequate as a medium for the speech of an infinite God."[11] In a similar vein, Bell writes, "Our words aren't absolutes. Only God is absolute, and God has no intention of sharing this absoluteness with anything, especially words people have come up with to talk about him."[12]

Such statements fly in the face of redemptive history and nearly every page of Scripture. The God of the Bible is nothing if He is not a God who speaks to His people. To be sure, none of us ever infinitely understand God in a nice, neat package of affirmations and denials, but we can know Him truly, both personally and propositionally. God can speak. He can use human language to communicate truth about Himself that is accurate and knowable, without ceasing to be God because we've somehow got Him all figured out.

We may all be, by nature, like blind men touching the elephant without knowing whether what we are feeling is a trunk, tail, or ear. But what if the elephant spoke and said, "Quit calling me crocodile, or peacock, or paradox. I'm an elephant, for crying out loud! That long thing is my trunk. That little frayed thing is my tail. That big floppy thing is my ear." And what if the elephant gave us ears to hear his voice and a mind to understand his message (cf. 1 Cor. 2:14–15)? Would our professed ignorance about the elephant and our unwillingness to make any confident assertions about his nature mean we were especially humble, or just deaf?

Because of the emerging church's implied doctrine of God's unknowability, the word *mystery*, a perfectly good word in its own right, has become downright annoying. Let me be very clear: I don't understand everything about God or the Bible. I don't fully understand how God can be three in one. I don't completely grasp how divine sovereignty works alongside human responsibility. The Christian faith *is* mysterious. But when we talk about Christianity, we don't start with mystery. It's some combination of pious confusion and intellectual laziness to claim that living in mystery is at the heart of Christianity.

Yet, time and again, emerging leaders brand Christianity as, above all things it seems, mysterious.

> Mystery is not the enemy to be [conquered] nor a problem to be solved, but rather, the partner with whom we dance—and dance we must. The call for the post-evangelical community is to dance and play the music. But we are also called to show each other the way into mystery. We would certainly be under providing if we didn't offer new ways to enter and live in mystery.[13]

> I don't think you can explain how Christian faith works either. It is a mystery. And I love this about Christian spirituality. It cannot be explained, and yet it is beautiful and true. It is something you feel, and it comes from the soul.[14]

> The Christian faith is mysterious to the core. It is about things and beings that ultimately can't be put into words. Language fails. And if we do definitively put God into words, we have at that very moment made God something God is not. . . . The mystery *is* the truth.[15]

So, Christian spirituality cannot be explained; we cannot use human language to speak truthfully about God; and the mystery of our unknowable, unfathomable God *is* the truth. That sounds more like the Hindu conception of Brahman than the Christian notion of God, revelation, and authority. True, there are secret things that belong to the Lord our God, but what about the things revealed that belong to us and to our children forever? (Deut. 29:29). What did Paul tell the men of Athens? "I see you worship an unknown God. Great! So do I." No. Paul declared, "Now what you worship as something unknown I am going to proclaim to you" (Acts 17:23 NIV).[16]

Mystery as an expression of our finitude is one thing. Mystery as a way of jettisoning responsibility for our beliefs is another thing.[17] Mystery as radical unknowing of God and His revealed truth is not Christian, and it will not sustain the church. As G. K. Chesterton observed, reflecting on the rationality of Christian commitment over two millennia, "People are not amused with a puzzle or a paradox or a mere muddle in the mind for all that time."[18]

IS UNCERTAINTY THE SAME AS HUMILITY?

The second problem with the emergent view of journey is that it suffers from a confusion of categories. Emerging leaders equate uncertainty with humility. Steve Chalke tells the story of a young man who finally got fed up with theologians telling him that he needed to search for the real Jesus. After one such speech, the young man shouted, "If you academics in your ivory towers have lost Jesus, that's your problem. I've not lost him. I know him. I love him. I don't need to search for him." Chalke's comments on the story are telling.

> However, as appealing as this kind of certainty might at first sound, it is in fact rather like the presumed familiarity of which Dallas Willard spoke. To assume that we have got Jesus "pinned down" or "summed up" is not simply arrogant but stupid, and in the end inhibits our ability to communicate his unchanging message to an ever-changing world.[19]

Certainty, for the emergent church, is the same as pinning down Jesus and summing up God, while uncertainty is a breath of fresh air. "Drop any affair you may have with certainty, proof, argument—and replace it with dialogue, conversation, intrigue and search," argues McLaren. Clarity, after all, is usually boring and wrong "since reality is seldom clear, but usually fuzzy and mysterious; not black-and-white, but in living color."[20]

But why do intrigue and search have to mean the end of all certainty? McLaren is guilty of a very modern error, insisting on *either-or* when a *both-and* is possible. There is a place for questions. There is a time for conversation. But there is also the possibility of certainty, not because we have dissected God like a freshman biology student dissects a frog, but because God has spoken to us clearly and intelligibly and has given us ears to hear His voice.

Listen to how Calvin confronted the postmoderns in his premodern day:

> But they contend that it is a matter of rash presumption for us to claim an undoubted knowledge of God's will. Now I would concede that point to them only if we took upon ourselves to subject God's incomprehensible plan to our slender understanding. But when we simply say with Paul: "we have received not the spirit of this world, but the Spirit that is from God . . . " by whose teaching "we know the gifts bestowed on us by God" [1 Cor. 2:12], how can they yelp against us without abusively assaulting the Holy Spirit? But if it is a dreadful sacrilege to accuse the revelation given by the Spirit either of falsehood or uncertainty or ambiguity, how do we transgress in declaring its certainty?"[21]

There is the possibility of certainty, because God has spoken to us clearly and intelligibly.

Who knew there were emerging Christians in sixteenth-century Western Europe! Apparently, this notion that only arrogance and rash presumption could lead one to speak of God with certainty is not a new idea. And it is not a mark of humility when we refuse to speak about God and His will except in the most ambiguous terms. It is an assault on the Holy Spirit and disbelief in God's ability to communicate rational, clear statements about Himself in human language. What we suffer from today, wrote Chesterton in the previous century, "is humility in the wrong place. Modesty has moved from the organ of ambition . . . [and] settled upon the organ of conviction, where it was never meant to be. A man was meant to be doubtful about himself, but undoubting about the truth; this has been exactly reversed. We are on the road to producing a race of men too mentally modest to believe in the multiplication table."[22]

The disdain for certainty in knowledge is built upon a false dichotomy. The false dichotomy says that you must know something omnisciently in order to know something truly. Stan Grenz, for example, wrote, "At the heart of the foundationalist agenda is the desire to overcome the uncertainty generated by our human liability to error and the inevitable disagreements that follow. Foundationalists are convinced that the only way to solve this problem is to find some means of grounding the entire edifice of human knowledge on invincible certainty."[23] But aren't we capable of knowing truth unambiguously without having to know it with invincible certainty? Carson calls it an asymptotic approach.[24] An asymptote is a curved line that gets closer and closer to a straight line without ever touching it. Likewise, our knowledge of the truth approaches the straight line of God's infallible, exhaustive comprehension of all things in such a way that it can be called true, reliable, and sure, while it is still not omniscient and invincible.

> **The false dichotomy says that you must know something omnisciently in order to know something truly.**

Paul did not claim to fully understand the depth of God's wisdom and mercy (Rom. 11:33–36), but that did not stop the apostle from chiding his fellow Jews for having a zeal for God "not based on knowledge" (Rom. 10:2 NIV). Indeed, Christianity is based upon, and the whole Bible assumes, a certain knowledge of and adherence to confident assertions about God and His Christ. That's why Paul preached in power and in the Holy Spirit and with full conviction (1 Thess. 1:5).

Arguing for the inherent uncertainty of knowledge causes problems when you write books trying to convince people to believe or behave in certain ways. That is to say, radical uncertainty sounds nice as a sort of protest against the perceived dogmatism of evangelical Christianity, but it gets in the way when you want prove your point. At some point, no matter how often you rag on certainty and boast in the great mysterious unknowability of God, you will want people to be clear about your beliefs.

Thus McLaren writes, "In one of my previous books, I said that clarity is sometimes overrated and that intrigue is correspondingly undervalued. But here I want to say—clearly—that it is tragic for anyone, especially anyone affiliated with the religion named after Jesus, not to be clear about what Jesus' message actually was."[25] So intrigue and ambiguity are good when the ideas in question are ones emerging leaders don't particularly care for or care about, but when it comes to making their point, clarity is key.

For all the talk of perspectives and uncertainty, McLaren still believes that some interpretations are good and some are bad. He has to. We all have to, if we are to have anything to say. No one writes books or preaches sermons or gives talks or converses in dialogue unless he believes that what he is saying is true, or at least truer than other options out there. What is frustrating, then, is when emerging authors claim the postmodern moral high ground that supposedly eschews reasons, logic, and certain truth claims.

On a related note, I'm not sure if it is rhetoric, intellectual laziness, humility, fear of criticism, consistent postmodernism, or all of the above, but much emergent writing is laden with disclaimers. McLaren's writings provide many examples. Here's one from an article about homosexuality: "I am no doubt wrong on many things. I am very likely wrong in my personal opinions on homosexuality (which, by the way, were never expressed in the piece, contrary to the assumptions of many responders)."[26] It may be a sign of humility to admit that your opinions are fallible, but admitting that your opinions on a particular subject are very likely wrong is odd to say the least. Why hold to your personal opinions if you think they are wrong?

Here's another example. At the beginning of *A Generous Orthodoxy*, McLaren describes himself as a lowly English major who snuck into pastoral ministry accidentally. "I am an amateur," he writes. "And even as an English major I'm a failure. The book is laced with overstatement, hyperbole, and generalizations. I am horribly unfair in this book, lacking all scholarly objectivity and evenhand-edness."[27] So *A Generous Orthodoxy* is unfair and full of misguided caricatures. But does recognizing these "egregious errors"[28] make them okay?

Here's yet one more example. McLaren admits that his unwillingness to speak candidly about his beliefs concerning the state of the wicked after death will frustrate many. "They'll say I'm being evasive, cowardly, afraid to take a stand, and write smoke." His response? "No one can blame them."[29] So is he admitting to being evasive and cowardly?

I have never met Brian McLaren. I bet that I would really like him and find him warm and thoughtful and kindhearted. Everyone I've talked to who has met McLaren has spoken highly of his kindness and sincerity. I believe him when he says repeatedly that he doesn't want to create controversy. But he is the most influential emergent writer and therefore the most controversial, no matter how many times he opines that he would rather his books be banned than stir up dissension. I hope McLaren takes seriously his own criticisms that his books are full of overgeneralizations, overreaching historical reconstruc-tions, and just plain overreactions. Just because he beats his critics to the punch in pointing these things out does not exonerate him from the charges.

At the end of McLaren's book *The Secret Message of Jesus*, he tries to counter objections some may have that his reading of Jesus is too new (which it is not) to be taken seriously. To counter these objections he argues that his reading of the Gospels is good because it "accounts for more of the details included in the text than a bad reading" and because "our reading here takes the whole text in all its wildness and intensity and seems to integrate political, social, theologi-cal, eschatological, and other themes into one coherent whole."[30] McLaren's stated hermeneutical approach does not bother me in the least. I use the same approach every week. What bothers me is all the other times McLaren chas-tises us supposed moderns for being too linear and too persuaded of our own fallible interpretations, when, at the end of the day, he reaches his conclusions like every other mortal studying the Bible. He asks, "Does this make sense with the context? Does this fit together with other parts of Scripture? Does this piece together a myriad of readings without internal contradiction?"

We can know some things after all, then. We are not trapped in a hermeneutical spiral pulling us down into the morass of "all we have are our interpretations." There is a meaning in the text. There are bad interpretations and good interpretations. Bell may list a series of stumper questions about the Bible to convince us that "the Bible is open-ended,"[31] but he *is* certain that the first three miracles in the book of John are directly related to Dionysus, Asclepius, and Demeter, and that the reference to women being saved in childbirth is a direct reference to Artemis, and that the first chapters of Revelation follow the sequence of the Domitian games.[32] It appears that the dance of uncertainty is fun but hard to keep up for a whole book, let alone a lifetime.

THE DANGER OF AMBIGUITY:
HOMOSEXUALITY AS A TEST CASE

The mantra "God is too big to understand and the truth too mysterious to know with certainty" is not just confused humility. It has dangerous pastoral implications. Humility, as Chesterton warned, was not meant to be moved to the organ of conviction. Uncertainty in light of our human limitations is a virtue. Uncertainty in light of God's Word is not.

Take homosexuality, for example. On one level, emerging church leaders offer a wise warning: Don't demonize homosexuals, and don't speak without thinking first. McLaren writes, "I hesitate in answering 'the homosexual question' not because I'm a cowardly flip-flopper who wants to tickle ears, but because I'm a pastor, and pastors have learned from Jesus that there is more to answering a question than being right or even honest: we must also be . . . pastoral."[33] That makes sense to me. Like McLaren, I get people asking me where our church stands on homosexuality. When the question arises, I try to be sensitive and cautious, because I don't know where the question is coming from.

But I eventually answer the question, something McLaren does not seem to do. McLaren's article, which has been understandably controversial, would be fine if he just said somewhere, "I believe the Bible teaches that homosexual behavior is wrong, but that's not all we have to know as pastors. We have to find the question behind the question." But he never says that. Because he doesn't know if it's wrong.

> Frankly, many of us don't know what we should think about homo-sexuality. We've heard all sides but no position has yet won our confidence so that we can say 'it seems good to the Holy Spirit and us.' That alienates us from both the liberals and conservatives who seem to know exactly what we should think. Even if we are convinced that all homo-sexual behavior is always sinful, we still want to treat gay and lesbian people with more dignity, gentleness, and respect than our colleagues do. If we think that there may actually be a legitimate context for some homosexual relationships, we know that the biblical arguments are nuanced and multilayered, and the pastoral ramifications are stagger-ingly complex. We aren't sure if or where lines are to be drawn, nor do we know how to enforce with fairness whatever lines are drawn.[34]

Later, in a response article, McLaren makes clear that the "we" is inten-tional.[35] Many, but not all, of his friends in the emergent conversation are unsure what to think about homosexuality. Steve Chalke, on the other side of the Atlantic, writes, "To what extent does the church model the spiritually and socially inclusive message of Jesus? Are we liberators of excluded people or simply another dimension of their oppression? We may not exclude tax-col-lectors or hemorrhaging women, but what about schizophrenics, divorcees, single people, one-parent families, drug users, transsexuals or those struggling with their faith?"[36] Similarly, Doug Pagitt comments,

> The question of humanity is inexorably linked to sexuality and gen-

der. Issues of sexuality can be among the most complex and convoluted we need to deal with. It seems to me that the theology of our history does not deal sufficiently with these issues for our day. I do not mean this as a critique, but as an acknowledgement that our times are different. I do not mean that we are a more or less sexual culture, but one that knows more about the genetic, social and cultural issues surrounding sexuality and gender than any previous culture. Christianity will be impotent to lead a conversation on sexuality and gender if we do not boldly integrate our current understandings of humanity with our theology. This will require us to not only draw new conclusions about sexuality but will force us to consider new ways of being sexual.[37]

New Testament scholar Ben Witherington believes Rob Bell has also been evasive (at best) when asked about homosexuality.[38] Witherington is largely positive toward Bell, but critical when it comes to his ethics. Without coming out and affirming homosexual behavior, Bell, speaking to a packed-out auditorium on his *Sex God* book tour, made all the usual arguments for acceptance of homosexuality. The arguments went something like this (with Witherington's response summarized in parentheses): We shouldn't speak on this issue unless we have gay friends (but didn't Paul speak to the issue?). Jesus never said anything about homosexuality (but didn't Jesus talk about God's design for marriage and celibacy for single persons?). We are hypocritical to ignore heterosexual sin (agreed, so let's stop ignoring it). The Bible says nothing about orientation (but it forbids homosexual behavior regardless).

Many emerging church leaders are loathe to even hint that homosexual behavior might be sin. Never has ambivalence sounded so courageous. But is their ambivalence really indecision? Take McLaren, for example. It seems as if he hasn't chosen sides in the debate, but for all practical purposes he has. He doesn't preach against it. He doesn't tell parishioners it's wrong. He doesn't draw any lines of right and wrong. We can all plead the humility of uncertainty, but on some issues our silence speaks volumes. Do we really need "a five-year moratorium on making pronouncements," so we can dialogue some more and listen to all the related academic fields before we make any decisions, which will be "admittedly provisional"?[39] My denomination has been talking about homosexuality for thirty years and are in an intentional three-year dialogue process presently. Tom Oden is right. "Much time has been wasted seeking traction in this swamp." Later he notes, "Confessing Christians have a long history of experience with the frustration and futility of such undisciplined dialogue not ordered under the written Word. It less often leads to questions of truth than to the question of how we 'feel,' and how we can accommodate or negotiate our competing interests."[40]

> The refusal to take a stance . . . hurts people—it hurts those struggling to overcome sexual temptation and those gently calling homosexuals to repentance.

I believe many emergent leaders are truly torn up inside over homosexuality. They don't want to hurt anyone. But their refusal to take a stance (and sometimes their decision to take an unbiblical stance) also hurts people—it hurts those struggling to overcome sexual temptation, it hurts those gently calling homosexuals (along with other sinners) to repentance, and it hurts those who dare to speak with certainty on this issue. After years and sometimes decades in pastoral ministry, is it too much to ask that emergent pastors have at least a working conviction on the issue? Maybe an opinion that is based on evidence, but open to reason?

When you are faced with one of the most explosive and controversial subjects facing any church and any pastor, it is good wisdom to search for questions behind the questions, but it is also prudent, helpful, and pastoral to tell your people what you actually think about the issue.

I don't doubt that there are many people like the couple in McLaren's article who ask about homosexuality because they have a family member who is gay and they want to know if he or she would be harshly condemned in their church. But McLaren and other emerging church leaders surely must realize that indecision is not pastorally helpful to most people. There are people in my congregation who struggle with same-gender attraction. To ostracize them for struggling with these desires would be pastorally damaging, but so would an unwillingness to encourage them in their fight against these desires.

I know a man whose mother left home and went to live with her lesbian partner. He used to go to the Methodist church, but stopped going to that church and church altogether after the pastor told him to stop being so judgmental about his mother. He figured, "I don't need a church to take the side of my lesbian mother and tell me to get over it." Another couple at our church is still dealing with the hurt from a previous marriage where the former husband ran off with a priest. I recently spoke with a man in our church who wants help overcoming same-gender attraction issues.

Such stories don't tell the whole story, of course. But they do remind us of what the emerging church often forgets, that some people need to know with certainty what we think about homosexuality.

I'm not impressed with the emergent claim to be a sanctified middle ground between conservative dogmatists and liberal bad guys. The emergent tendency to wind up as the fresh and sane third option between two caricatures is unfair. I trust that McLaren and others realize that it's not just fire-breathing conservatives who know what emergent leaders should think about homosexuality. It's also Peter Akinola, primate of Nigeria, and Archbishop Livingstone Mpalanyi Nkoyoyo of Uganda who sacrificed financial aid from the West rather than be implicated in the Episcopal church's homosexual scandals, and the rest of the global South who know exactly what emerging leaders should think about homosexuality, not to mention nearly two thousand years of Christians who were also certain about God's opinion on the subject.[41] Martyn Lloyd-Jones, writing in a different context, could have been speaking about the emerging church when he said, "First, these people generally object to clear-cut definitions; they dislike clarity and certainty. We need not at this point go into the specific reason for this. I think they object to clarity of thought and definition because of its demands. The most comfortable type of religion is always a vague religion, nebulous and uncertain, cluttered up with forms and rituals."[42]

To all the pastors reading this book who will encounter questions about homosexuality, please be sensitive and ask good questions, but do not be silent and do not be uncertain.

WHAT ABOUT DOUBT?

The third problem with the emergent view of journey is that it establishes doubt as the essence of faith. McLaren is more balanced than most in admitting that doubt is not always good.[43] But then he turns around and lauds the value of doubt. "It's ironic: the more free I am to doubt a specific belief, the more free I become to hold on to that person-to-Person faith in God. . . . After all, to trust our beliefs about God more than we trust God—wouldn't that be missing the point?"[44] Or as Peter Rollins puts it, "In contrast to the modern view that religious doubt is something to reject, fear or merely tolerate, doubt not only can be seen as an inevitable aspect of our humanity but also can be celebrated as a vital part of faith."[45]

Tomlinson makes the same point: "Post-evangelicals also want room to express doubt without having someone rush around in a mad panic trying to 'deliver' them from unbelief. Far too often doubt is portrayed simply as an enemy rather than a potential friend; as something mature Christians should not suffer from, rather than a vital means by which Christians mature."[46]

Doubt, for Tomlinson, is the opposite of the "neat schemes in which we think we have truth wrapped up. Doubt creates a 'holy insecurity.'"[47] For emergent leaders, faith is a personal trust commitment despite the uncertainty of our knowledge and the doubt we all experience. In other words, doubt is the good friend of faith.

The key to the emergent appreciation for doubt is the distinction made between trusting in God versus trusting in doctrines about God. Doubt is good because it turns our attention from our fallible, man-made beliefs about God, which we can't trust, to a personal God whom we can trust. Instead of relying on religion, Christ bids us to trust Him.[48]

But isn't this a distinction without a difference? If I trust Frank, or to use religious language, have faith in Frank, what does that mean? How would I explain my faith in Frank to a friend who doesn't have faith? I would explain that I believe Frank will keep his promises. I know that he is a trustworthy person. I have faith in his ability to do what he says. I might even point to instances in the past where he proved faithful. In explaining my trust in Frank in these ways, have I not also explained my faith in certain beliefs about Frank? I believe he is trustworthy. I believe he has acted in certain ways in the past. I believe he is capable of doing what he promises. Can my trust in Frank really be distinguished from the confidence I have in my beliefs about him? If I doubt all that I believe to be true about Frank, how does that make me more able to trust Frank the person?

> **Doubt is something we are supposed to work through ... rather than embrace as the great friend of faith.**

Don't misunderstand; doubt is not the unforgivable sin. All the great books on spiritual warfare (or spiritual direction or spiritual formation, as they might be called today) understand that Christians, very often tremendous Christians, go through seasons of doubt. They question their faith. They don't sense God's presence. They doubt their salvation. Most of us will feel these things at some point in our lives, which is why Jude says, "Have mercy on those who doubt" (Jude 22).

But if we are to show mercy to those who doubt, doesn't this suggest that doubt is something we are supposed to work through and fight against rather than embrace as the great friend of faith? Faith is, after all, being sure of what we hope for and certain of what we do not see (Hebrew 11:1). True faith, to quote the Heidelberg Catechism (Q/A 21), "is not only a knowledge and conviction"; it is also a "deep-rooted assurance." To be sure, Jesus had mercy on those who struggled. Sometimes the only prayer we can muster is "I believe; help my unbelief!" (Mark 9:24). But Jesus also rebuked those who doubted and chided His disciples for having little faith (Matt. 6:30; 21:21; John 20:27; cf. James 1:6).

Tomlinson would have us break free from our "rigid frameworks of certainty" and "climb out of the little boat of our settled certainties and join Jesus in walking on the waters of uncertainty and vulnerability."[49] But let's look at that story for a moment. Peter took a risk when he came to Jesus on the water. Way to go, Peter. That took faith—we have all heard sermons how you can't walk on water until you get out of the boat. But Peter saw the wind and was afraid. He doubted. And what was Jesus' response? "O you of little faith, why did you doubt?" (Matt. 14:31). Doubt was not the friend of Peter's faith but its enemy. Jesus did not applaud Peter for his struggle to believe, but rebuked him for his doubt and lack of faith, for his uncertainty.

Perhaps in some churches, people need room to question without fear of disapproval. Perhaps some Christians need permission to think again. But being tossed to and fro by the waves and carried about by every wind of doctrine is not the goal. Perhaps some of us on the journey need to be reminded of the destination, that we are moving toward a place where the faith will become sight.

And until we reach that destination, let us rest confidently in the certain truth that God is knowable and can make Himself and His ways known. Maybe Lloyd-Jones—in his typical Welsh, Calvinist, authoritarian, overstated way—was on to something. "Come to the Word of God," he says. "Stop asking questions. Start with the promises in their right order. Say: 'I want the truth whatever it costs me.' Bind yourself to it, submit yourself to it, come in utter submission as a little child and plead with Him to give you a clear sign, perfect vision, and to make you whole. . . . We are not meant to be left in a state of doubt and misgiving, of uncertainty and unhappiness."[50]

Notes

1. Spencer Burke with Colleen Pepper, *Making Sense of the Church* (Grand Rapids: Zondervan, 2003), 45.
2. Dave Tomlinson, *The Post-Evangelical* (Grand Rapids: Zondervan, 2003), 138.
3. Peter Rollins, *How (Not) to Speak of God* (Brewster, Mass.: Paraclete, 2006), 6.
4. Rob Bell, *Velvet Elvis* (Grand Rapids: Zondervan, 2005), 27.
5. David F. Wells, *Above All Earthly Pow'rs* (Grand Rapids: Eerdmans, 2005), 122 (emphasis original).
6. Doug Pagitt and the Solomon's Porch Community, *Reimagining Spiritual Formation* (Grand Rapids: Zondervan, 2004), 23–24.
7. Brian D. McLaren and Tony Campolo, *Adventures in Missing the Point* (Grand Rapids: Zondervan, 2003), 43.
8. Quoted in *The Church in Emerging Culture*, Leonard Sweet, ed. (Grand Rapids: Zondervan, 2003), 249.
9. Donald Miller, *Blue Like Jazz* (Nashville: Nelson, 2003), 103.
10. D. A. Carson, *The Gagging of God* (Grand Rapids: Zondervan, 1996).
11. Tomlinson, *The Post-Evangelical*, 113–14.
12. Bell, *Velvet Elvis*, 23.
13. Doug Pagitt, as quoted in Tomlinson, *The Post-Evangelical*, 85.
14. Miller, *Blue Like Jazz*, 57.
15. Bell, *Velvet Elvis*, 32–33 (emphasis in original).
16. See D. A. Carson, *Becoming Conversant with the Emerging Church* (Grand Rapids: Zondervan, 2005), 188ff., where he lists page after page of biblical passages where we are said to *know* things with certainty.
17. Doug Pagitt remarks, "To be honest, I am not sure how useful this sense of mystery is. I am not saying Dan [Kimball] is dishonest, not at all. I am suggesting that at times, there is a bit of word play going on that allows Dan to simultaneously believe (with full assurance of authority) but not have to be responsible for that belief"; in Robert Webber, ed., *Listening to the Beliefs of Emerging Churches* (Grand Rapids: Zondervan, 2007), 112–13.
18. G. K. Chesterton, *The Everlasting Man* (San Francisco: Ignatius Press, 1925), 231.
19. Steve Chalke and Alan Mann, *The Lost Message of Jesus* (Grand Rapids: Zondervan, 2003), 18–19.
20. McLaren and Campolo, *Adventures in Missing the Point*, 84.
21. John Calvin, *Institutes of the Christian Religion* (Louisville: Westminster John Knox, 1960), III.ii.39.
22. G. K. Chesterton, *Orthodoxy* (New York: Doubleday, 1959), 27–28.
23. Stanley J. Grenz and John R. Franke, *Beyond Foundationalism: Shaping Theology in a Postmodern Context* (Louisville: Westminster John Knox, 2001), 30.
24. Carson, *Becoming Conversant*, 119.
25. Brian McLaren, *The Secret Message of Jesus* (Nashville: Nelson, 2006), 7.
26. http://blog.christianitytoday.com/outofur/archives/2006/01/brian_mclaren_o_3.html
27. Brian McLaren, *A Generous Orthodoxy* (Grand Rapids: Zondervan, 2004), 38.
28. Ibid., 43.
29. Ibid., 42.
30. McLaren, *The Secret Message of Jesus*, 210–11.
31. Bell, *Velvet Elvis*, 46.

32. Ibid., 64–65.
33. "Brian McLaren on the Homosexual Question," January 23, 2006; in "Out of Ur," a *Leadership Journal* blog, at http://blog.christianitytoday.com/outofur/archives/2006/01/brian_mclaren_o.html
34. Ibid.
35. "Brian McLaren on the Homosexual Question 4: McLaren's Response," January 30, 2006, in "Out of Ur," a *Leadership Journal* blog, at http://blog.christianitytoday.com/outofur/archives/2006/01/brian_mclaren_3.html
36. Chalke and Mann, *The Lost Message of Jesus*, 94.
37. Webber, *Listening to the Beliefs*, 140.
38. "Rob Bell Hits Lexington and a Packed-Out House," February 15, 2007, http://benwitherington.blogspot.com
39. http://blog.christianitytoday.com/outofur/archives/2006/01/brian_mclaren_o.html
40. Thomas C. Oden, *Turning Around the Mainline* (Grand Rapids: Baker, 2006), 64, 67.
41. It's no secret that the global South, especially African leaders in the Anglican church, have responded in dismay over the confirmation of Gene Robinson by the Episcopal Church USA (ECUSA is the Anglican branch in America) as the first actively gay bishop. For example, Akinola concluded his statement: "A clear choice has been made for a church that exists primarily in allegiance to the unbiblical departures and waywardness of our generation; a Church that enthrones the will of men over and above the authority of God and His revealed and written Word. Such a church is bound to become a shrine for the worship of men rather than God" (http://www.ekk.org/articles.php?id=12&page=8). Nkoyoyo's words were even stronger. When the ECUSA wanted to send a delegation to Uganda in order to offer financial assistance to the people, the Archbishop explained why he could not accept such a delegation. "If we fall silent about what you have done—promoting unbiblical sexual immorality—and we overturn or ignore the decision to declare a severing of relationship with ECUSA, poor displaced persons will receive aid. Here is our response: The gospel of Jesus Christ is not for sale, even among the poorest of us who have no money. Eternal life, obedience to Jesus Christ, and conforming to his Word are more important. The Word of God is clear that you have chosen a course of separation that leads to spiritual destruction. Because we love you, we cannot let that go unanswered. . . . As a result, any delegation you send cannot be welcomed, received, or seated. Neither can we share fellowship nor even receive desperately needed resources. If, however, you repent and return to the Lord, it would be an occasion of great joy."
42. D. Martyn Lloyd-Jones, *Spiritual Depression* (Grand Rapids: Eerdmans, 1965), 44.
43. McLaren and Campolo, *Adventures in Missing the Point*, 243ff.
44. Ibid., 251.
45. Rollins, *How (Not) to Speak of God*, 33.
46. Tomlinson, *The Post-Evangelical*, 25–26.
47. Ibid., 103.
48. Dwight J. Friesen in *An Emergent Manifesto of Hope*, Doug Pagitt and Tony Jones, eds. (Grand Rapids: Baker, 2007), 211.
49. Tomlinson in *An Emergent Manifesto*, Pagitt and Jones, eds., 88.
50. Lloyd-Jones, *Spiritual Depression*, 48.

"Find the father."

— **NICHOLAS RAY,** *director of* Rebel Without a Cause, *when asked the point of the film*

CHAPTER 2

REBEL WITHOUT A CAUSE:
WHAT IS WORTH SUBMITTING TO?

IT'S ONE OF THOSE idyllic, northern Michigan summer afternoons where the lake is bluer, the grilled whitefish is whiter, and the beautiful people are even more beautiful than they normally are. My wife and I are spending a few days at a lavish cottage with some of her extended family, where everyone is complaining about not sleeping well. Perhaps we didn't sleep well because we didn't do anything to get tired the night before. Leisure can be a very stressful thing.

There is the usual smattering of Christian books on various end tables and deck chairs—topics like "A Christian Woman and Her Pain," "Praying through the Hard Times," "What Would Jesus Eat," etc. It's a good illustration of what we do up here—we sit, we read, we worry, we eat.

TOUCHING VELVET

This is the setting in which I am reading *Velvet Elvis*, by Rob Bell, for the first time. It's part of a little informal research I am doing on the emergent church. I certainly haven't read everything the movement has produced, because to do so might take forever. The brown, hand-woven Central American canvas deck chair ($88, Pottery Barn) creaks every so slightly under my weight as I sit down with the book. With its art-decoish cover and orange-rimmed pages, *Velvet* has the look and feel of a hard-copy blog.

Bell's image half-smiles at me from the back cover. He has the requisite black-framed glasses that everyone our age who considers himself learned has these days. I have them too.

Rob Bell tells me to wrestle with the book—more than 200,000 readers have—and he gives the usual emergent disclaimer on page 87: "Just because I'm a Christian and I'm trying to articulate a Christian worldview doesn't mean I've got it nailed. I'm contributing to a discussion." The discussion costs $19.99—a little steep for a good, frugal (read: cheap), Michigan-based reformer—and is filed under the category "religion/practical life/general."

I also learned online that Bell has just embarked on a Zondervan-sponsored speaking tour called "Everything Is Spiritual," which makes me even more interested in reading what he has to say here. Most of the tour stops—hip theatres in college towns and small cities—are already sold out. Who would have thought spirituality would be the toughest ticket in town?

My first impression of the book is that it has lots of white space. It's kind of like reading a list of bullet points regarding what Bell finds interesting at the time. He compares the Christian life to a velvet Elvis painting in his basement. And a trampoline. He says that like artists, we need to be constantly "repainting" the faith (theology, etc.) to keep time with a changing culture.

He describes starting a church with no vision statement and no goals that now numbers in the ten thousands, so he must be doing something right, I guess. The new church meets in an old mall, and doesn't look like a church.

This is a good time to interject that I feel that I understand, in some sense, why Rob Bell wrote this book and with reservations salute him for doing so.

Living in Michigan is perhaps the only way one can understand the culture in West Michigan, which is where Rob lives and ministers. To say that it is "conservative" and "steeped in tradition" would be an understatement. It has been called "stifling." While there are a great many wonderful Christian families there, there is also a lot of what I would call pressure to fit in.

There are seven chapters in the book—the biblical number for completeness. A nice touch. They have ambiguously intriguing titles like "Jump," "Yoke," "True," "Tassels," "Dust," "New," and "Good."

The main theme, if I can pick one out already, is that we need to question everything. Spirituality is everywhere. Mystery is good.

My wife's extended family, who knew Rob's family when they both shared a suburb of Lansing, Michigan, is surprisingly unaware of the book, save for my brother-in-law, who catches me reading it on the deck.

"Do you feel spiritually refreshed and nonconformist?" he asks, picking it up and turning it over in his hands.

I feel the need, now, to come up with something really clever. Ryan is in his late twenties and has just spent the last four years in Panama working with poor indigenous peoples and generally doing the work that people like Rob Bell and myself write about doing. And he is a really smart guy. He's not "emergent" per se, but I'm feeling like one of the hallmarks of the movement is that being thought of as a Really Smart Guy is very important. And one of the tenets of being a Really Smart Guy is questioning everything.

"As nonconformist as I felt when I wasn't conforming to the last thing," I reply. Weak.

REBELS IN THE CHURCHES

I love James Dean, the actor. I think *East of Eden, Rebel Without a Cause,* and *Giant* are among the best films ever made. I love the fact that he is from Fairmount, Indiana, which is just a few miles down the road from where I grew up in Hartford City. I love the fact that we both come from the middle of nowhere. In central Indiana one can stop at a gas station anywhere along Interstate 69 and pick up James Dean memorabilia (along with fireworks, any time of the year—weird). Usually the T-shirts involve a cheesy silk screen of Dean pursing his lips and looking pensive, with the word "Rebel" screened underneath it.

Dean the 1950s rebel. Not much has changed. Today our economy turns on rebellion. Watch television at any time of the day and you'll learn that the can of Coke you're drinking is more than a can of Coke—it's a way to distance your-self from the masses. A way to communicate the fact that Nobody Keeps You Down. Nobody tells you what to do because, friend, you're unique and special. In spite of your khakis and polo shirt, gray cubicle, and Ford Taurus, you are a spicy, flavorful, expressive human being with lithe hips and lots of feelings.

You'll also learn that rebellion is sexy. It's a thrill to turn your 2007 Jeep Grand Cherokee with the leather package off the beaten path and into a mud-filled valley, while the buxom brunette with the Nalgene bottle in the passen-ger's seat bleats her excitement.

I see the marketing of churches in much the same way.

In the 1980s we became disillusioned with organs, pews, and little old ladies, so we built churches with stadium seating that looked like small arenas, put together praise bands that looked like Barbie and Ken, and sold millions of books. We made Christian superstars out of people who claimed to be able to "do it better." And may have reached lots of people with the gospel. (That's the good part.)

In the early 2000s the offspring of the 80s generation got disillusioned with their dads' arenas (where you can get a Christian haircut, a Christian oil change, and buy Christian clothes) and started blogging about their feelings. Let's meet on a beach (nothing wrong with that), let's meet in an empty ware-house with exposed brick and ductwork (nothing wrong with that either), and let's start a movement that won't have any leaders and that we won't actually call a movement. Instead of pastors we might have discussion leaders and worship gathering facilitators. Because non-movements are the new movements. Tell your neighbor. And then they also sold millions of books, but the books were about things like the spiritual journeys of Bono and Bob Dylan. Christianity was getting hip.

TED THE REBEL

In 2002 I was at the height of my personal "church is irrelevant" rebellion phase. My wife and I had just gone to Little Rock, Arkansas, for her high school reunion, and visited a church there that used to be her church, years ago, as a kid. Now, in the new millennium, this place had put the "glitz" in "glitzy." You could get everything there. Gourmet coffee. CDs. An array of books. There was a climbing wall for the teens. Beepers for the parents of young children. Lots of Cadillacs and Benzes in the parking lot, and a sermon on reaching your potential after a fabulous performance by an all-white praise band in matching polos. Their smiles were blinding. It was all so fabulous that I almost got sick to my stomach.

And nobody said hello.

So on the flight back I wrote a short film (fifteen minutes) called *Behind the Praise Band: Manna from Heaven* that got made and, truth be told, was probably a little irreverent. It was made by other disillusioned twentysomethings like me who all thought they were hilarious and all thought they were sticking it to the man. It showed at a couple of film festivals, and we got fifty copies of *Manna* printed on DVD, with slick packages and everything. Forty-eight of those copies are still in my basement.[1]

I was done with conventional church, and done with what I perceived as a bunch of middle-class Christian whites who didn't care about social justice and just wanted health, wealth, and prosperity. But I didn't yet know anything about the emergent church movement (namely because I didn't live in Portland, Oregon, or Minneapolis, Minnesota); instead, I was challenged by someone who communicated that no church is perfect, that we will find ourselves at church with people who don't look, act, and think like us, that we need, at some point, to commit ourselves to a body. Actually the challenges came from a number of someones—people who knew my critiques, respected them, and still challenged me to dig into theology, learn what I believed, and hang my hat in a camp—theirs.

I think, in general, it's easier to be against something than stand for something. For years, I knew I was against evangelical cheesiness—I was the first guy to rant about Christian music, the shallow books, and megachurches—but I didn't have a clue what I was for. After going to a Christian college, it seemed as if it was almost a requirement, when meeting with college friends, to serve alcohol (note: I have no problem with this), talk about how newly open-minded we were, and how oppressive our school had been. Shock value was king. It was almost an unspoken race to see who could shock who the most. Questions were the new answers.

And I think that rebellion starts from the top down—that it's much easier to get traction for a movement when there's an easily vilifiable figure in the Oval Office. During the Clinton regime the religious right bandwagon was never fuller, as some Christians concluded that they had to lock up their wives and daughters and protect the homestead from a morally bankrupt Prez. That if we didn't Do Something, by the end of Clinton's presidency people were going to be fornicating (or worse yet, dancing) in the streets of Grand Rapids and Wheaton. It was heady stuff.

Now it is President Bush who is feeding the beast, as emergent types blog about social justice, Bush's perceived lack of concern for the poor, the arts, and the English language, and his perceived desire to bomb the daylights out of any country without a state named Texas. The anti-Bush bandwagon is a sexy sell, inhabited by Hollywood stars, college professors, and the coolest guy and girl on your campus. This, also, is heady stuff.

DOING CHURCH DIFFERENTLY

During my "church is shallow" phase I was approached by a great guy with a plan. What if we did church differently? What if we let the artists in our congregation be artists? What if we lit candles and embraced the mystery of our faith? He outlined a worship service that would include projected images, sofas, performance art, and new teaching that was more like a discussion group than one guy on a dais "preaching." I would be hard-pressed to find anything our generation hates more than "preaching." When talking about our faith we're careful to not sound "preachy." The word carries great baggage. It is especially important, too, to lead us to believe that we've figured something out on our own, rather than telling us anything.

"Nobody Is Going to Tell Me What to Do" could well be the motto of my generation. Thus, the logic goes, it's hard to file into a pew and listen to someone teach.

The approach was interesting. And truth be told, I was more interested in supporting the guy than his ideas—because I loved the guy, but the ideas I wasn't crazy about. At my essence, I am pretty stodgy when it comes to worship.

So we ended up taking lunch meetings in a greasy spoon pizza place in East Lansing. Him trying to sell me on the emergent plan. Me wondering if I should climb aboard, while also wondering if it would hurt our friendship to decline. We were two hip guys ready to leave a bunch of lame suckers behind. We'll have church at home and discuss books and movies. I like books and movies. Hey, I made a movie. This is making sense. We'll repaint Christianity in a light that will make it appeal to postmoderns.

For a while it was just us in the pizza joint, and then we were joined by a couple of other guys who were disillusioned with our church. They were both older, in their late thirties, and were intrigued by the emergent ideal. Books were passed around, highlighted, and dog-eared. We read *A New Kind of Christian* as well as Dan Kimball's *Emergent Worship*. "Who are we to think we know what the Bible is trying to say?" insisted one of the new guys. "It was put together and interpreted by men over the years, so how can we fully trust it?" Diagrams were drawn about how the world was out here. (Don't diagrams seem awfully "modern" and therefore bad?) Meanwhile, we were in here, in our church bubble with bad carpet, bad coffee, and lots of dogma. There were discussions about how church shouldn't be about the building, and how worship should and could take place in people's homes, in coffee shops, and in pubs.

There was a real "saving the world" quality about the whole thing. A real sense that we had it figured out and the rest of the evangelical world was mired in modernism and all of its heavy-handed, un-mysterious trappings.

But then a funny thing happened. It didn't take. I thought *A New Kind of Christian* was an entertaining read, and enjoyed McLaren's account of Pastor Dan Poole making his first black friend, but ultimately was uncomfortable with some of the liberties he took with Scripture. And while I enjoy watching (and making) movies very much, I couldn't accept them as a part of worship.

As I entered my thirties and adopted a child, rebellion and starting a movement that would take people away from my church seemed less and less plausible for me. I was really enjoying my church and the friendships I'd made there with people who weren't like me—people who were older and sat in cubicles for a living, people who knew nothing about movies, and people with or without advanced college degrees. I felt as if there was real diversity there—a diversity that I would miss if I started meeting with other white, college-educated artsy types at a coffee-shop church. And even though we were in the midst of a pastoral search, I trusted our search committee to make a wise decision that was in accordance with what we believed as a church.

There were logistical reasons as well, like what to do with our three-year-old while I was sipping a latte and trying to have church in a coffee shop. The fact that I don't like finger-painting in front of people. And as terrible as it felt, I had to tell my friend that I wouldn't be able to join him in his journey. It felt terrible because I love and respect this guy, and know that whatever he's involved in will be thoughtful, reasoned, and probably successful.

As it turned out, I wasn't as rebellious as I thought I was.

= = = =

There is a great scene in *Rebel Without a Cause* where Jim Stark (Dean) comes home from a knife fight to find his father clad in an apron and cleaning up after a spill upstairs. "I bet you thought I was Mom," he says, as the Dean character approaches him on the landing. Dean has been cut on the torso and is bleeding a little bit, and his dad, Frank (still wearing the apron, and portrayed brilliantly by Jim Backus who later played Thurston Howell on *Gilligan's Island*), is having a meltdown about the whole thing.

Jim (the James Dean character) is explaining why he needs to go back out into the night, to play "Chickie"[2] with a local thug named Buzz Gunderson who challenged his manhood earlier in the film. Stark is a new kid in town and is having trouble fitting in. We get the idea that his family moves around a lot, and whenever there is trouble they just bolt to a new town where Jim (despite being ridiculously good-looking) has trouble making friends. We also get the idea that Jim isn't really a bad kid who loves chaos; rather, he just wants his dad to understand him and his needs to prove himself. But Jim is finding it hard to believe in a father who wears an apron and who seems to be completely "whipped" by his domineering mother.

"I wouldn't make a hasty decision," says Frank. "Nobody can make a snap decision. We've got to consider the pros and cons, make a list, get advice. . . . Have I ever stopped you from doing anything?"

As you know if you've seen the film (and if you haven't I definitely recommend it), Jim goes back out and something terrible happens. The cops get involved and there comes a point of no return for Jim, his red jacket, and the rest of the Stark family. Jim wants to go to the police station to turn himself in, while his mother wants to move again and start over. He says of his father, "He always wants to be my pal. . . . If he had guts to knock Mom cold once,[3] then maybe she'd be happy and then she'd stop picking on him. Because they make mush out of him! Just mush!"

Rather than running, Jim just wants a father who will go to the gallows with him—a father who will crucify his own need for acceptance in the community and esteem and stand up for his son. Jim doesn't want to rebel; he wants somebody worth submitting to, who makes demands on his character in the name of truth.

While years of lunchboxes, T-shirts, and other bad kitsch have made James Dean into the face of rebellion, the more I watch the film, the more I'm convinced that he is the picture of us—Christians struggling to figure out what is worth submitting to. Jim wasn't looking for a cool buddy, for a dad who would roll cigarettes up in his shirtsleeves and drive his car fast; he was looking for someone with a backbone. Someone who stood for something that was right. Someone to believe in.

And I guess that's what I was looking for in a church. I wasn't looking for the guys with the biggest projection screens, the coolest "gathering place," or the best film discussions. I was looking for a theology and a body that I could give my life to and entrust with my children. The reason I love Christianity and the Bible is that I think they are really the only things in this world that don't need to be periodically "repainted" or reframed.

= = = =

It's taken a few days of intense cottage laziness, but I am at the epilogue of *Velvet Elvis* now. In it, Bell tells a story of being in a church where a pastor makes an altar call and lies about the fact that there are hands going up all around the room when there actually aren't any. Bell talks about how crushed he was, and uses that as an illustration of the things that have been done in the name of God that God wouldn't want anything to do with. It is, in my opinion, the best writing in the book. I wish it had come earlier.

He is, in essence, saying, "Don't throw the baby out with the bathwater." Don't lump Jesus and the gospel in with the *Left Behind* movies, TBN, Joel Osteen, Joyce Meyer, or whatever else you may be using as your reason to be disillusioned with Christianity.

Bell asks me to reclaim my innocence with him, to retain my ideals and my confidence in big ideas. It's all pretty vague, but it's the kind of speech that reminds me of Jerry Maguire's "memo" in the movie *Jerry Maguire*.[4] This is the talk that you would give at the end of a conference—the kind of thing that makes people clap and fill out a card saying that, yes, they would like more information. It reaffirms my place in the center of my own universe. It's about me and my journey.

And then Bell does a funny thing—he gets modern. His last words are, "We need you to join us. It's better that way. It's what Jesus had in mind." I am taken aback by this. So much so that I put down the book and take a swim. After 177 pages of pro-questioning, he claims to know what God had in mind, and calls us to join his movement, which in ten years (when Bell would be forty-six) might very well be the establishment.

I look around me at all of the wealth here in paradise, and wonder if innocence is really possible in this place. I wonder if it's possible in my own heart and pray that it is, and that it will be so for my wife and son as well.

Being up here makes me miss my church—a place where truth is spoken, where people are diligent in prayer, and where the church, both as individuals and a collective, is about giving to the poor and meeting the needs of the oppressed both here and abroad. It's a small church that flies under the radar most of the time, but good things are happening. Things that are worth committing to. I think my church, in the broadest sense, helps people find the Father, and it is a Father who is loving and kind, but also demanding and true. The greatest version of the father that Jim Stark, Plato, and the rest of the cast of *Rebel* were looking for.

NOTES

1. Please take them off our hands. My wife would be glad to send you a copy. Or twenty. The film features the author wearing a blue nylon jumpsuit and lots of gold medallions. I play a Christian record producer with loose morals.

2. A game where two guys get into cars and drive toward a cliff—the guy who jumps out of the car first is the loser. This kind of thing, along with knife fights and rumbles, seems like it was a staple of 1950s teen dramas.

3. I'm not advocating spousal abuse here. I think Jim wanted his father to stand up to his mother, and perhaps "knocking her cold" could be taken as just disagreeing with her and sticking to his guns as the head of the household.

4. "Fewer clients, less money, more personal attention." And it's not a memo; it's a mission statement. *Jerry Maguire* is another movie you should see.

In addition to these helpful postures, we refer to the Bible as a member of our community of faith—an essential member that must be listened to on all matters on which it speaks. . . . We believe the Bible because our hopes, ideas, experiences, and community of faith allow and require us to believe.

—DOUG PAGITT, *Reimaginging Spiritual Formation*

Therefore let God-inspired Scripture decide between us; and on whichever side be found doctrines in harmony with the word of God, in favour of that side will be cast the vote of truth.

—BASIL OF CAESAREA (CA. 329–379), *Letter to Eustathius*

CHAPTER 3

BIBLE: WHY I LOVE THE PERSON AND PROPOSITIONS OF JESUS

I'VE NEVER MET a Christian who didn't like the Bible. No matter how liberal or conservative, mythical or literal, text-critical or traditional—no matter the approach, every Christian of every persuasion whom I have ever known or read has liked the Bible. And so do emerging Christians.

"I believe it [the Bible] is a gift from God," writes Brian McLaren, "inspired by God, to benefit us in the most important way possible: equipping us so that we can benefit others, so that we can play our part in the ongoing mission of God. *My regard for the Bible is higher than ever*." Elsewhere he writes, "The Bible is an inspired gift from God—a unique collection of literary artifacts that together support the telling of an amazing and essential story."[1] Similarly, Rob Bell affirms that "the Bible is the most amazing, beautiful, deep, inspired, engaging collection of writings ever."[2] Doug Pagitt calls it "a member with great sway [in our community] and participation in all our conversations."[3]

Emerging Christians dig the Scriptures.

But they also confess to having "mixed feelings" about the Bible.[4] Emergent leaders want to move away from seeing Scripture as a battleground. They don't want to use the traditional terms—*authority, infallibility, inerrancy, revelation, objective, absolute, literal*—terms they believe are unbiblical. They would rather use phrases like "deep love of" and "respect for."[5] And they bemoan the fact that evangelicals, as they see it, employ the Bible as an answer book, scouring it like a phone book or encyclopedia or legal constitution for rules, regulations, and timeless truths.

The net result is that the Bible has taken on a different role in emergent communities. The Bible is not the voice of God from heaven and certainly not the foundation (foundationalism being a whipping boy among emerging Christians of a philosophical bent). Rather, the Bible spurs us on to new ways of imagining and learning. It is "not reduced to a book from which we exact truth, but the Bible is a full, living, and active member of our community that is listened to on all topics of which it speaks."[6] The Bible, for many emerging Christians, has been rediscovered "as a human product."[7] "The Bible is still in the center for us," Bell explains, "but it's a different kind of center. We want to embrace mystery, rather than conquer it." Rob Bell's wife, Kristen, continues the train of thought. "I grew up thinking we've figured out the Bible, that we knew what it means. Now I have no idea what most of it means. And yet I feel like life is big again—like life used to be black and white, and now it's in color."[8]

During this time of reimagining the Bible, Kristen Bell credits Brian McLaren with directing their thinking on Scriptural authority. "Our lifeboat," Kristen continues, "was *A New Kind of Christian*." It's here that McLaren first introduces us to his protagonist, Neo, who helps the bewildered pastor Dan Poole discover a new kind of Christianity and a new kind of biblical authority. Neo explains, "When we let it [the Bible] go as a modern answer book, we get to rediscover it for what it really is: an ancient book of incredible spiritual value for us, a kind of universal and cosmic history, a book that tells us who we are and what story we find ourselves in so that we know what to do and how to live. That letting go is going to be hard for you evangelicals."[9] Through the lips of Neo, McLaren argues for a postmodern understanding of the Bible's role in our churches—a role that is above propositions, beyond inerrancy, and behind the text.

POOH-POOHING THE PROPOSITIONS

Few things are so universally criticized in the emerging church as propositions. For too long, emerging leaders argue, evangelicals have approached the Bible as an encyclopedia, a rule book, an answer book, a scientific text, an easy-step instruction book instead of the book that tells our family story.[10] Consequentially, we end up looking at the Bible like an Easter egg hunt looking for propositions. This ends up killing the very book that is supposed to give us life. McLaren argues, "When we theological conservatives seek to understand the Bible, we generally analyze it. We break it down into chapters, paragraphs, verses, sentences, clauses, phrases, words, prefixes, roots, suffixes, jots, and tittles. Now we understand it, we tell ourselves. Now we have conquered the text, captured the meaning, removed all mystery, stuffed it and preserved it for posterity, like a taxidermist with a deer head."[11]

There is one thing right with this statement and two things wrong. McLaren is right to criticize the impulse some of us have to dissect the Bible but not be transformed by it. That does happen. And no doubt, there are scores of freshly minted seminary-trained pastors who bore their congregations with endless word studies and the ins and outs of genitive absolutes.

But there are two things wrong with McLaren's chastisement. The first is historical. Conservative American evangelicals didn't invent parsing or versification or the minutia of exegesis. Read the early church apologists, the Latin fathers or the Greek fathers, the medieval churchmen, the Scholastics, the Reformers, the Puritans, or the Pietists and you will find Christians of all time everywhere pulling apart the words of Scripture. They are harmonizing texts, analyzing Greek and Hebrew words, and expounding on the jots and tittles of the Word of God. If evangelicals' approach to Scripture makes them biblical taxidermists, then the hall of Christian history is lined with head after head of stuffed animals, because wherever Christians have considered the words of the Bible to be the words of God, they have sought to understand those words with every exegetical tool at their disposal.

McLaren considers our love affair with finding doctrinal formulations in Scripture to be an unfortunate product of the Enlightenment. "Our sermons tended to exegete texts in such a way that stories, poetry, and biography (among other features of the Bible)—the 'chaff'—were sifted out, while the 'wheat' of doctrines and principles were saved. Modern Western people loved that approach; meanwhile, however, people of a more postmodern bent (who are more like *premodern* people in many ways) find the doctrines and principles as interesting as grass clippings."[12]

Curiously enough, Hughes Oliphant Old, whose monumental series *The Reading and Preaching of the Scriptures in the Worship of the Christian Church* now runs into the thousands of pages, frequently comes to the opposite conclusion: it's modern people who can't stomach doctrine, not the premodern. For example, in commenting on the preaching of Cyril of Alexandria (ca. 375–444), Old writes,

> No doubt there will be those who will abhor these heavily doctrinal sermons. Our day and age, still under the shadow of the Enlightenment, naively imagines that the doctrinal sermon is boring and that sermons like these must have been tedious. A less beclouded day will probably recognize this prejudice as a rather peculiar form of pietistic agnosticism. The history of preaching is filled with examples of great doctrinal preachers who drew enthusiastic, thoughtful, and, indeed, large congregations.[13]

Why can we only affirm the Bible as family story by denigrating the Bible as a book to be analyzed and theologized? Why not go the more historically responsible route and uphold the Bible as both?

The second problem with McLaren's criticism is that it reveals the broader emergent distaste for propositions. Tomlinson's sentiments are typical: "Post-evangelicals are less inclined to look for truth in propositional statements and old moral certitudes and more likely to seek it in symbols, ambiguities, and situational judgments."[14] But why pooh-pooh propositions?

A proposition is simply a statement that can be either true or false. "The lights are on." "My name is Kevin." "God is love." These are statements that we can either affirm or deny. That's the definition of a proposition. The Bible is certainly more than propositions; it has commands and questions too. But the vast majority of the Bible —whether in laws, letters, poems, or narratives—is made up of propositions. Some are doctrinal formulations ("there is no one righteous"), and others are units of a larger story ("he took his staff in hand and chose five smooth stones from the brook"). On nearly every page of Scripture we read propositional sentences. So this cannot be what emergent leaders are objecting to.

> The vast majority of the Bible—whether in laws, letters, poems, or narratives—is made up of propositions.

I trust also that they are not objecting absolutely to any kind of proposition. For a statement rejecting propositions is, in itself, a proposition, just like a statement coming out against statements of faith (as per Tony Jones) is a kind of statement of faith.

The concerns with propositions, I fear, run deeper. "Christianity is a relationship with a person, not affirming a set of propositions" is how the concern is usually voiced. Or, "We worship the Word made flesh, not the words on a page."[15] This is the emergent concern.

And it's not new. In the first half of the twentieth century there was a group of theologians who fell under the broad heading of "neoorthodox"—men like Karl Barth, Emil Brunner, Rudolf Bultmann, and H. Richard Niebuhr. They were saying things like revelation "cannot be expressed in the impersonal ways of creeds or other propositions" and "faith is not a relation to. . . a truth, or a doctrine . . . but it is wholly a personal relationship."[16] The neoorthodox theologians of the last century, in their pre-emergent way, thought God could not properly be the subject of human knowledge and that belief in doctrinal revelation eroded personal faith in Christ. In many ways, when it comes to their understanding of Scripture, emergent leaders are the new neoorthodoxy.

THREE PROPOSITIONS FROM JESUS

But the Bible forces no such distinction between faith in the Jesus revealed in the Bible and trust in the propositional statements revealed about Him. Consider a few examples from John's gospel. All three come from the lips of Jesus.

"I told you that you would die in your sins, for unless you believe that I am he you will die in your sins" (John 8:24).

Personal faith in Christ, for it to be genuine and saving, must have propositional content. We must believe that Jesus is the One ("I am he"). We must believe He is from above (8:23), the light of the world (v. 12), and sent from the Father (v. 16). We may think we have a wonderful relationship with Jesus, and we may even love Him, but unless we believe He is the Christ, the Son of God, we will not have life in His name (20:31).

"If you abide in me, and my words abide in you, ask whatever you wish, and it will be done for you" (John 15:7).

The two are put side by side—Jesus abiding in us and His words abiding in us. They are two sides of the same coin. We cannot have an abiding relationship with Jesus without having His words abide in us too. And if we allow His words—commands, sentences, and propositions—to abide in us, He will abide as well.

"But now I am coming to you, and these things I speak in the world, that they may have my joy fulfilled in themselves" (John 17:13).

Our fullness of joy is dependent on believing, embracing, and treasuring sentences that Jesus spoke. The sentences do not save us. The life, death, and resurrection of Jesus save us. But without truth-corresponding propositions like "this is eternal life, that they know you the only true God, and Jesus Christ whom you have sent" (17:3) and "I have manifested your name to the people" (v. 6) and "I am praying for them" (v. 9) and "all mine are yours, and yours are mine, and I am glorified in them" (v. 10)—without these precious theological statements communicated and understood by verbal utterances, the joy of Jesus will not be fulfilled in us.

I'm convinced that a major problem with the emerging church is that they refuse to have their cake and eat it to. The whole movement seems to be built on reductionistic, even modernistic, either-or categories. They pit information versus transformation, believing versus belonging, and propositions about Christ versus the person of Christ. The emerging church will be a helpful corrective against real, and sometimes perceived, abuses in evangelicalism when they discover the genius of the "and," and stop forcing us to accept half-truths.

> **Every word in every sentence in the Bible is inspired by God, is authoritative, trustworthy, true, useful, and aids our joy in God.**

Carl Henry is right: "The antithesis of 'person-revelation' and 'proposition-revelation' can only result in an equally unscriptural contrast of personal faith with doctrinal belief. It is now often said that belief in Christ is something wholly different from belief in truths or propositions. But to lose intelligible revelation spells inescapable loss of any supernatural authorized doctrinal assertions concerning God."[17]

It is possible for Christians to esteem the Bible wrongly and equate the Bible with God. But it is not possible for Christians to esteem the Bible too highly. Every word in every sentence in every proposition or command or question in the Bible is inspired by God, is authoritative, trustworthy, true, useful, and aids our joy in God. Despite their differing interpretations on some matters, Christians of various theological stripes in all ages have believed wholeheartedly in this previous sentence. My hope is that emerging Christians are not departing from it.

THE IRRELEVANCY OF INERRANCY

Inerrancy is the conviction that the Bible makes no mistakes. There are metaphors in the Bible, approximations, observational comments on the universe, free quotations, and various types of literature that must be read according to their own "rules," not to mention questions of application, but there are no mistakes. The Bible is true in all that it affirms. Whenever we believe the Scriptures, we believe what is true.

That, in a nutshell, is the doctrine of inerrancy—no errors. Emerging Christians have little patience for inerrancy. This doesn't mean they think the Bible is full of errors (though it could). They don't outright reject inerrancy. They just find it a waste of time. Some prefer the term *inherency* to describe the Bible instead of *inerrancy*, because the Word of God is inherent in the Bible (the implication being the Bible in itself is not the Word of God). The goal, then, is to move beyond inerrancy.[18]

Again, let's affirm that the Bible reveals God to us and that the central piece of that revelation is in the person of Jesus Christ—whom we know next to nothing about apart from the Bible. And let us go on to affirm that we want more than information about God, we want to know God Himself. But why go out of our way to go out of the way of inerrancy? The once (and briefly) credible idea that Charles Hodge and B. B. Warfield invented inerrancy has been shown to be resoundingly false. Scholars like John Woodbridge and Richard Muller have demonstrated convincingly that the doctrine of complete biblical truthfulness is not a Princetonian invention.[19] Clement of Rome (30–100) described "the Sacred Scriptures" as "the true utterance of the Holy Spirit." Polycarp (65–155) called them "the oracles of the Lord." Irenaeus (120–202) claimed that the biblical writers "were incapable of a false statement." Origen (185–254) stated, "The sacred volumes are fully inspired by the Holy Spirit, and there is no passage either in the Law or the Gospel, or the writings of an Apostle, which does not proceed from the inspired source of Divine Truth." Augustine (354–430) explained in a letter to Jerome, "I have learnt to ascribe to those Books which are of the Canonical rank, and only to them, such reverence and honour, that I firmly believe that no single error due to the author is found in any of them."[20] It was not modernism that invented inerrancy. It was modernism that undermined inerrancy.

And postmodernism is avoiding it altogether. This is a mistake. The emergent church ought to pay attention to the wisdom of J. I. Packer.

> What can we say about the Bible that we cannot say about any other book?

Once I too avoided the word *inerrancy* as much as I could, partly because of the tendencies mentioned, and partly because the word has a negative form and I like to sound positive. But I find that nowadays I need the word. Verbal currency, as we know, can be devalued. Any word may have some of its meaning rubbed off, and this has happened to all my preferred terms for stating my belief about the Bible. I hear folk declare Scripture *inspired* and in the next break say that it misleads from time to time. I hear them call it *infallible* and *authoritative*, and find they mean only that its impact on us and the commitment to which it leads us will keep us in God's grace, not that it is all true. This is not enough for me. I want to safeguard the historic evangelical meaning of these three words . . . So I assert inerrancy after all. I think this is a clarifying thing to do, since it shows what I mean when I call Scripture inspired, infallible, and authoritative. In an era of linguistic devaluation and double-talk we owe this kind of honesty to one another.[21]

It's all well and good to speak of the Bible as a wonderful, rich story, or an amazing collection of deep writings, or an honored conversation partner, or an in-living-color book that is mysteriously beyond our comprehension, but what does all of this actually mean? Is the Bible the final word in matters of faith and practice? Can it be trusted in all that it affirms? Is it intelligible and knowable? Is it from God? What is its practical authority in the believer's life? Is it ever mistaken? What can we say about the Bible that we cannot say about any other book?

The emerging church thrives on eschewing definition, of itself and of its theology. But doctrinal formulations happen for a reason. People wonder, "What do they mean by that?" And so we respond, with words, sometimes even ones that don't appear in the Bible, in order to clarify what we think the Bible says. "This is what we mean, not this."

I'm not sure what the emerging church believes about the Bible. And this concerns me. Burned-out evangelicals who go emergent and talk squishy about the Bible may still basically treat the Bible as if it were completely true and authoritative. This would be a fortuitous inconsistency. But what happens in the second generation? What happens when an erstwhile church planter with a few Neo books under his belt starts doing church with a radical skepticism about the authority of the Bible and forms a people by musing on about how his community affirms the Bible (in part?), therefore making it "welcome" in their conversation? We can wax eloquent about the beauty of the story and how the Scriptures read us, but unless people are convinced that the Bible is authoritative, true, inspired, and the very words of God, over time they will read it less frequently, know it less fully, and trust it less surely.

TEXT MESSAGING

Seventy years ago Karl Barth argued, "The Bible is God's Word to the extent that God causes it to be His Word, to the extent that He speaks through it."[22] At the time, Barth was calling liberalism back to the Word, which was a good thing, but he pioneered a new approach in establishing biblical authority, which was not as good. The Bible, according to Barth, was not in itself the Word of God, but as God spoke in and through the Bible, it became for us the Word of God.

The Bible is only "derivatively and indirectly" God's Word, he wrote.[23] The authority of the Word, therefore, resides not in the Scriptures that contain the very words of God, but in Him who speaks through the words of the text.

This neoorthodox view of Scripture is, wittingly or unwittingly, the view of many in the emerging church. Tomlinson explicitly relies on Barth, noting appreciatively that "Barth spoke of the Bible *becoming*, rather than *being*, the word of God."[24] The late Stan Grenz, one of the most influential theologians in the emerging movement, wrote, with John Franke, something similar: "As we noted earlier, it is not the Bible as a book that is authoritative, but the Bible as the instrumentality of the Spirit; the biblical message spoken by the Spirit through the text is theology's norming norm."[25] According to Grenz and Franke, the text has its own intention, which begins in the author's intended meaning but is not exhausted by it. We must start with the original meaning of the text, but we are not bound by it. For God has spoken, but He still speaks. The words of Scripture, therefore, are not the norming norm but the Spirit speaking through the Scripture becoming the Word of God.

As a result, theology, for many in the emerging church, becomes something different from speaking the truth about God as revealed in Scripture. The task of theology, in the emergent model, is to express communal beliefs and values, to set forth that community's particular "web of significance" and "matrix of meaning." Christian theology, therefore, is the task of speaking about the God known in the Christian community. The church is really the new foundation. Christian theology is done by and for the Christian community as an ongoing conversation among those who have been encountered by God in Christ and are attempting to clarify a mosaic of beliefs that comprise the interpretative framework of the community that the aforementioned encounter has called forth.[26]

Confusing, isn't it? That's actually one of the flaws of the neoorthodox/emerging view of Scripture. What does this mean for the person in the pew? When they hear Scripture, are they hearing God speak?

Might they also get the Word of God just as authoritatively somewhere else?

Does that make the Bible one of many authorities in the community?

If the "norming norm" is the Spirit speaking through the text as understood by the Christian community, is the basis for what we believe and do as Christians nothing more than what our particular community says we should believe and do? And if so, is all knowledge nothing more than a social construct rather than a reflection of reality?[27]

Does doctrine speak of what is objectively true and corresponds to reality, or does it merely set the rules of discourse and explain our belief mosaic?

> Does doctrine speak of what is objectively true and corresponds to reality, or does it merely set the rules of discourse?

Grenz and Franke are trying to answer the question, "How do we know what we know about God?" The old answer, which they find hopelessly modern, is, "We know because it's in the Bible, which is God's self-revelation in divinely inspired words." The new postmodern answer, it seems to me, is less certain and less absolute. The postmodern answer is, "We know what we know about God because it is the expression of our community's understanding of the biblical message that the Spirit is speaking through the Bible in our called-out community." We end up with functional authority for the Bible that is dependent upon the community rather than intrinsic authority that is based on God having spoken.

At first blush, it sounds like a mark of piety to make the Spirit speaking through the Word (and creation and each other and other venues perhaps) the authority rather than the text of Scripture. It always scores a rhetorical victory to accuse evangelicals of bibliolatry, of worshiping the Bible rather than the Christ of the Bible, but it almost always misses the point. Every Christian I know who believes the Bible is the Word of God worships the Christ he finds in the Bible, believes in this Christ, and prays to this Christ. These Christians also happen to believe that God not only speaks to them through the Bible, but that God's words are recorded in the text of Scripture. Isn't this what Paul meant when he called the Scriptures "the oracles of God" and breathed-out by God (Rom. 3:2; 2 Tim. 3:16)? Isn't this what Hebrews means when it quotes from the Old Testament, saying, "The Holy Spirit says" (Heb. 3:7)? Didn't Peter hold to a verbal, plenary view of inspiration when he asserted that no prophecy of Scripture came from the will of man, but men spoke from God as they were carried along by the Holy Spirit (2 Peter 1:20–21)? Didn't Jesus assume intrinsic authority in the actual texts of Scripture when He quoted Deuteronomy to the Devil in the wilderness with the words "it is written" (Matt. 4:1–11)? Wasn't Jesus trusting that the words of Scripture were the very words of God when He quoted Genesis 2:24 and assumed that words of the text were the words of the Creator (Matt. 19:4–5)?

For every fundamentalist who loves the Bible more than Christ, I'm willing to bet there are several emergent Christians who honor the Bible less than Christ did. I fear that what starts out as a fancy way of coupling postmodern jargon with biblical authority quickly leads to a loss of confidence in the Word of God—a lost confidence that prevents preachers and evangelists from establishing doctrine, ethics, and gospel truth with the words "It is written."

BEYOND FOUNDATIONALISM

All of the philosophical wrangling aside, this is all I mean, and most non-philosophers mean, by saying the Bible is our foundation.[28] We mean the Bible settles our disputes. The Bible tells us what is true. Our thinking about God, ourselves, and the Word should start with the Bible and never contradict the Bible. In that sense, what's so wrong with calling the Bible our foundation?

McLaren claims (via Neo) that what's wrong is that the Bible never speaks of itself as the foundation. In one case the church is, in the second Jesus is, and in the third Peter is, "but unless I'm mistaken, the Bible never calls itself the foundation."[29] Besides betraying the kind of biblicism McLaren elsewhere decries—can't we call the Bible the foundation without finding the word in Scripture?—the fact of the matter is the Bible is called the foundation. Or at least that's how Protestants since the Reformation have understood Ephesians 2:20. The "household of God" is "built on the foundation of the apostles and prophets," Paul writes. The Reformers understood that in one sense only Christ is the foundation (1 Cor. 3:11), but they also believed that the church is built on the once-for-all, non-repeatable foundation of the teaching of the apostles and prophets which we have preserved in sacred Scripture.[30] So yes, the Bible is the foundation of truth for the church.

A FIRM FOUNDATION?

Not only do many emergent leaders reject the Bible as the foundation of Christian theology and reflection, they are also skeptical of our ability to understand the original intent of the biblical authors. Since words are only symbols, the truth in the Bible must be seen as ambiguous and in need of constant reinterpretation.[31] The Bible is open-ended. All we can do is tell people what we think the Bible means—give them our version.[32] Somebody has to decide which Bible verses apply and which don't.[33] "The real authority does not reside in the text itself, in the ink on paper, which is always open to misinterpretation—sometimes, history tells us, horrific and dangerous misinterpretation. Instead, the real authority lies in God, who is there behind the text or beyond it or about it, right? In other words, the authority is not in what I say the text says but in what God says the text says."[34] All we have are interpretations.[35]

Of course, in one sense this is true—a truism, in fact. It's like the old preacher's joke, "Sorry to use so many personal stories about myself, but they're the only kind of stories I have about myself." As soon as we open our mouths or punch our keyboards with an original thought, we are giving our version of things. Every sermon and every commentary and every blog that has ever been written about the Bible has been an interpretation of sorts. And sometimes those interpretations are wrong or tentative. Occasionally in my preaching I will admit, "I'm not exactly sure what this means, but I think this is the best option." Postmodernism, if it has done nothing else good (and it has), has reminded us of our own finitude. But does this mean we are left with a Bible that is completely open-ended, practically unknowable, and subject to constant change?[36]

Obviously, my answer is no. In his classic work defending authorial intent in the text, E. D. Hirsch points out, "Certainty is not the same thing as validity, and knowledge of ambiguity is not necessarily ambiguous knowledge."[37] In other words, just because you are sure about something doesn't make you right, and just because you know you could be wrong doesn't mean you are. To be sure, words and sentences and paragraphs are sometimes ambiguous and open to different understandings, which is why humans disagree on so many things (although words are still the most precise means of communicating ideas that we have). But this doesn't mean that one understanding is not the right one or at least better than the others. Nor does this mean that we can't plausibly determine which is the correct understanding, even if we can't determine the meaning of a text with complete omniscience.

FINDING THE RIGHT AND WRONG MEANINGS

So for emergent leaders to keep mentioning slavery and all the things Christians have gotten wrong from the Bible is self-defeating. They are demonstrating their belief that texts have meaning and that they have determined what is that correct meaning (namely, that slavery is wrong). Unless we are God, we must always hold out the possibility that we have understood something incorrectly. Christians have misread the Bible before, and we'll do it again, I'm afraid. But that doesn't mean we can't hold on with firmness to biblical truth, nor even that we can't consider some matters of interpretation settled. The biblical authors were humans who grew and changed and learned, and yet they didn't hesitate to write about what they *knew* and were *convinced of*.

Emergent authors are really no different. They still write books. They still use language to communicate ideas and trust implicitly that the people reading their books and blogs will understand what they mean to say. McLaren has uncovered "the secret message of Jesus," and Chalke has found "the lost message of Jesus," so these guys must be figuring something out from the Bible. When McLaren wants to make a point about creation, he argues that we need to read the story as a Jew, not a Greek—that's the right way to read the text.[38] When Bell reads "I am the way, the truth, and the life," he knows that Jesus was not making claims about one religion being better than others; He was just showing the best possible way for a person to live.[39] So there are still right and wrong meanings from the text. It seems that when emergent authors want to contest traditional beliefs (in, say, hell, exclusivism, and propitiation) they cry, "All we have are interpretations," but when they want to make their points (say, about hell as a metaphor, inclusivism, and kingdom living) they argue, "You've been misreading the Bible, can't you see?" It seems there is a meaning in the text after all.

TRUTH IN MEANINGFUL WORDS

The heart of the matter is this: Does the God who created us also know how to speak to us? Is He able to communicate truth to us through words in a way that is meaningful and understandable? The answer assumed on every page of Scripture is "yes." God spoke to patriarchs, prophets, and priests, and when the words God spoke were written down, the people treated those words as the sacred oracles of God. When the people were taught the meaning in those inspired texts (and they obeyed), there was rejoicing (Neh. 8:1–12). When no one instructed them from those words, the people suffered (2 Chron. 15:3). At one point this written revelation was called the Law, then the Law and the Prophets; then the Gospels were added, and then the Epistles, until we finally have what we call the Bible.

At each of those stages what was written was considered by God's people to be authoritative and demanding of our obedience, because the words written down came from the very mouth of God.

Isn't it strange, C. S. Lewis wondered, that the Law would be the Psalmist's delight (Ps. 1:2)? Respect or reverence we might understand, but delight? Who delights in law? And why? Lewis explains: "Their delight in the Law, is a delight in having touched firmness; like the pedestrian's delight in feeling the hard road beneath his feet after a false short cut has long entangled him in muddy fields."[40]

In our world of perpetual squishitude, why offer people more of what they already have—vague spirituality, uncertainty, and borderline interpretative relativism? Why not offer them something hard and old like the Law in which we delight, and dare to say and believe "Thus saith the Lord"?

NOTES

1. Brian McLaren, *A Generous Orthodoxy* (Grand Rapids: Zondervan, 2004), 177; Brian D. McLaren and Tony Campolo, *Adventures in Missing the Point* (Grand Rapids: Zondervan, 2003), 75.
2. Rob Bell, *Velvet Elvis* (Grand Rapids: Zondervan, 2005), 42.
3. Dave Tomlinson, *The Post-Evangelical* (Grand Rapids: Zondervan, 2003), 114.
4. Ibid., 107.
5. Ibid., 74.
6. Doug Pagitt, *Reimagining Spiritual Formation* (Grand Rapids: Zondervan, 2004), 32.
7. Rob Bell quoted in *Christianity Today*, "The Emergent Mystique," November 2004, 38.
8. Ibid.
9. See Brian D. McLaren, *A New Kind of Christian* (San Francisco: Jossey-Bass, 2001), 52.
10. Ibid.
11. McLaren and Campolo, *Adventures in Missing the Point*, 79.
12. Ibid., 77.
13. Hughes Oliphant Old, *The Reading and Preaching of the Scriptures in the Worship of the Christian Church*, vol. 2 (Grand Rapids: Eerdmans, 1998), 119.
14. Tomlinson, *The Post-Evangelical*, 94. Mark Galli, who writes one of the sidebars for the book, makes the point that post-evangelicals like Tomlinson are "less inclined to look for truth in propositional statements and old moral certitudes," and then Galli adds, "except when making statements like this!"
15. For example, Sally Morgenthaler (in *Exploring the Worship Spectrum: 6 Views* (Grand Rapids: Zondervan, 2004, 224), in arguing for "knowing-by-narrative" instead of "knowing-by-notion," says, "And in entering the drama of their stories, we engage with the person of God, not just the principles of God."
16. Niebuhr and Brunner, respectively, quoted in Carl F. H. Henry, *God, Revelation and Authority* (Wheaton, Ill.: Crossway, 1979), 3:431, 436.

17. Ibid., 436. From the Roman Catholic side, Avery Cardinal Dulles ("The Orthodox Imperative," *First Things* [August/September 2006], 33) sounds the same note. "The Scriptures and the creeds testify to certain essential facts: that Jesus was born of the Virgin Mary, that he suffered under Pontius Pilate, rose from the dead, and sent the Holy Spirit upon the community of believers. These and other events, committed to language, belong to the Christian creeds and are inseparable from the Christian faith. A non-propositional understanding of revelation contradicts the tenor of Holy Scripture and the earliest confessions of faith, which describe particular historical events of crucial importance for faith. "

18. See Carl Raschke, *The Next Reformation: Why Evangelicals Must Embrace Postmodernity* (Grand Rapids: Baker Academic, 2004), 115–143.

19. See John Woodbridge, *Biblical Authority* (Grand Rapids: Zondervan, 1982); Richard Muller, *Holy Scripture: The Cognitive Foundation of Theology, Post-Reformation Reformed Dogmatics,* vol. 2 (Grand Rapids: Baker, 1993).

20. The string of quotations come from Carl F. H. Henry, *God, Revelation and Authority*, vol. 4 (Wheaton, Ill.: Crossway, 1979), 368ff.

21. J. I. Packer, *Truth & Power* (Wheaton, Ill.: Shaw, 1993), 50–51.

22. Karl Barth, *Church Dogmatics* (Edinburgh: T&T Clark, 1975), I.1.109.

23. Ibid., 117.

24. Tomlinson, *The Post-Evangelical*, 113.

25. Stanley J. Grenz and John R. Franke, *Beyond Foundationalism* (Louisville: Westminster John Knox, 2007), 69.

26. Ibid., 232–33. For a critique of Grenz and the "postconservative" school of theologians and philosophers, see *Reclaiming the Center: Confronting Evangelical Accommodation in Postmodern Times*, Millard J. Erickson, Paul Kjoss, and Justin Taylor, eds. (Wheaton, Ill: Crossway, 2004), especially D. A. Carson's essay "Domesticating the Gospel: A Review of Grenz's *Renewing the Center*" (33–58).

27. Carson, "Domesticating the Gospel," 51.

28. *Foundationalism* is an epistemological term that philosophers and theologians use to describe how we know what we know. Postmoderns reject foundationalism, while conservative evangelicals tend to be comfortable with a modest foundationalism. The technical use of the term is not necessary for this discussion.

29. Brian D. McLaren, *A New Kind of Christian* (San Francisco: Jossey-Bass, 2001), 53.

30. As D. A. Carson has pointed out, emerging church leaders, unlike the Reformers, are calling for change because the culture has moved. The Reformers, by contrast, were calling for change because the church had moved away from the Bible. "Reformed and always reforming" was not a motto giving license for continual doctrinal innovation, which is how I've heard *semper reformada* used a hundred times. It was a rallying cry to keep going back to the Scriptures so that by them the church may be reformed and always reforming.

31. Tomlinson, *The Post-Evangelical*, 115.

32. Bell, *Velvet Elvis*, 46, 55.

33. Ibid., 58.

34. McLaren, *A New Kind of Christian*, 50.

35. According to Bell, nobody really gives you the Bible straight. They just tell you what they think it means (54). At times, Bell seems to be simply advocating some interpretive humility. At other times he makes the whole process of discerning biblical truth sound willy-nilly and downright impossible. "Somebody in your history decided certain Bible verses still

apply and others don't" (56). Scripture alone sounds nice, "but it is not true" (67). Bell's reason for rejecting *sola scriptura*? The fact that "we got the Bible from the church voting on what the Bible even is . . ." In one sentence Bell brushes aside centuries of the Protestant understanding of the canon—the church did not vote on the books of the Bible, but it recognized the authority these books already possessed in the churches by virtue of apostolic authorship or connection.

36. For example, McLaren argues that the Bible is so rich and multilayered that new resources are constantly drawn out, "so that the message itself changes because the message changes its context, which is to say that the message itself changes by addressing new situations and problems and opportunities in new ways"; McLaren, *The Church in Emerging Culture*, Leonard Sweet, ed. (Grand Rapids: Zondervan, 2003), 210. Therefore, it's an insult to the riches and depths of the gospel to say that it cannot change. But as Horton points out in the same book, is there no catholicity? Does *multilayered* have to mean multiple or changing message?

37. E. D. Hirsch, *Validity in Interpretation* (New Haven: Yale, 1967), ix.

38. Brian D. McLaren, *The Story We Find Ourselves In* (San Francisco: Jossey-Bass, 2003), 52.

39. Bell, *Velvet Elvis*, 21.

40. C. S. Lewis, *Reflections on the Psalms* (Glasgow: Collins, 1961), 55.

That's the beauty of argument—if you argue correctly, you're never wrong.

—NICK NAYLOR, *protagonist of* Thank You for Smoking[1]

CHAPTER 4

THANK YOU FOR SMOKING: ON DIALOGUE, FUTURISM, AND HELL

DOES IT MAKE ME less intelligent to admit that the pictures are my favorite part? I'm reading another emergent book, *The Church in Emerging Culture: Five Perspectives*, edited by Leonard Sweet, which is set up as a discussion among a handful of Christian heavyweights, supposedly spanning the emergent spectrum. And I'm finding myself oddly distracted by how people look. The book is interspersed with black and whites of the group sitting around a living room, gesturing wildly with manuscript pages and takeout coffee cups littering the table. They are shots that seem to say: "This is a vibrant discussion between the cutting-edge intellectual minds of our day. Don't you wish you were here?"

I almost put the book down for good after reading Len Sweet's intros of each of the speakers, as he made them all sound like intellectual demigods. I felt that if, somehow, Christ failed to redeem the culture, the world was safe in the hands of (in no particular order) Frederica Matthewes-Green, Erwin

Raphael McManus, Brian McLaren, Michael Horton, and Andy Crouch.

I don't know what I'm expecting, but for whatever reason, they don't look the part. I think I was expecting aging hipsters[2] with soul patches and graying ponytails, and—with the exception of Len Sweet's sort of tweed sports-jacket, college-professor vibe—they all, despite their own descriptions, look pretty ordinary. I'm learning that for a movement that supposedly hates being put "in a box" and being tied down to modern descriptives, each of their Web sites provides much of the same. Sweet's describes himself as a "theologian, author and futurist." McManus describes himself as a "husband, father, writer, futurist, activist, artist, consultant and spiritual and cultural leader." Not too shabby. Brian McLaren, according to his Web site, is an "author, speaker, networker, and Christian Activist."

Matthewes-Green, refreshingly, doesn't have a Web site (at least that I can find) and looks remarkably non-NPRish—like someone who might live in my hometown, immediately predisposing me to liking her (I also liked her chapter, but more on that later). Michael Horton, I think, is the token conservative and, I suppose, looks like what you might envision the token conservative looking like.

McManus recently wrote a book called *The Barbarian Way* in which one of the main points is that "the greatest enemy to the movement of Jesus Christ is Christianity,"[3] a sentiment I've also seen ascribed to Bono, before it became the exclusive territory of billboards, bumper stickers (seen often with "God is not a Republican"), and other leaders in the emergent movement. According to the book's back flap, McManus partners "with a team of dreamers and innovators who specialize in the field of developing and unleashing personal and organizational creativity." Though McManus doesn't consider himself emergent, and explained as much in one of his books.

WHAT'S A FUTURIST?

While I had heard of the term *futurist* I, admittedly, didn't know much about it.[4] According to three minutes of research on that great postmodern mash-up of information, Wikipedia, "*Futurism* was a 20th century art movement," not to be confused with Futurist–trend watching. . . . The Italian painter and sculptor Umberto Boccioni (1882–1916) wrote the *Manifesto of Futurist Painters* in 1910 in which he vowed:

> We will fight with all our might the fanatical, senseless and snobbish religion of the past, a religion encouraged by the vicious existence of museums. We rebel against that spineless worshipping of old canvases, old statues and old bric-a-brac, against everything which is filthy and worm-ridden and corroded by time. We consider the habitual contempt for everything which is young, new and burning with life to be unjust and even criminal. [5]

Futurists dubbed the love of the past "pastism," and its proponents "pastists" (*cf.* Stuckism, a recent art movement also catalogued on Wikipedia). They would sometimes even physically attack alleged pastists, in other words, those who were apparently not enjoying futurist exhibitions or performances. Not that Len Sweet is going to attack any of us with a lemon scone anytime soon.

Regarding futurists (also from Wikipedia):

> *Futurists* is a term often used to describe management consultants who advise corporations on a wide range of global trends, risk management and potential market opportunities. In some countries the equivalent word used is *futurologist*.
>
> A key element of all management is being able to anticipate what competitors, employees and customers are likely to do next, in the context of a rapidly changing wider world. Thus it is true that to some extent all effective leaders are futurists.[6]

A quick Google search of "futurist" revealed a guy named David Zach who is available to speak to your corporation about the future; another guy, Glen Hiemstra, who wrote a book called *Turning the Future into Revenue;* and a Libertarian Futurist Society promoting Libertarian Science Fiction (where, ostensibly, all of the aliens make lots of money in entrepreneurial ventures, pay no income taxes, and also grow their own pot). There was nothing mentioned about religion whatsoever.

DRIVING MR. D. A. ISY

I am sitting in my Toyota Echo with D.A. Carson, author of over forty-five books and professor of theology at Trinity Evangelical Divinity School. Carson is in town to present a weekend's worth of talks on "postmodernism," and I am hearing him tell me, with a slightly British accent that makes him sound even more intelligent, that he is already sick of talking about postmodernism and the emergent movement.

Carson looks and sounds the part of the old-school Christian intellectual. When he says names like "Derrida" and "Foucault," he says them correctly. I detect, at times, a Scottish brogue, a French accent, and shades of "Hockey Night in Canada." I have asked him whether he regularly interacts with leaders in the emergent movement.[7]

"I don't blog," he says. I can tell saying "blog" is uncomfortable for him. Like when your dad tries to sing lyrics from one of your favorite songs. "What would I have to give up for two hours each day if I started posting responses to these guys on their Web sites?" he asks.

I briefly imagine what D. A. Carson's Web site might look like if he had one. Would it include the obligatory artsy-hip-pensive-scholarly black-and-white photos? Perhaps one of Carson with his glasses off, pondering a point. Would he describe himself as a "thinker, rebel, revolutionary, speaker, writer, scholar" like some of his emergent contemporaries?

"I'm very easy to get ahold of," he continues. "After my book on the emergent church came out, I got a blistering twenty-page response from an emergent leader via e-mail. . . . He was very angry. Stuff to the effect that I was trying to ruin him and ruin his ministry. So I replied, point by point, with my own twenty-pager, and at the end said I'd be delighted to meet him to work out some of these differences in person."

Well?

"He wrote me back a very short e-mail and said that he had nothing more to discuss."

We ride on in silence and both ponder the sadness of that anecdote for a moment. I don't consider myself a Carson fan or admirer, like many in the young orthodox movement. I would like to think that I try to stay away from groupieism on either side. But I appreciate his candor here, in my car.

I am reminded of a story I was told earlier this week by my pastor. An emergent leader named Tony Jones called reformed icon John Piper's comments "smart-[expletive]" on his blog earlier in the week, in response to Piper's invitation to a recent conference. To his credit though, Jones invited Piper and several other reformed heavyweights to coffee, ostensibly for a sort of evangelical peace summit, complete with caramel lattes and biscotti. Piper went, but first he asked Jones, "Do you always call someone a smart-[expletive] before asking him to coffee?"[8]

"The feedback on blogs is immediate," Carson continues. "You have a thought and then three minutes later it's published for the world to digest. And then in another three minutes you have anonymous folks posting messages about how wonderful you are. It tends to inflate one's sense of importance."

We agree that there is something good about the editing process, the idea that your work sits for a while and is evaluated before being thrust before the world.

"One of these emergent guys—who is really quite sharp and has written extensively on the Old Testament—recently posted anecdotes about how often he has to go to the loo [that's British-guy talk for toilet, can, or potty] now that he's getting older."

"What did you think of that?" I asked D. A. Carson, with a straight face. "I mean, it is authentic."

"Too much information."

ON TOLERANCE

Unfortunately, my experience with Voltaire is limited to the scene in *Swingers* where the John Favreau character, after seeing an ad for "breakfast anytime," orders the "pancakes, in the age of Enlightenment." He frets as the waitress walks away, feeling like he has somehow intellectually upstaged her. After all, what would a waitress in a Las Vegas diner know about French philosophers? He catches her eye a moment later, to which she replies, "Hang on, Voltaire."

Voltaire, says Carson during the session, also gave us a working definition of tolerance when he said, "I may disagree with everything you say, but I will defend to the death your right to say it."

However, tolerance today, in Carson's estimation, is more of an outright refusal to say that anyone else is wrong. It is a core value of the emergent non-movement.

"Leonard Sweet recently wrote on his Web site that he would rather be wrong with Brian McLaren than right with D. A. Carson," says Carson. I expect a scathing word to follow, but there is none. Carson just leaves the comment to hang in the air and speak for itself.

"Postmodernism turns to the 'I,'" he says, "where premodernism commonly began with God."

He points out that the emergent movement sees itself as the shape of things to come, with regards to changing culture, and that most people in the move-ment see it as a reaction to either the traditional church with its propositions and teaching, or the seeker-sensitive church with its entertainment-oriented shallowness.[9] But he adds that the movement—with its ever-growing library of books, its own conferences, its own journals and, sadly, its own celebrities—

has itself become a pretty reasonable facsimile of the church-growth movement that it so vehemently opposes.

"The emergent church says that 'you belong in order to believe,'" Carson explains. "Why exclude someone from the Lord's Table? They might meet Him there."

Of course, the Bible itself limits who can come to the Lord's Table, but Carson also reveals that reading the Bible "literally" has become something of a dirty concept.

"Under the impact of the Enlightenment," he continues, "emergents argue that people became way too concerned with questions of truth."

= = = =

One of the potentially cool things about writing books is the idea that someday people will come to interview you and ask your thoughts on things. A few weeks after being interviewed about my boxing book by *Infuze Magazine*, one of several online Christianity-and-culture mags that have popped up of late, I was intrigued by an interview there with the aforementioned Erwin McManus, or Erwin Raphael McManus as he sometimes goes.

After reading the McManus piece, I jotted the following e-mail to a friend:

Total subject change here, but read this interview[10] that ran in Infuze Mag today. . . . It's on a pastor named Erwin McManus. . . . I can't believe people are buying this stuff.

Here are some quotes from him:

. . . focus on unleashing the potential in every human being . . .

There is more within you than you can imagine . . .

Soul Cravings, to me, is very much a human story. It's the story of finding God inside of yourself.

What happens is that these people don't feel they need permission to get the future they want, but Christians sit back and hope God will create the future.

But all of that because there's a sense of urgency at Mosaic. People know I am willing to sacrifice and do whatever is necessary to be a significant voice and influence in Los Angeles and allow this to permeate across the world. And this is exciting, let me tell you. When there's a crisis with Katrina, we were there. And the crisis in Bande Ache, we were there days after the crisis. We mobilize within days of a crisis. We take this stuff seriously. We redirect, we move on a dime, and we draw people who want to make a difference in the world . . .

"This is the subject today" because I got 20 questions on "Is it okay to be gay?" And I just tell them, "Look, I'm not telling you that I'm gonna give you the best answer. I'm not even telling you that my answer is adequate. But I am gonna engage you in a conversation you will want to continue. . . .

Rather than piquing the interest of the little Christian Revolutionary/ Barbarian inside me, it got my inner Midwestern Working Stiff asking questions. Is my faith about getting, as McManus says, "what I want out of life" or "finding God inside of myself"? And what's wrong with "hoping God will create the future"? Perhaps one has to be a "futurist" to really know what creating the future is all about.

My friend's reply was telling:

Ted,

This is rich stuff (in the wrong way). . . . I hear better theology from (Chicago Bears DT) Tommie Harris in post-game interviews.

Harris the so modern—linear, logical, coherent. How bothersome.

Defensive tackle Tommie Harris: "When a quarterback throws a ball on a three-step drop, or if he's letting the ball go quick, the D-linemen cannot get a penetration on a pass rush. . . . You're not getting through there with all those guys staying in to block, so it was very difficult for us to get in there. They game-planned us well, they played us well at first, but we found a way to win.

= = = =

Nick Naylor, the protagonist in the novel and movie *Thank You for Smoking*, is convinced that arguing well (or for our purposes "dialoguing," the Christian/academic version of arguing) trumps the actual message. He believes so strongly in this that he works as the mouthpiece for perhaps the most hated group in Washington—Big Tobacco.

Naylor works his magic throughout the film in offices, courtrooms, restaurants, and the home of a former "Marlboro Man," who is now dying of lung cancer. "Charles Manson kills people. Michael Jordan plays basketball. I talk," he says. "You know that guy who can walk into a room and pick up any girl? I'm that guy, on crack."

Watching the film, I'm struck by how similar the tobacco argument is to the emergent "discussion." By and large, I think right now, at least, the emergent movement has the best mouthpieces. Ask a college student if they would rather read a book by Donald Miller or Chuck Colson, Rob Bell or John Piper, Doug Pagitt or J. I. Packer. The youngest, best-looking, and snappiest writers among us are now cranking out their wares under the emergent umbrella, a fact that hasn't gone unnoticed by the book publishing industry and its salespeople.

After reading McLaren, Bell, Sweet, and other emergent leaders via their Web sites, I am beginning to develop a very rough sketch of my observations of the movement, and its relationship to evangelical Christianity. I think it's safe to say that some emergents think

. . . evangelicals don't care about the poor. And don't even get evangelicals started on diversity, which they clearly want nothing to do with.

. . . the evangelical church is about pushing right-wing politics. Jim Wallis aside, a good bit of emergent literature is laced with the Bush/church connection and how disastrous that particular connection is.

. . . evangelicals promote an "in or out" type of salvation experience.

. . . the evangelical church has participated in a variety of ills that it somehow hasn't adequately apologized for.

. . . evangelicals are "fake" and for many the worship experience is somehow "inauthentic."

. . . evangelicals are artistically challenged and uncreative. They watch lame movies, listen to lame music.

I'm almost through with McLaren's *A Generous Orthodoxy*. He does some things well in the book, and I am most appreciative of a diagram on pages 72–73, which quickly and pretty concisely sums up seven "types" of Christians,[11] along with brief descriptions of what the "good news" looks like to each group. I am less appreciative of another diagram, appearing on page 315, in which McLaren likens *emergent thinking* to the cross-sectioned trunk of a tree, in a chapter called "Why I'm Emergent." After 300-plus pages of McLaren, some of it really engaging, lots of it probably over my head, I am left wondering who the audience is for this book. Here's a paragraph near the end of *Orthodoxy*:

> In Christian theology, this anti-emergent thinking is expressed in systematic theologies that claim (overtly, covertly, or unconsciously) to have final orthodoxy nailed down, freeze-dried, and shrink-wrapped forever. Emergent Christians (post-liberal, post-conservative) see pluralistic relativism as a dangerous treatment for Stage 4 absolutist/colonial/totalitarian modernity (to use language from cancer diagnosis), something that saves a life by nearly killing it. It's dangerous medicine—but stagnancy, getting stuck too long in the cocoon, is dangerous too.

I live in a college town but still know very few people, even pastors, who would think of their lives, or the lives of others, in terms like "Stage 4 absolutist/colonial/ totalitarian modernity."

= = = =

I'm sitting in a coffee shop in East Lansing, hoping to pick the brain of a philosophy major and a friend, when an acquaintance—a woman who left our church to join a local emergent cohort—sits down at the table next to ours. We exchange awkward hellos, and I can tell that she is listening to every word my friend says because he is—and I'm being kind—a bit of a loud talker. Of all the coffee shops in the greater Lansing area, I pick this one. Nice.

It reminds me of how sad this all is—this us/them mentality—and how writing a book titled *Why We're Not Emergent* probably won't help at all in the "further alienating friends and acquaintances" department. And it reminds me that I am still young and impressionable enough to be really sad when somebody leaves our church. Actually, I hope this always matters.

At any rate, my friend David is more than eager to talk about postmodernism, emergent, theology, and the like. I think every church probably has a David or two—he is the rare college student who is passionate about theology, and feels a little bit like an outsider because of it. I wouldn't go so far as to put him in the "rabid young John Piper groupies" department, but if he met a beautiful young girl wearing glasses, no makeup, and an indie-rock T-shirt, reading *Calvin's Institutes*, he probably wouldn't hesitate to ask her to "court."

As a third-year philosophy student, he is conversant in the names and theories surrounding postmodernism but isn't ready to anoint his/our generation as overtly postmodern as some in the movement would believe.

"Donald Miller, Brian McLaren, and Rob Bell especially have been big influences, especially in the Campus Crusade group," he says. "I think a lot of it has to do with the 'we just want Jesus' mentality. People who think more theologically seem to college students to be narrow-minded or judgmental. They see 'I just want Jesus' as kind of an oppositional view to the theological camp. But to know the Lord is to know Him through propositions," he continues. "Being in a relationship—and people who like the emergent movement like to focus on the relationship aspect of Jesus—but to be in a relationship with someone, it's imperative that you know specific things and true things about the person you're in the relationship with.

"Even in my own mind I see myself as someone who really loves theology, but it shouldn't be that you're a 'mind' person or a 'hands' person," he says. "But even in studying philosophy it makes me think about the passage in Matthew, 'you didn't visit me when I was in prison . . . you didn't clothe me' [cf. Matt. 25:34–40]. But there has to be a way that theology is the fuel, or the belief that causes us to take action. But that's not a very popular thought with college students."

I ask David if there is a dichotomy among young people between experience and belief. Or experience and bearing fruit.

"There seems to be an obsession with the experience aspect," he says, "but where is the focus on the fruits of the Spirit?"

At this point the acquaintance approaches our table on her way out and says that she couldn't help but overhear our conversation, and that it sounded really interesting. Gulp. Am I writing an article or something? Gulp again.

She leaves and we again start to discuss postmodernism, and I communicate that while the movement assumes a level of postmodern among all younger people, I theorize that perhaps it's less prevalent than some in the movement would think. The idea that "young people don't want answers" and "young people don't like to think in linear ways" is painting with pretty broad strokes.

"In my experience talking with other philosophy students, it seems like people are still asking for evidence," David says. "Within student ministries, or my Christian friends, I feel like people have the mind-set of wanting to hear what other people think, but not just for the purpose of immediately approving it as 'different but good.' Truth is still important."

He communicates that there are "underlying little rumbles" of interest in the movement among his group of young, reformed Christians. He mentions the proximity of Mars Hill and Rob Bell as a major influence.

"I'd never heard of Mars Hill a year ago, and now I know a lot of people who go there," he says, when asked on what levels the movement is succeeding. "So people who consider themselves postmodern, who aren't Christian, are being exposed to some ideas through that. But it needs to just be more than the Bible as narrative, or now I know Jesus and I have a better life. I was dead before I had Jesus. . . . Loving people and ministering to the person should always be a priority, but I don't think we need to change church to fit the culture."

The Good News as opposed to no news.

"Tolerance is something we should maybe talk about, because it's something I'm really like . . . grrr . . . about," he says.

Okay, we can talk about that.

"Let's say somebody is talking about their religious beliefs, and I go up to them and say, respectfully, 'I disagree with you,'" he says. "Most people would say that respectfully disagreeing is an intolerant act. Now tolerance means just agreeing with someone. But by definition tolerance implies some disagreement. There's a huge misconception surrounding that."

I ask him if he thinks maybe the emergent movement is just theological liberalism in "MTV" clothes, for lack of a better term (and I really do lack a better term)—specifically, though, is it liberalism with regards to a soft position on hell and the inerrancy of Scripture?

"Personally, when I was a senior in high school, I would have considered myself a Christian, but if you had asked me if I believed in hell I would have said no," he says. "I grew up in a theologically liberal church. I was never taught about hell . . . it was an off-limits kind of topic."

Rob Bell says about hell, on page 147 of *Velvet Elvis*:

Now if there is a life of heaven, and we can choose it, then there's also another way. A way of living out of sync with how God created us to live. The word for this is hell: a way, a place, a realm absent of how God desires things to be. We can bring heaven to earth; we can bring hell to earth.

Bell repaints hell as something we experience in this life:

When people use the word *hell*, what do they mean? They mean a place, an event, a situation absent of how God desires things to be. Famine, debt, oppression, loneliness, despair, death, slaughter—they are all hell on earth.

What's disturbing then is when people talk more about hell after this life than they do about hell here and now. As a Christian, I want to do what I can to resist hell coming to earth. Poverty, injustice, suffering —they are all hells on earth, and as Christians we oppose them with all our energies. Jesus told us to.[12]

"On the emergent end I think people are afraid that Christians are using hell as a sales tool to get people to buy into Christianity, and I think that should be avoided," David continues. "But that's not the only reason we preach about hell. Jesus doesn't avoid speaking about weeping and gnashing of teeth."

NOTES

1. As quoted in Christopher Buckley, *Thank You for Smoking* (New York: Random House, 1994). In this novel, Nick Naylor is the PR spokesman for the Academy of Tobacco Studies, who spins on the merits of tobacco smoking. Later played by Aaron Eckhart in the 2006 movie of the same name.
2. Not so. See Doug Pagitt at Dougpagitt.com.
3. Erwin Raphael McManus, *The Barbarian Way* (Nashville: Nelson, 2005), 6, as cited in "Special Report: The Barbarian Way," at http://www.lighthousetrailsresearch.com/erwinmcmanus.htm
4. This could be my McLarenian disclaimer. The part where I tell you up front how unqualified I am to write this book . . . but you probably know that already.
5. http://www.cassiopedia.org/wiki/index.php?title=futurism_(art).
6. http://en.wikipedia.org/wiki/futurist
7. Though there are no leaders, per se. And it's not a movement, for the record; rather, a discussion.
8. "Reformed?" August 28, 2006, at http://theoblogy.blogspot.com/ 2006_08_01_archive.html
9. From my notebook comes a running list of words that are *verboten* in emergent circles: *propositional, metanarrative, assertions,* and *foundational.*
10. http://www.infuzemag.com/interviews/books/erwinmcmanus
11. The seven are listed as Conservative Protestant, Pentecostal, Roman Catholic, Eastern Orthodox, Liberal Protestant, Anabaptist, and Liberation Theology (nonviolent).

12. Rob Bell, *Velvet Elvis* (Grand Rapids: Zondervan, 2005), 148.

Ikon [community] has no substantial doctrinal centre.

—PETER ROLLINS

Indifferentism about doctrine makes no heroes of the faith.

—J. GRESHAM MACHEN

CHAPTER 5

DOCTRINE: THE DRAMA IS IN THE DOGMA

IT IS NOT HARD to find emergent leaders questioning the importance of doctrine. Doctrine is derided as logical, sterile, and exclusive. Instead of saying, "Here is truth; take it or leave it," the emergent crowd calls Christians to declare, "Come and experience the story of God in the life of this community."[1] Too many Christians want to put down their anchor in doctrinal truth, rather than being free to explore other ports, according to emergent leaders.[2] As Tomlinson writes, "Ultimately, our church pedigrees, spiritual experiences, or creedal affirmations do not impress God. St. Peter will not be asking us at the pearly gates which church we belonged to or if we believed in the virgin birth."[3]

Brian McLaren, at least, admits that people can be sincere and still believe untrue things.[4] He also acknowledges that "sound doctrine is very, very, *very* important." And though he is suspicious of highlighting doctrinal distinctives, he does affirm the Apostles' and Nicene creeds.[5] But on the other hand,

McLaren is critical of those who claim to have final orthodoxy "nailed down, freeze-dried, and shrink-wrapped forever."[6] He resists "nauseating arguments about why this or that form of theology (dispensational, covenant, charismatic, whatever) or methodology (cell church, megachurch, liturgical church, seeker church, blah, blah, blah) is right (meaning approaching or achieving timeless technical perfection)."[7] He caricaturizes typical orthodoxy as "the hard mental work of holding in one's mind an increasing bank of complex opinions about a lot of things before breakfast."[8]

Carla, a member of Doug Pagitt's church, Solomon's Porch, probably speaks for many in the emergent movement when she says, "I feel like dogma never works, like people are hungry to see a better life."[9]

It would be unfair to say that every emergent leader has thrown doctrine out the window. But I think it is fair to say that even for those who affirm core doctrinal beliefs, and that does not include everyone in the movement, orthodoxy as a set of immovable theological assertions is largely downplayed, if not completely rejected. What animates emerging leaders and holds them together is not a set of defined and defended doctrines. What invigorates the emergent church is a way of life, or inclusion, or something else entirely. To turn Dorothy Sayers's famous saying on its head, the drama is no longer in the dogma.

JUST GIVE ME JESUS

In emergent circles, spirituality is hot and religion is not. Barry Taylor goes so far as to suggest that "there may not be a future for 'Christianity,' the religion of Christian faith." By "religion," Taylor means "the institutional and organizational form around faith," which may no longer be "necessary for the future of faith."[10] Religion is all about certainty and sanctity, while spirituality, or faith, lives in inquiry and fluidity. "The reason traditional faiths are having a hard time of things," offers Taylor, "is that the present situation is one in which certainty is suspect and sanctity is being redefined." Taylor's alternative is a commitment to "nondogmatic specificity."[11]

But is it really the traditional faiths that are having a hard time of things in our postmodern world? Of course, we want to be careful "proving" church theology by growth and size, but it is worth pointing out what is now common knowledge; namely, that conservative churches are growing in America, and liberal churches—those committed to nondogmatic specifity—are not. Over the past decade among liberal churches, declines in attendance have ranged from 5.3 percent to as much as 14.8 percent. By comparison, conservative denominations have been growing over the past ten years, ranging from 5 percent (the Southern Baptist Convention) to more than 50 percent (57.2 percent in the Evangelical Free Church).[12]

> "All we need is Jesus," many emerging Christians cry, "not these doctrinal formulations."

The mainline church bent over backward to accommodate modernism, and its members have budget crunches and shrinking churches to show for it. Will the emerging church go down the same nondoctrinal path as the mainline church relative to postmodernism? If it is really true that wherever you are finding "passion and love and exhilaration" there "you are finding God,"[13] Christianity has no unique message to give the world.

I have no doubt that non-Christians find some of the emergent literature very appealing. The literature often describes who they already are—nondogmatic, ambiguously spiritual postmoderns interested in making the world a better place. But where is there mention of the hard edges of Christian faith—God's holiness, divine judgment, the uniqueness of Jesus Christ, human depravity, the necessity of new birth?

Where is the offense in the gospel? J. Gresham Machen observed seventy-five years ago "this curious fact—when men talk thus about propagating Christianity without defending it, the thing that we are propagating is pretty sure not to be Christianity at all. They are propagating an anti-intellectualistic, nondoctrinal Modernism; and the reason why it requires no defense is simply that it is so completely in accord with the current of the age."[14] Nobody objects to a nondoctrinal Christianity because there is nothing to object to.

"All we need is Jesus," many emerging Christians cry, "not these fancy theologies and doctrinal formulations." Thus Erwin McManus writes, "The power of the gospel is the result of a person—Jesus Christ—not a message. The gospel is an event to be proclaimed, not a doctrine to be preserved."[15] Granted, this sounds good, and McManus may mean something good by it. But the argument is overstated. How is the gospel event we proclaim different than a message? And how is a message about Jesus—say, who He is and what He did on earth—different than doctrine? We can tell people about Jesus every day until He returns again, but without some doctrinal content filling up what we mean by Jesus and why He matters, we are just shouting slogans, not proclaiming any kind of intelligible gospel.

Jonathan Campbell, an emerging leader in Seattle, says about following Jesus:

> We have come to see that it is all about Jesus and not just a methodology. It is not about mission, not about church, but it's about Jesus and his glory, his life. To know Jesus is not an event, a ritual, a creed, or a religion. It is a journey of trust and adventure. We don't believe in any religion anymore—including Christianity—but we do believe in following Jesus. We no longer need religion with its special buildings, dogmas, programs, clergy, or any other human inventions that displace genuine spirituality. Why do we need a name and address to be a church? We've come out of religion and back to God.[16]

"It's all about Jesus" is certainly true. But what is it about Jesus that we are all about? If we have no events, no creeds, and no ritual, what do we have? His glory and His life, Campbell suggests. But once we say something about why Jesus is glorious and what His life was like and what it accomplished, aren't we settling back into dogma and religion again? The Jesus-versus-theology mantra is centuries old, and it makes no more sense and no more converts today than a hundred years ago.

Emergent leaders like to point out Paul's accommodating missional strategy among the Athenians at Mars Hill. "Paul began with what they had and built from there," writes Taylor. He adds:

> His declaration that God is not far from any one of us (see Acts 17:27) is a profound missional lesson for us all; we don't have to take God anywhere; we just have to discover where he is already at work.
>
> *God is nowhere. God is now here.* God is present; God is absent. The future of faith rests in the tension between these words, and it is from this place of discomfort and complexity that new life emerges.[17]

This is the kind of paragraph that drives "normal" Christians bonkers. It sounds cool to say that God is present and absent, nowhere and now here, but once the "tension" and "complexity" of these epigrams wear off, you're left wondering, "Uh?" Maybe that's the point. New life will emerge from the "Uh?" But this is so unlike Paul's actual sermon at Mars Hill. After Paul did his cultural engagement thing, he proclaimed the gospel in no uncertain terms. "The times of ignorance God overlooked, but now he commands all people everywhere to repent, because he has fixed a day on which he will judge the world in righteousness by a man whom he has appointed; and of this he has given assurance to all by raising him from the dead" (Acts 17:30–31).

The apostles never preached with the double-talk and ambiguity you find in so many emergent books. Dorothy Sayers critiqued the notion of a contentless Christ in her devastating rebuff of the modernists (or were they postmodernists?) running rampant in the 1930s and 40s:

> Christ, in His Divine innocence, said to the Woman of Samaria, "Ye worship ye know not what"—being apparently under the impression

that it might be desirable, on the whole, to know what one was worshipping. He thus showed Himself sadly out of touch with the twentieth-century mind, for the cry today is: "Away with the tendentious complexities of dogma—let us have the simple spirit of worship; just worship, no matter of what!" The only drawback to this demand for a generalized and undirected worship is the practical difficulty of arousing any sort of enthusiasm for the worship of nothing in particular.[18]

ORTHODOXY AS A WAY OF LIFE

Historically, Christians have affirmed the importance of orthodoxy, right belief, and orthopraxy, right living. The emergent church often redefines the two so they are one. Or to put it more accurately, they conflate the two so that orthodoxy equals right living, and right belief, if it matters at all, flows from right living instead of the other way around (cf. Rom. 12:1). When asked what is orthodoxy and who gets to define it, McLaren answered, "It's virtue, and it's Christlikeness. . . . Orthodoxy itself is a practice. . . . So ethics comes first, then doctrine comes second, and witness flows out of that."[19] Peter Rollins goes even further:

> Instead of following the Greek-influenced idea of orthodoxy as right belief, these chapters show that the emerging community is helping us rediscover the more Hebraic and mystical notion of the orthodox Christian as one who believes in the right way—that is, believing in a loving, sacrificial and Christlike manner. . . . Thus orthodoxy is no longer (mis)understood as the opposite of heresy but rather is understood as a term that signals a way of being in the world rather than a means of believing things about the world.[20]

The creeds, then, do not mark out the borders of faith. The creeds—don't tell Athanasius, who apparently wasted his life fighting the Arians over a diphthong—are only "conversation guides."[21] The church is not meant to solve the big questions of life, but to help people understand who they are, when and where they are, while imagining a glorious future together with the Father, Son, and Holy Spirit.[22] How we help people understand who they are and what a glorious future with the Trinity looks like without answering any big questions is unclear to me, but that's our task.

Rob Bell is also suspicious of orthodoxy, putting it several notches below orthopraxy. For example, Bell admits that he believes in the virgin birth, but it is not as important as living like Jesus.

> What if tomorrow someone digs up definitive proof that Jesus had a real, earthly, biological father named Larry, and archaeologists find Larry's tomb and do DNA samples and prove beyond a shadow of a doubt that the virgin birth was really just a bit of mythologizing the Gospel writers threw in to appeal to the followers of Mithra and Dionysian religious cults that were hugely popular at the time of Jesus, whose gods had virgin births? But what if as you study the origin of the word *virgin*, you discover that the word *virgin* in the gospel of Matthew actually comes from the book of Isaiah, and then you find out that in the Hebrew language at that time, the word *virgin* could mean several things. And what if you discover that in the first century being born of a virgin also referred to a child whose mother became pregnant the first time she had intercourse? What if that spring was seriously questioned? Could a person keep jumping? Could a person still love God? Could you still be a Christian? Is the way of Jesus still the best possible way to live?[23]

This emphasis on right living over against right belief is nothing new. It is, in fact, quintessentially modern. Adolf Harnack, the brilliant and popular promoter of Protestant liberalism, said the same thing at the turn of the last century: "True faith in Jesus is not a matter of creedal orthodoxy but of doing as he did."[24] There are only two problems with this liberal/emergent view of orthodoxy. One, it isn't true. And two, it isn't helpful.

It simply isn't true that orthodoxy as right belief is nothing but a perverted Greek idea. John wrote his gospel, not that people might follow Jesus' exemplary way of life, but that they might believe Jesus was the Christ and by believing have life in His name (John 20:31). As John wrote elsewhere, any spirit that does not confess that Jesus Christ has come in the flesh is not from God but is the spirit of the antichrist (1 John 4:2–3).

There are certain truths that must be affirmed in order to be a Christian. Whoever does not believe that Jesus was God's own Son, for example, is condemned already (John 3:18). Here are three more fundamental truths about right belief:

- *People go to hell for believing the wrong things.* "But even if we or an angel from heaven should preach a gospel other than the one we preached to you, let him be eternally condemned" (Gal. 1:8 NIV).

- *People within the church should be corrected when they believe the wrong things.* "[An elder] must hold firmly to the trustworthy message as it has been taught, so that he can encourage others by sound doctrine and refute those who oppose it" (Titus 1:9 NIV).

- *People are sometimes to be kept out of your house for believing the wrong things.* "Anyone who runs ahead and does not continue in the teaching of Christ does not have God; whoever continues in the teaching has both the Father and the Son. If anyone comes to you and does not bring this teaching, do not take him into your house or welcome him" (2 John 9–10).

There's no question that Paul believed in orthodoxy. "Follow the pattern of the sound words that you have heard from me, in the faith and love that are in

Christ Jesus," he told Timothy. "By the Holy Spirit who dwells within us, guard the good deposit entrusted to you" (2 Tim. 1:13–14). Paul's message undoubtedly had a doctrinal center. There were certain propositions of fact regarding election, the incarnation, the resurrection, and the atonement that Paul had passed along to Timothy that absolutely had to be preserved and protected at all costs, even if it meant suffering and death (1:8–11).

Doctrine was to die for because it was the heartbeat of Paul's saving message about saving historical facts.[25] Machen writes, "But if any one fact is clear, on the basis of this evidence, it is that the Christian movement at its inception was not just a way of life in the modern sense, but a way of life founded upon a message. It was based, not upon mere feeling, not upon a mere program of work, but upon an account of facts. In other words it was based upon doctrine."[26] As soon as you say Jesus died and rose again for your sins according to the Scriptures, you have doctrine. You have a message about what happened in history and what it means. That's theology. There is no gospel without it.

Besides being untrue, orthodoxy as orthopraxy is monumentally unhelpful. It sounds wonderful at first. Jesus is the best way to live. Where's the harm in that? After all, it is true that Jesus taught good ethics and set a good moral example. But if orthodoxy means I live the right way, the way of Jesus, I have no hope. Where do I turn after I've screwed up the beatitudes for the fiftieth time? Where do I find peace when I realize I fail the Sermon on the Mount daily? What do I tell the Devil when he reminds me that I don't do justly and love mercy and walk humbly with my God (see Mic. 6:8) as I should?

And what about my family and friends? What comfort do I give a loved one who is dying with cancer and feels no assurance of salvation because she hasn't loved God or her neighbor enough? I hope I can read Ephesians 2 and tell her that though she was dead in her trespasses and sins, by nature an object of wrath, now she has been made alive together with Christ and that by grace alone her sins have been forgiven, not according to works lest anyone should boast.

Now, I'm sure that many in the emergent church would also talk about grace, but I don't read much about grace in their books. Certainly, there's grace as a general inclusiveness, but not grace as the only hope for sinners deserving of God's judgment. I despair when I hear Pagitt say, "The good news is not informational…. Instead we have an invitation into a way of life—life we constantly realize is not ours alone."[27] If the good news is an invitation to a Jesus way of life and not information about somebody who accomplished something on my behalf, I'm sunk. This is law and no gospel.

What Machen wrote about liberalism could be said of many in the emergent church. "Here is found the most fundamental difference between liberalism and Christianity—liberalism is altogether in the imperative mood, while Christianity begins with a triumphant indicative; liberalism appeals to man's will, while Christianity announces, first, a gracious act of God."[28] Isn't this what we are left with when we have an orthodoxy stripped of doctrinal content and informational good news? We have no more glorious indicatives. Only damning imperatives.

REPAINTING OUR THEOLOGY

According to old-school liberals like Friedrich Schleiermacher, religion had an inner piety at its core that always took shape in a specific religious tradition. In other words, there was a kernel of timeless spirituality (absolute dependence in Schleiermacher's language) and a husk of temporal and changing doctrines surrounding the kernel. Our culturally bound religious formulas spring out of our religious experiences. This allows doctrines to come and go as we dig deeper into the same religious experience and then reemerge with different formulations appropriate to our times. Harry Emerson Fosdick, the popular liberal preacher of the early 1900s, said the "first step [of liberalism] is to go through old formulas into the experiences out of which all religious formulas must come."[29] Christianity, then, to quote Machen explaining liberalism, "is a life or an experience that has doctrine merely as its symbolic intellectual expression, so that while the life abides the doctrine must necessarily change from age to age."[30]

I doubt that many emergent leaders are reading Schleiermacher or Fosdick, but their approach to theology is strikingly similar.[31] "Whether 'Christianity' has any future at all as a vibrant expression of faith in the Man from Galilee is a matter of debate as far as I am concerned," writes Taylor. "Perhaps the times call for something else, something other, not merely the repackaging of old metaphors (playing the 'relevant' game), but a new incarnation of what it means to follow Jesus."[32] Since all our theology is socially constructed and heretical, as I've read often in emergent books, it is only fitting that it would change with the times. Malleability of doctrine is good because it shows that we aren't absolutizing our theology. Or to use Rob Bell's metaphor, doctrines are like springs on the trampoline. The springs aren't the point. They just help us keep jumping. In a line that could have been ripped out of a Fosdick sermon, Bell suggests, "The springs help make sense of these deeper realities that drive how we live every day. The springs aren't God. The springs aren't Jesus. The springs are statements and beliefs about our faith that help give words to the depth that we are experiencing in our jumping."[33]

> **What begins as a freeing exercise in doctrinal exploration ends up an expression of not much in particular.**

This liberal (in the strict theological sense of the word) way of thinking has been labeled by Robert Sanders "the ecstatic heresy." The term *ecstatic* comes from Paul Tillich. The perspective claims that God can only be known in feeling, in ways that transcend human language, so that God can never be the object of observation and described like you would describe an electron, a tree, or a cat. To do so would be to profane God.[34] Sanders is an Episcopalian who sees the ecstatic heresy underlying many of the divisions in the mainline Protestant churches. His analysis is worth reading and can apply to the emergent church as well.

Ecstatic: God in himself, or in his revelation as Word and words, is never really verbal. He always transcends language.

Orthodox: God is transcendent in his essence, but God can speak to human beings who can actually understand him. Above all, God is known in the words and deeds of Jesus Christ, the Word made flesh . . .

Ecstatic: The task of theology is to reinterpret the faith as relevant to new cultural contexts. The context of faith evolves since culture evolves.

Orthodox: The task of theology is first and foremost to clarify and preserve the faith once delivered to the saints and to transfer intact to each succeeding generations. Certain aspects of revelation never evolve. . . .

Ecstatic: Doctrines do not literally refer to God but to feeling, the depth of reality, or the horizon of being. Therefore doctrines can be radically reinterpreted in terms of ecstatic categories, and pastoral experience can carry more weight than doctrine.

Orthodox: Doctrines teach truths about God—his moral will and his saving acts. They can be variously understood. They deal with mysteries, but they cannot be reinterpreted in categories that have no literal reference to a God who speaks.[35]

The ecstatic view of doctrine and revelation that has dogged the mainline churches sounds eerily similar to the view of many emergent books I read. This is worrisome. What begins as a freeing exercise in doctrinal exploration ends up an expression of not much in particular. I know that some in my generation have a hard time with truth claims. But I'm convinced there are just as many of us—Christian and not—in our postmodern world who are tired of endless uncertainties and doctrinal repaintings. We are tired of indecision and inconsistency reheated and served to us as paradox and mystery. Some of us long for teaching that has authority, ethics rooted in dogma, and something unique in this world of banal diversity. We long for Jesus—not a shapeless, formless, good-hearted ethical teacher Jesus, but the Jesus of the New Testament, the Jesus of the church, the Jesus of faith, the Jesus of two millennia of Christian witness with all of its unchanging and edgy doctrinal propositions.

THE BOUNDARY PROBLEM

If the emerging church struggles to find a theological center, it struggles even more to define theological boundaries—not just what are they, but whether any even exist. In an interview with *Relevant* magazine, Tony Jones, the national coordinator of Emergent, explained "that the very nature of theology is one of conversation and dialogue, not one of setting boundaries and safeguards from elusive historic orthodoxy." This means that Jones finds statements of faith seriously alarming.

> Statements of faith are about drawing borders, which means you have to load your weapons and place soldiers at those borders. You have to check people's passports when they pass at those borders. It becomes an obsession—guarding the borders. That is simply not the ministry of Jesus. It wasn't the ministry of Paul or Peter. It started to become the ministry of the early Church, and it abated somewhat in the Middle Ages and blew back to life in the time of modernity. For the short duration of time that I have on this planet to do my best to partner with God and build his kingdom, I don't want to spend it guarding borders. I'd like to spend it inviting people into the kingdom. Statements of faith don't do they [sic]. They're a modernistic endeavor that I'm not the least bit interested in.

Later, when the magazine interviewer asked whether lesbian pastors and conservative absolutists can both be a part of the emergent church, Jones answered, "We haven't yet found that there's anything that justifies us breaking fellowship with somebody else who loves and is trying to follow Jesus."[36] Can this really be? Are there no doctrinal beliefs (besides believing in statements of faith) or ethical behaviors (besides undefined lovelessness) that put one outside the camp? The issue then becomes: Is there anyone who says "I love Jesus and am trying to follow Him" whom we would not call brother or sister?

Jones, it seems, would say no. But what about Mormons? Arians? Hardcore Pelagians? Those who disbelieve in the resurrection? Those who love Jesus while also worshiping Krishna, Shiva, and Vishnu? Those who deny the personhood of God?

Christianity cannot and does not exist without boundaries. Being a Christian in any biblical sense requires that we not only say yes to many things, but that we also are willing to say no to a number of beliefs and behaviors.[37]

The question is whether the emerging church has the ability to correct its own abuses and challenge the massive theological errors coming from fellow conversation partners. More importantly, the question is whether the emerging church even has the category of theological error. Some do, but many, I fear, do not. As long as we try to live out justice as Jesus modeled and love in community as Jesus taught, that's all that really matters—if the emerging church refuses to stand for more than this, it will quickly lose any semblance of being evangelical, any semblance of being historically orthodox, and eventually any sense of being decidedly Christian.

The emergent problem with boundaries is illustrated in two recent books: *A Heretic's Guide to Eternity*, by Spencer Burke and Barry Taylor, and *How (Not) to Speak of God*, by Peter Rollins. I have chosen to deal with these books separately because they are so far removed from "mere Christianity" that I didn't think it fair to assume their ideas speak for the whole emerging church. I pray to God they do not. If these two books signal the future of the emerging church, the future is bleak, for they deviate widely from the faith presented in the Scriptures.

BOUNDARIES AND THE *HERETIC'S GUIDE*

Spencer Burke has been one of the formative voices in the emergent conversation. He is the creator of theooze.com and the host of *Soularize*, which he calls the original postmodern/emergent annual conference. It's not clear how influential Burke's ideas are,[38] but they seem to be a welcome part of the emerging movement, even if they don't form the center. Far from distancing himself from *A Heretic's Guide to Eternity*, Brian McLaren actually wrote the foreword to the book. Granted, you can write a foreword and not agree with everything in the book, but introducing a book, unless clearly stated otherwise, is an implicit sign that you are at least broadly sympathetic with its ideas. McLaren thanks "Spencer and Barry" for their "courage and charity" in raising the issues that are "driving away millions of people." In *Heretic's Guide*, McLaren believes "any honest reader can find much truth worth seeking."[39]

The problem lies not in emerging Christians seeking the truth, but in their refusal to find and call out falsehood. Burke, who denies the importance of the visible church and has removed himself from it,[40] pushes past the orthodox edge "when he affirms a quasi-universalism where everyone is in unless they want out:

Could it be that—beyond religion, reason, and conventional wisdom—grace is something to be opted out of rather than opted in to? Is it not something you get but something you already have?

When I say I'm a universalist, what I really mean is that I don't believe you have to convert to any particular religion to find God. As I see it, God finds us, and it has nothing to do with subscribing to any particular religious view.

The God I connect with does not assign humans to hell.[41]

He rejects the cross of Christ as an atoning sacrifice for sin, quoting approvingly from the journalist Polly Toynbee: "Of all the elements of Christianity, the most repugnant is the notion of the Christ who took our sins upon himself and sacrificed his body in agony to save our souls. Did we ask him to?" Burke continues, reintroducing the old liberal notion of Jesus as the great moral example. "Although the link between grace and sin has driven Christianity for centuries, it just doesn't resonate in our culture anymore. It repulses rather than attracts. People are becoming much less inclined to acknowledge themselves as 'sinners in need of a Savior.'" A better approach is to see Jesus as "the model of sinless living, the ultimate example to which all humanity should aspire."[42]

Burke has little (no?) place for doctrinal belief. What you believe about Jesus or the work He accomplished is irrelevant. Jesus' vision of God is "for anyone and everyone—Jewish, Christian, Buddhist, whatever. . . . What counts is not a belief system but a holistic approach of following what you feel, experience, discover, and believe; it is a willingness to join Jesus in his vision for a transformed humanity."[43]

Moreover, in Burke's *Guide to Eternity*, faith itself is irrelevant. "Faith is many things, but it is not a requirement. It is faithfulness, the giving of oneself, trust in God, and belief that something greater than the material world exists for all of us. . . . In reality, nothing stands between us and God's grace."[44]

This is maybe the biggest difference between emergent Christianity and historic evangelical Christianity. Being a Christian—for Burke, for McLaren, for Bell, for Jones, and for many others in the emerging conversation—is less about faith in the person and work of Jesus Christ as the only access to God the Father and the only atonement for sins before a wrathful God, and more about living the life that Jesus lived and walking in His way.

Burke also rejects the most basic doctrines about the Christian God.

What's more, I'm not sure I believe in God exclusively as a person anymore either. . . . I now incorporate a panentheist view, which basically means that God is "in all," alongside my creedal view of God as Father, Son, and Spirit. . . . As I see it, we are in God, here on earth. This is how our relationship is defined. God does not just have to be reached up to; he is here as the surrounding Spirit.[45]

Finally, Burke's conception of the Christian life (I'm not sure Burke would even call it Christian) is completely removed from the gospel of Christ's life, death, resurrection, ascension, exaltation, and coming again. His idea of discipleship is no different from that of your run-of-the-mill self-help guru.

The challenge of the spiritual life is to live fully connected here and now. A commitment to mystical responsibility is a commitment to an evolutionary journey toward personal, social, and communal transformation, where we pay attention to life, listen to its messages, and discover its opportunities.[46]

Of course, others in the emergent conversation will be quick to say, "We don't agree with everything our friend Spencer Burke writes." That's fine, but we need to hear what exactly they don't agree with, and are any of the disagreements so serious as to put Burke outside the boundaries of Christianity? Or is emergent not a conversation about the church and Christianity? Scot McKnight, who is sympathetic to the emerging church, provides a wise summary of the book and a good example of the boundary setting we need more of in the emerging conversation.

Is Spencer a "heretic"? He says he is, and I see no reason to think he believes in the Trinity from reading this book. That's what heresy means to me. Denial of God's personhood flies in the face of everything orthodox. To say you believe in the creedal view of God as Father, Son, and Spirit and deny "person" is to deny the Trinitarian concept of God.

Is Spencer a "Christian"? He says he is. What is a Christian? Is it not one who finds redemption through faith in Christ, the one who died and who was raised? If so, I see nothing in this book that makes me think that God's grace comes to us through the death and resurrection of Christ. Grace seems to be what each person is "born into" in Spencer's theses in this book. That means that I see no reason in this book to think Spencer believes in the gospel as the NT defines gospel (grace as the gift of God through Christ by faith).[47]

BOUNDARIES AND *TALK OF GOD*

Of the two books, *How (Not) to Talk of God* is probably the more important. Peter Rollins is a young, rising voice in the emergent conversation. Intelligent, creative, and iconoclastic, Rollins holds multiple degrees and is the founder of the Ikon community in Belfast. His first book has definitely struck a nerve with several key emergent leaders. Brian McLaren, who writes the foreword for the book, beams with praise for Rollins. His book "makes one of the most important contributions to date to that [emergent] conversation. I am a raving fan of the book you are holding," writes McLaren, who deems *Talk of God* "one of the two or three most rewarding books of theology I have read in ten years." He adds: "I loved reading it. I have already begun widely recommending it. . . . It helped me understand my own spiritual journey more clearly, and it gave me a sense of context for the work I'm involved in."

Tony Jones gives an equally ringing endorsement. He calls Rollins's book "the best [expletive] book yet on the emerging church!" He goes so far as to make the proclamation: *"I will no longer respond to any critics of Emergent who have not read* How (Not) to Speak of God. *If you want to get the emerging church, read this book."*[48]

So I did. And I was impressed and deeply disturbed. I was impressed because Rollins's book is more than souped-up blog entries. It is an intelligent attempt—part theory and part liturgical examples from the Ikon community—

to understand God from a mystical-emergent-deconstructionist perspective. I was disturbed because what Rollins (does not) say(s) about God from his mystical-emergent-deconstructionist perspective turns out to be profoundly unbiblical, unevangelical, and even—I'm not sure what other word to use—un-Christian. I can only hope that Rollins's book is not indicative of the direction of the emergent church.

Let me mention just a few concerns with *How (Not) to Speak of God*.[49] First, Rollins posits a radical skepticism about knowing anything about God. This doesn't mean we have nothing to say about God, for "that which we cannot speak of is the one thing about whom and to whom we must never stop speaking."[50] So we talk about God, but we don't make Him known. We render God known as unknown,[51] refusing to "colonize the name 'God' with concepts."[52] We believe in God but remain dubious concerning what we believe about God, to the point that we disbelieve the God we also believe in, "holding atheism and theism together in the cradle of faith."[53] Therefore, idolatry is not worshiping the wrong God but believing "that our ideas actually represent the way that God and the world really operate."[54] "In short, an emerging discourse acknowledges that *speaking of God is never speaking of God but only ever speaking about our understanding of God.*"[55]

This is one way to understand our relationship to God and His revelation, but it is not Christian. After all, the Psalms "colonize" God with all sorts of concepts—goodness, might, power, sovereignty, and omniscience, to name a few. The prophets claimed to know exactly how the people of Israel should live and what their God was like. Peter, Paul, James, and John, not to mention Jesus, knew a thousand times more about God—and wanted others to understand what they knew—than Rollins's brand of Christianity.

I keep wondering, am I missing something here? Yes, yes, a thousand times yes; we do see through a glass dimly; we do not fully understand God; we don't know God as God knows Himself; our words can't capture the essence of God. God *is* greater than we can conceive—but what about the 1,189 chapters in the Bible? Don't they tell us lots of things about God that we are supposed to do more with than doubt and not understand? Aren't the Scriptures written so that we might believe and be sure of what we hope for and certain of what we do not see and even proclaim this faith to others?

It's hard for me to believe that the apostles went off into the world telling people about the God they couldn't speak of and inviting the people to journey with them as they grew in their mutual un/knowing about the God they disbelieved in. The book of Acts paints the complete opposite picture. Peter preached an exegetical sermon at Pentecost. Peter and John thunder "let it be known" as they herald the gospel message. Stephen rebukes the people from their own history. Philip explains what a text means to the Ethiopian eunuch. Paul reasons in the synagogues. He lectures in the hall of Tyrannus. He tries to persuade Felix. He makes known the true God in the face of Christ that the Athenians only worshiped as unknown.

> **Don't the 1,189 chapters in the Bible tell us lots of things about God that we are supposed to do more with than doubt?**

A second concern: Rollins seems to reduce Christianity to little more than love. "To love is to know God precisely because God is love."[56] Therefore, orthodox refers to someone who engages the world in the right way, the way of love.[57] After quoting 1 John 4:7–16 Rollins argues, "Here John equates the existence of religious knowledge with the act of love. Knowledge of God (the Truth) as a set of propositions is utterly absent; instead he claims that those who exhibit a genuine love know God, regardless of their religious system, while those who do not love cannot know God, again regardless of their religious system."[58] If you read all of 1 John 4, however, you see that this conclusion is staggeringly wrong.

In the first six verses of chapter 4, John indicates there are wrong beliefs about Christ, false prophets, antichrists, and worldly voices that lead us away from God. We must test the spirits and discern the truth from error. Love is not the only orthodoxy.

And, I would argue, love is not a sufficient hermeneutical or ethical guideline, unless it is filled up with 1,189 chapters' worth of meaning. "What is important about revelation," Rollins argues, "is not that we seek to interpret it in the same way but rather that we all love it and are transformed by it."[59] But isn't the desired transformation a product itself of how we interpret revelation? For example, transformation looks very different for someone who reads the Bible as affirming homosexual behavior than it does for someone who reads the Bible as affirming one man–one woman as the definition of marriage.

Rollins allows for competing interpretations, but not all interpretations are equally good. When we need a good reading out of the text, we should do so with a prejudice of love, by reading with the poor, weak, and marginalized in mind, Rollins argues.[60] This sounds nice, but is it really workable as an interpretative key? Rollins's hermeneutical grid is a moving target. For instance, do we read the text with the poor in rural Alabama in mind or the poor in Sudan, the weak in power or the weak in moral resolve, the marginalized in Rollins's Ireland or marginalized fundamentalists in a secular university?

> Rollins's hermeneutical grid is a moving target.

Rollins wants to have it both ways. He wants the text to be open to a multitude of meanings, but he wants the text to still say certain things about compassion and poverty and justice. When it comes to "God is love" Rollins wants to affirm that this obviously doesn't mean we are called to hate. But what if God's love means He hates sin? Shouldn't "holy, holy, holy" and "our God is a consuming fire" obviously not mean something too, like that God is indifferent toward impurity?

It seems that Rollins has managed to assert a new foundationalism. God is love—that's all we know and everything else is unknown and therefore can only be un/known by the fact that God is love. But what love means is by no means clear without knowledge of what God is like; yet, this is precisely the sort of knowledge Rollins won't allow.

Third, Rollins, in his praise of doubt, has created a Christianity devoid of good news. He suggests that the movie *The Passion of the Christ* would have been more poignant if it hadn't included a brief scene of the empty tomb, because the Saturday before Easter is where faith really happens. We should not love Christ for the gain we receive. In one of his liturgies, Rollins imagines a group of Jesus' followers who left Jerusalem after the crucifixion, but still committed themselves to "protect the memory of Jesus and live by his teaching."[61] Centuries later, missionaries came to the people to tell them the rest of the story. But when they hear the "good news" one of the elders mourns because he fears that his people will now follow Jesus because He has value for them and not simply because Jesus has value in Himself. Rollins goes so far as to say that it is not "loving if I act in order to gain a reward."[62]

Rollins should read Jonathan Edwards or John Piper, both of whom demonstrate from Scripture that it pleases God most when we treasure Him as that which is most valuable to us.[63] As Piper puts it, "God is most glorified in us when we are most satisfied in him." It is not wrong to seek reward in God, provided that the reward we seek is ultimately God Himself. If self-interest (rightly conceived) has no place in the Christian life, why did Jesus tell His disciples to store up treasures in heaven (Matt. 6:19–20), and to be last that they might be first (Mark 9:35)? Why does Hebrews tell us that "without faith it impossible to please him [God], for whoever would draw near to God must believe that he exists and that he rewards those who seek him" (11:6)? This is a far cry from an a/theistic approach to faith that dis/believes in God regardless of whether He was raised from the dead, rewards His people, or even exists.

I'm sure that some people reading this book will say, "I've never even heard of Peter Rollins. He sounds whacked out to me. He certainly doesn't represent the emergent church I'm a part of." Hopefully not, but once again this illustrates the problem of boundaries. When the front cover has a quote from Brian McLaren declaring, "I am a raving fan of [this] book . . . one of the most important contributions to date to the emergent church conversation," it doesn't seem like this book has been relocated to the extreme fringe of the movement. Indeed, the endorsements of McLaren and Jones suggest that Rollins is a respected voice in the conversation.

BUILDING BRIDGES AND BUILDING WALLS

When people find out I'm writing on the emerging church, they often ask me, "Where is this going to end up?" I'm neither the prophet nor the son of a prophet, so I can't say. I doubt it will drop off the radar screen, though I could be mistaken. I hope the movement corrects itself, because there are voices within the conversation that are theologically orthodox and truly want to reform the evangelical church from some of its reductionistic, seeker-driven, arrogant, tradition-shunning errors. My fear, however, is that the movement will pick up steam and chug along in an increasingly biblically ill-informed, doctrine-less direction. There are lots of good intentions and plenty of whimsically stated paradoxes, but is there a message with doctrinal content that forms the center of the movement? As Lionel Trilling rightly warns, "When the dogmatic principle in religion is slighted, religion goes along for a while on generalized emotion and ethical intention . . . and then loses the force of its impulse, even the essence of its being."[64]

Young people will give their lives for an exclamation point, but they will not give their lives for a question mark, not for very long anyway. Once the protest runs out and the emerging church has its own blogdom, and conferences, and church networks, and book deals, there will be no exclamation point, and all that's left will be ethical intentions and passionate appeals for kingdom living. This will not sustain a movement—the protest will for a while, but once that's gone there will be no great vision of God, no urgent proclamation of salvation, no eternal judgment or reward at stake, just a call to live rightly and love one another. That message will sell on Oprah, Larry King, and at the Oscars, but it won't sustain and propel a gospel-driven church, because it isn't the gospel. Art, community, creativity, the environment, and a living wage are all nice things to be "for," just like family values, patriotism, school vouchers, faith-based initiatives, and a strong military, but isn't the church of Jesus Christ supposed to be mainly about the Father, Son, and Holy Spirit, the death and resurrection of Jesus, His atonement for our sins, the promise of eternal life, and the threat of coming judgment? In the rush to welcome people in we mustn't forget what "in" means.

Building bridges can be good, but so can building walls. Once in a while, we do need some "brickianity," to use Bell's pejorative noun. As Chesterton observed, doctrine may make walls, but they are the walls of a playground.

> We might fancy some children playing on the flat grassy top of some tall island in the sea. So long as there was a wall round the cliff's edge they could fling themselves into every frantic game and make the place the noisiest of nurseries. But the walls were knocked down, leaving the naked peril of the precipice. They did not fall over; but when their friends returned to them they were all huddled in terror in the centre of the island; and their song had ceased.[65]

In other words, walls are good if they keep us safe and free.

We must never forget that the story we have to believe and live in and proclaim is a story of glorious doctrinal assertions. "It is the dogma that is the drama," penned Sayers, "not beautiful phrases, nor comforting sentiments, nor vague aspirations to loving kindness and uplift, nor the promise of something nice after death—but the terrifying assertion that the same God who made the world lived in the world and passed through the grave and gate of death. Show that to a heathen, and they may not believe it; but at least they may realize that here is something that a man might be glad to believe."[66]

Notes

1. Doug Pagitt in Dave Tomlinson, *The Post-Evangelical* (Grand Rapids: Zondervan, 2003), 84.
2. This is Pagitt's critique of Dan Kimball in *Listening to the Beliefs of Emerging Churches*, Robert Webber, ed. (Grand Rapids: Zondervan, 2007), 114.
3. Tomlinson, *The Post-Evangelical*, 70.
4. Brian McLaren, *The Secret Message of Jesus* (Nashville: Nelson, 2007), 6.
5. Brain McLaren, *A Generous Orthodoxy* (Grand Rapids: Zondervan, 2004), 36.
6. Ibid., 325.
7. Ibid., 25.
8. Ibid., 33.
9. Quoted in Doug Pagitt, *Reimagining Spiritual Formation* (Grand Rapids: Zondervan, 2004), 43.
10. As quoted in Doug Pagitt, *An Emergent Manifesto of Hope*, Doug Pagitt and Tony Jones, eds. (Grand Rapids: Baker, 2007), 166, 168. Apparently, Fuller Theological Seminary, where Taylor teaches, and Zondervan, which published the book, do not qualify as organizations or institutions.
11. Ibid., 168, 169.
12. Statistics are from Dave Shiflett, *Exodus: Why Americans Are Fleeing Liberal Churches for Conservative Christianity* (New York: Sentinel, 2005), xiii–xiv. Shiflett reported double-digit growth for the Assemblies of God (18.5 percent), Conservative Christian Churches and Churches of Christ (18.6 percent), the Christian and Missionary Alliance (21.8 percent), the Church of God (40.2 percent), and the Presbyterian Church in America (42.4 percent). In their book *The Churching of America, 1776–2005* (New Brunswick, N.J.: Rutgers Univ. Press, 2005), Roger Finke and Rodney Stark come to the opposite conclusion of Taylor and many in the emergent church. Finke and Stark's working thesis is this: "To the degree that denominations rejected traditional doctrines and ceased to make serious demands on their followers, they ceased to prosper. The churching of America was accomplished by aggressive churches committed to vivid otherworldliness" (xiv).
13. Rob Bell, *Velvet Elvis* (Grand Rapids: Zondervan, 2005), 92.
14. D. G. Hart, ed., *J. Gresham Machen: Selected Shorter Writings* (Phillipsburg, N.J.: P&R Publishing, 2004), 144.
15. Erwin Raphael McManus in *The Church in Emerging Culture: Five Perspectives*, Leonard Sweet, ed. (Grand Rapids: Zondervan, 2003), 248.
16. As quoted in Eddie Gibbs and Ryan K. Bolger, *Emerging Churches: Creating Christian Community in Postmodern Culture* (Grand Rapids: Baker, 2005), 47.
17. Barry Taylor in Pagitt, *An Emergent Manifesto*, 170.
18. Dorothy Sayers, *Creed or Chaos? Why Christians Must Choose Either Dogma or Disaster (Or, Why It Really Does Matter What You Believe)* (Manchester, N.H.: Sophia Institute Press, 1999), 19.
19. Brian McLaren, *Modern Reformation*, July/August 2005, 49.
20. Peter Rollins, *How (Not) to Speak of God* (Brewster, Mass.: Paraclete, 2006), 3.
21. Dwight J. Friesen in *Emergent Manifesto*, 210. Athanasius was the fourth-century champion of Nicene orthodoxy. He maintained, against the Arians and at times against the world (*contra mundum*), that Christ was *homoousios* (of the same substance) with the Father, not simply *homoiousios* (of similar substance).
22. Ibid., 210.

23. Rob Bell, *Velvet Elvis* (Grand Rapids: Zondervan, 2005), 26–27.

24. Adolf Harnack, as quoted in James D. G. Dunn, *A New Perspective on Jesus: What the Quest for the Historical Jesus Missed* (Grand Rapids: Baker, 2005), 18.

25. Cf. G.K. Chesterton, *Everlasting Man* (San Francisco: Ignatius Press, 1925): "All that is condemned in Catholic tradition, authority, and dogmatism and the refusal to retract and modify, are but the natural human attributes of a man with a message relating to a fact" (267–68).

26. J. Gresham Machen, *Christianity and Liberalism* (Grand Rapids: Eerdmans, 1923), 21.

27. Doug Pagitt, *Preaching Re-Imagined: The Role of the Sermon in Communities of Faith* (Grand Rapids: Zondervan, 2005), 103.

28. Machen, *Christianity and Liberalism*, 47.

29. Harry Emerson Fosdick as quoted in *J. Gresham Machen: Selected Shorter Writings*, 460.

30. Ibid., 93.

31. The exception is Peter Rollins, who explicitly mentions, approvingly, Schleiermacher, Barth, Bultmann, Tillich, and Rosenzweig in *How (Not) to Speak of God*, 23.

32. Barry Taylor in Pagitt, *Emergent Manifesto*, 165.

33. Bell, *Velvet Elvis*, 22. Cf. Bell's second book, *Sex God: Exploring the Endless Connections Between Sexuality and Spirituality* (Grand Rapids: Zondervan, 2007), where he says, "God meets people where they are and invites them to the next stage of enlightenment" (136).

34. Robert Sanders, "The Ecstatic Heresy," *Christianity Today*, October 2004, 55.

35. Ibid., 56–57.

36. All three quotes come from http://www.relevantmagazine.com/beta/issue_21_missing-pointA.php

37. Caroline Westerhoff writes, "If anyone and everyone are too easily included, we are saying in effect that anything goes. We are disclaiming boundaries. And as our membership is more and more made up of those who will not or cannot confirm some measure of adherence to the core practices and values of the defined community, that community as we have known it will disappear. . . . If even initial membership is without qualification, then we stand for little other than being nonsensically 'inclusive.' If belonging is without obligation and accountability, then we finally have not joined much of anything at all, and any significance that community might have held for us evaporates like mist" (*Good Fences* [Harrisburg, Pa.: Morehouse, 1999], 29).

38. Because Burke is the main author of *Heretic's Guide*, I will refer to the ideas in the book as his, rather than going the more cumbersome route of always mentioning Burke and Taylor.

39. Spencer Burke and Barry Taylor, *A Heretic's Guide to Eternity* (San Francisco: Jossey-Bass, 2006), ix, x.

40. He writes, "To be honest, religion doesn't really work for me anymore. Being aligned with an institutional church or a particular system of worship seems increasingly irrelevant to my ongoing journey with God," *Heretic's Guide*, 6.

41. Ibid., 52, 197, 199, respectively.

42. Ibid., 64–65.

43. Ibid., 130–31.

44. Ibid., 184–85.

45. Ibid., 195.

46. Ibid., 211.

47. "Heretic's Guide to Eternity 4." Jesus Creed. August 8, 2006; a blog by Scot McKnight at http://www.jesuscreed.org/?p=1319. To be fair, McKnight mentions that Burke told him over the phone that all are included in God's grace because of Jesus' death and resurrection. McKnight wonders, as I do, why not put that in the book then?

48. "I Am (Not) as Smart as Peter Rollins," December 5, 2006, http://theoblogy.blogspot.com/ (emphasis in original).

49. By and large I am not even touching on his liturgies, one of which includes a time where people forgive God's faults and pronounce judgment on God (94–95) and another where a bare-chested man has words like "gay," "queer," "homo," and "fag" painted on him (134). See Ted's chapter 8 for more discussion.

50. Peter Rollins, *How (Not) to Speak of God* (Brewster, Mass.: Paraclete, 2006), xii.

51. Ibid., 17.

52. Ibid., xii.

53. Ibid., 25. See 26 on keeping doubts about what we believe about God.

54. Ibid., 21.

55. Ibid., 32. Emphasis in original.

56. Ibid., 3. Chesterton wisely remarks, "If there is one thing that the same liberals always offer as a piece of pure and simple Christianity, untroubled by doctrinal disputes, it is the single sentence 'God is love'" (*The Everlasting Man*, 227).

57. Ibid., 66.

58. Ibid., 57.

59. Ibid., 17.

60. Ibid., 61.

61. Ibid., 80.

62. Ibid., 68. Rollins's detachment philosophy leads him to utter statements like this: "Here we are presented with three criteria for the perfect, loving gift—that is, one that we would not use in order to get a reward: (1) the receiver does not know he or she has been given a gift; (2) nothing is actually given; and (3) the giver does not know he or she has given anything" (70).

63. All of Piper's books deal with this theme. See for example: *Desiring God: Meditations of a Christian Hedonist* (Sisters, Ore.: Multnomah, 1999); *God's Passion for His Glory: Living the Vision of Jonathan Edwards* (Wheaton, Ill: Crossway, 1998); *God is the Gospel: Meditations on God's Love as the Gift of Himself* (Wheaton, Ill.: Crossway, 2005).

64. Lionel Trilling as quoted in Richard John Neuhaus, "How We Got to Where We Are," *First Things*, January 2007, 172.

65. Chesterton, *Orthodoxy*, 153.

66. Sayers, *Creed or Chaos*, 25.

See to it that no one takes you captive through hollow and deceptive philosophy, which depends on human tradition and the basic principles of this world rather than on Christ.

—COLOSSIANS 2:8 (NIV)

CHAPTER 6

A FUNERAL FOR A FRIEND: ON CHURCHES, STORY, AND PROPOSITIONAL LANGUAGE

AS THE STORY GOES, a young schoolteacher, new in town, repeatedly visited a bank to make deposits into his savings account. He would come to the same window each time, where there happened to work an attractive young woman with dark hair and a nice smile. The man was always smiling. He always had a kind word to say to her, and one day, breaking protocol, she asked: "What are you going to do with all of that money you're saving?"

"I'm going to give it all to you," the man replied. Three years later they were married. They remained married, happily, for forty years, until the man passed away.

Today I am showing my wife the church and preschool of my youth, as we are more than thirty minutes early for an 11 o'clock funeral—the funeral of the schoolteacher who married the attractive teller. The church, Grace United Methodist Church in Hartford City, Indiana, is, as it always was, immaculately clean. There are stained glass windows throughout, and while fashions and movements have come and gone, the church—adjacent to a used car lot, a funeral home, and the city firehouse—has stayed the same. Same red carpet. Same understated beauty. It's probably been over twenty years since I've been in this building—and twenty-five years since I was a student at the Helen Lieber Preschool in the basement of the church. Nothing much has changed about Lieber Preschool, either.

Walking through the church is like taking a walk back in time. I hug people I haven't hugged in two decades. I visit a fellowship hall downstairs that would give Dan Kimball a heart attack—complete with folding tables, a drop ceiling, bad carpet, and a potluck lunch. As I catch up with people, my mother, ever the cheerleader, tells them that I am writing a book on the emergent church. They nod politely and wish me well. I'm quite certain they have no idea what the emergent church is—or who Dan Kimball is. I estimate the number of people in this room who have read Brian McLaren's *A Generous Orthodoxy* to be zero. Ditto for D. A. Carson's *Becoming Conversant with the Emergent Church.* This pleases me to no end.

This church, like many in America, has survived a great deal. Car wrecks, cancer, extramarital affairs, some bad theology, and the like. But, much like the small town that it's in, it has taken care of its own. It has mourned with those who mourn. It has delivered meals. It has made countless hospital visits. It has, for the most part, spoken truth and preached the gospel of Christ crucified. It has come alongside single mothers, of which there are many in Hartford City. I find myself, this morning, very proud of the church and its people.

Those here today come to honor the life of a man who lived largely because of a proposition—the sometimes outmoded belief that Christ paid the penalty for our sins, and that we are, because of that, compelled to live for Him, and like Him. Brian McLaren would call this view of Christ incomplete, somehow, asserting that there must be more.

In each of the photos set along the front of the sanctuary, the schoolteacher was smiling. Smiling with Janie, his wife (the bank teller), and smiling with his boys, who were my friends through school.

THE FRUITS OF JOE'S LIFE

As I look around the church, in what is thought to be an insignificant small town in an insignificant part of the country—rural Indiana—I see the fruits of Joe's life. He has brought together diverse populations: Six-figure administrators from the university where he worked as a professor are sitting shoulder to shoulder with six-dollar-an-hour workers from Hartford Concrete, who he may have visited in the hospital. He has championed the oppressed—the inner-city basketball player who probably should have flunked out of Taylor University, but who is now the principal of a large and thriving high school.

I am reminded that there are still churches and places in this country where one doesn't have to work at being "authentic." Authentic isn't a look you put on in the morning, or a new and snappy way to bathe the sanctuary in "mystery" through the strategic arrangement of candles and projected images. Authentic is bearing one another's burdens. Authentic is people coming to a funeral in their work clothes—Carhartts, hospital scrubs, etc.—on a Friday morning.

Later in life Joe taught an education course at Taylor University. He taught people how to be teachers—and in my case he encouraged some of us to go in different directions when he saw talents being underutilized. He spoke often of his "girlfriend"—his wife, the bank teller. He was unwittingly showing us how to be married. How to love our wives as Christ loved His church.

"In all things, He must be preeminent," he would say, from the front of the classroom. He was small of stature, with graying hair. In a way he was probably the meekest guy I knew, because I had never heard him say a harsh word about anyone. He wouldn't do much in a fight, I thought then. I never saw him pound his fist on the table. I knew what he believed because of the way he lived, not because of what he said in a message board debate or in a journal article or a series of books.

At the time I was a two-hundred-forty-pound college football player on crutches. He came to see me in the hospital, and later at home while I rested a surgically repaired leg that would never be any good for football again. "Have you considered doing something with writing?" he asked, by my bedside. He graded all my papers, he said, and thought I had a knack. *Screw writing*, I thought to myself. *I'm a football player*. Now, ten years later, I am a writer. It's the only thing that has ever come easily.

Three pastors stand at the front of the sanctuary, sharing their thoughts about Joe. There are the usual funny stories, and some touching ones. Rev. Lloyd Hall tells of a time when he asked Joe to be on the congregational care staff, and Joe, so moved, wept because, he said, he had been waiting for someone to ask him to serve in that capacity. Hall tells of the ministry Joe had to small churches—often serving country congregations as an interim pastor. Serving the churches that the church industry considers to be "dead" or "dying" because they aren't innovating, embracing change, engaging the culture, building new wings, etc.

We sing "Amazing Grace," and then a song called "Hymn of Promise," which I'd never heard before. Hall then reads Philippians 1:22–23 and Hebrews 4:16 on living for Christ and coming to the throne of grace. Last, he reads some thoughts that Joe had prepared, in the weeks leading up to his death:

> In dying, Christ destroyed our death, and in rising, Christ has restored our life. Christ will come again in glory. As in faith Joe put on Christ, so in Christ Joe is clothed with glory. Here and now we are God's children. What we shall be has not yet been revealed; but we know that when he appears, we shall be like him, for we shall see him as he is. Those who have this hope purify themselves, as Christ is pure.
>
> Jesus said, "I am the resurrection and I am life. Those who believe in me, even though they shall die, yet shall they live, and whoever lives and believes in me shall never die. . . . I am the Alpha and Omega, the

beginning and the end, the first and the last and I hold the keys of hell and death. . . . Because I live, you shall live also."

JOE'S PRAYER

Finally, we are asked to do something that feels a little strange, probably because I have been in the city too long, where it is uncommon for people to actually say what they mean.

"Joe didn't want anyone to leave here without considering praying this prayer," says Hall. "In the bulletin it's called a *Personal Prayer of Belief and Acceptance.*" For any emergent here who knew Joe, alarms and whistles may be sounding in fear of more impending propositions. But this is the proposition that was at the heart of the stuff in Joe's life—all the deep-felt truths that made Joe, Joe.

So we all stood together—my mom next to me on one side, all of the college administrators behind us, the cops, the old ladies, and everybody else—and prayed this prayer, penned by Joe before his death. I could see and hear him in it, so much so that I got a little choked up.

"Dear Father, I believe that Jesus Christ is Your only begotten Son, and that He became a human being, shed His blood and died on the cross to cleanse away my sin that was separating me from You. I believe that He rose from the dead, physically, to give me a new life. Lord Jesus, I invite You to come into my heart. I accept You as my Savior and Lord. I confess my sins and ask You to wash them away. I believe that You have come and are living in me right now. Thank You, Jesus! Amen."

= = = =

"They don't like any propositional language," says Neil, a philosophy student at Michigan State University, of his summer spent dialoguing on The Ooze, a popular emergent Web site and online community (run by Spencer Burke). I give him a lot of credit, I tell him, for engaging in the message board wars that inevitably happen on these sites.

"I'm not a fan of the message board at all," he says. "I don't think it's a good way to be in a 'discussion,' but I really wanted to engage the movement and see what people were thinking." Again, more credit given. This is because Neil did more than the author was willing to do. I would rather take a beating than argue (dialogue) on message boards all day, where people are regularly brave and full of convictions without actually being brave and full of convictions.

"There was a lot that I would bring up, just to see where people were at," he says. "Mainly to see if there is an importance in theology."

Neil describes an encounter in which he was in a discussion with another Ooze member, who accused him of using propositional language when talking about Jesus.

"I asked him to describe his relationship with Jesus without using propositions," he says. "The guy wrote back and just said 'relationship, relationship, relationship—it's all about relationships.' Which on one hand is true, but on the other hand you can't have a relationship with someone without knowing about—and wanting to know more about—that person. I mean, we worship in spirit and in truth, and I think they're willing to accept the spirit part, but not as much interested in truth."

"Surprisingly with my generation, I think there seems to be a trend back toward being more conservative again, when it comes to this stuff," he says. "At least in the circles that I've been in with young Christians, they want something solid to grasp and hold on to. But I will say that there is a group—a lot of the Campus Crusade kids on campus—that is grasping onto these new ideas. I think at some level they like the worship style and atmosphere, but I was talking to a friend who said, 'If I want to take somebody to church, I take them to Mars Hill, but if I want to go and be fed with solid theology, I'm going to go somewhere else.' So they feel like it's a place that they might think is more appealing to new believers or young people."

Our conversation works back around to his experiences on The Ooze.

"This is what I've gathered. There are members of the emergent church who do have solid theology. The majority that I encountered didn't seem to. The big things they get caught up on are semantics—a lot of people see language as a stumbling block. It's about conversation but ironically they have trouble engaging in any conversations because of getting tripped up on words.

"The majority of people on The Ooze seemed to me to be people who have had bad experiences in the church. Somehow they felt unwelcomed or their ideas were rejected. I think they're looking for acceptance and affirmation. There's a lot of bitterness . . . and that's translated into equating dogmatism and spiritual discipline with things that are bad. So all of the good things that are affirmed in dogmatic creeds are immediately labeled as 'bad.'

"I eventually had to stop, because I was getting angry, more than anything."

= = = =

This project has made me realize how easy it is to write sports books. People love sports. People think I'm cool for having spent time with people who play sports, and telling their stories in a compelling way. This book, however, is a completely different ball game. It's having an interesting effect on my friends and family, whose reactions have ranged from "Why are you so mean?" to "This book really needs to be written, and I'm glad you're doing it."

I have been exchanging e-mails with Ben, a friend for whom I have a great deal of respect. Ben is a science teacher in the public schools, and has felt less than welcome at his church because of his stance on creation. This has led him to look into the emergent church. Below are a couple of our e-mails, reprinted with his permission (and including the casual terms, punctuation, and style we love to use in our e-messages):

From: Ben
To: Ted
Subject: RE: howdy
Date: Wed, 20 Dec 2006 04:26:46 -0800 (PST)

Hey I was wondering if you have read anything by Brian McLaren (A new kind of Christian, or others)? I guess you could say the last couple of years I have been a little rebellious in terms of my theology. Our church here is great, but I think my rebel streak is in association to our church body. So anyways I have been doing quite a bit of reading and thinking and have been looking for others who have read any of his material or similar things to see what they think.

Our church body is very homogenous, and none of these things are really preached, it is more of an assumed culture within the church that Republicans are good, Democrats are of the Devil, home school your kids to keep them from those sinful schools and teachers teaching evolution (oops! that's me), and the list goes on.

I respect these views and thoughts but it isn't a church of dialogue, more so of ridicule for those on the other side, because they really don't know anyone on the other side. I always felt URC was conservative on many issues, but there was a certain type of respect or caution about making blanket statements that I think came from being located in a college town. Our church is a great community and I don't mean to bash it, although it makes me think. Ben

- - -

Hey Ben,

Man, it's crazy that you bring this up—I'm so glad you did!! I've been doing a ton of reading on the emergent church movement. . . . I started a couple of years ago when URC was between pastors. At that time we had been (unsuccessfully) recruited to join an emergent group here in Lansing.

Wow, where to start on all of this. I think your assessment of a lot of affluent, suburban churches is dead-on accurate. I always hated that "wealthiness is next to godliness" "Republican party/homeschool" ethic. There's so much pride wrapped up in that stuff. Makes me ill.

That said, based on a lot of the reading I've done on Emergent—stuff like McLaren's books, Erwin McManus, Pete Rollins, Rob Bell, etc., I don't think Emergent is the answer. What I'm feeling more and more is that Emergent is just a new set of conceits—a love of philosophy, leftist politics, and a theology that is more man-centered than God-centered. To the Emergent, Christianity is a story from which ethics are gleaned, rather than a life-saving proposition. That's my take on it at least . . . although I'm still doing lots of reading. Check out D. A. Carson's "Becoming Conversant with the Emergent Church."

Ted

- - -

Hey Ted,

It was great to talk the other day, and it would be great to get together some time after the Holidays for sure. . . .

As I reflect on the Emergent movement, I agree with you. It is a total knee jerk reaction to the culturally driven conservative church. I really don't like the idea of going and starting new "emergent" churches, but I think the idea of churches having "emergent" thinkers is more beneficial. Starting whole new churches is like throwing the baby out with the bath water. But I understand why it is done as many churches don't want to compromise on any issues in fear of the slippery slope. And you are right in that we do need to stand on scripture and we do need to realize that sometimes scripture says things that don't feel right and don't seem good but God said them.

I mentioned before that we had a meeting with our pastor over the whole evolution thing and that it really went quite well. But during the course of our talk he mentioned a meeting he had had a few weeks earlier with a couple that had visited our church.

The husband was one of the leaders of the democratic party for the county, and he came to the pastor asking if it was still OK for him to be involved with the church!!! Of course he replied yes, and it frustrated him. But shouldn't that send off huge warning sirens that the Church is headed in the wrong direction? And again, it isn't that anything is preached pro-Rep. but just the overall atmosphere and culture of the people in today's church leads to this. It is sad. So I think when these people are given a choice, Church A—They quote, "God is the same yesterday, today. . ." and then say they are not changing (not realizing that the way their church runs and functions is totally different than anything else in the past)—or Church B—"Everything is good! have a good time, grab a mocha on your way into the entertainment room"—then I think they choose Church B.

I want the middle ground. I don't mind having a church that I disagree with on certain issues, I know my stance and the churches may even flip flop in the next 50 years. I like it when the church takes a stand on issues, but then again, I want a situation where I can feel free to be who I am and not scorned for these thoughts. I want to be able to bring visitors and have them be loved, not focused on how they will be judged. I can't wait to hear more about the book you guys are doing,

Ben

= = = =

Almost everyone here looks like Sufjan Stevens—which is to say skinny,[1] hip, and misunderstood. This is something that almost everyone here would probably also consider a huge compliment. *Here* is Grand Rapids, Michigan, the city that invented conservative, on the campus of Calvin College, the Christian college that is trying very hard to shed the conservative label.

If you don't know who Sufjan Stevens is, you must, like, live under a rock or something. All kidding aside, he's the pomo[2] guy that pomo Christian kids have latched on to, much like my college classmates latched on to U2 for being interesting without being too naughty back in the day. Christian music for people who wouldn't admit to liking Christian music. And he's also, by the way, a truly great and creative musician.

Sufjan is here to perform this weekend, as well as "engage in an ongoing discussion of Christianity and the arts"—a discussion that has been going for at least ten years now, since I left a Christian college a lot like this one, filled with well-to-do artsy Christian kids trying to "out-dishevel" one another at gatherings like this one. The conference is called FFM, or the Festival of Faith and Music. Its official purpose, I'm told, is to "explore what is worthwhile in today's popular music scene."

The event's emcee is a faculty member at Calvin, who explains that the conference, in essence, is "a profound apology from the Christian community for doing such a poor job of engaging art and culture in the public square." He adds, "We don't have a lot of answers."

This is an apology I've heard made several times before, and I'm still a little unclear as to the reason. Is it because churches aren't displaying art on their walls? Neither are insurance companies, but nobody is up in arms about that. My hunch is that there is this feeling that churches aren't adequately "supporting" artists (musicians, writers, visual artists) in their midst. However, I don't exactly see churches "supporting" software designers, salesmen, or farmers either. That's not the church's purpose. And it seems that the artists who are making the most noise about "not being supported" are the ones who may not have the talent to really cut it in the marketplace anyway. I don't know of any working artists (musicians, actors, writers, painters) who complain that their church doesn't "support" their efforts. Art is tough. Making a living at art is tough. It's tough on families and marriages. That's simply the nature of the game.

The emcee continues by asking the crowd to be on guard against "the cult of personality, or the cult of celebrity." Though they have all paid a premium to be here, he asks the conferees not to "ask for autographs, take pictures, or gawk" at the celebrities in their midst. "Treat them like colleagues," he says, before introducing the keynote speaker, Lauren Winner. There is a tension here, because it is celebrity that sells Sufjan Stevens's albums, Lauren Winner's books . . . and my books, for that matter. It's why musicians and writers tour. It's why people pay good money to come to something called the "Festival of Faith and Music."

I don't know if Lauren Winner considers herself emergent. Probably not, but I think she, Anne Lamott, and the male Anne Lamott, Donald Miller,[3] may have unwittingly been the first emergents. The emergent church is big on story, and no stories have made a bigger ripple in Christian publishing than theirs. She wrote a memoir in her late twenties called *Girl Meets God.* I think it made waves in the Christian book business in part because it didn't read like a Christian book. This is a compliment.

I am fully prepared to not like Lauren Winner, but actually end up enjoying her talk very much. She avoids the usual clichés at these sorts of things—jokes at the expense of people like Thomas Kinkade, rants about how the church doesn't support anything worth supporting, and the like. She is almost comfortingly boring, as a speaker, and I don't mean that in a mean way. She is straightforward and avoids the irony and cynicism that infuse almost any interaction with almost any person under age forty-five.

The Q and A time at the end of her talk is especially enjoyable, mostly because of the questions from attendees, who are all trying to "out-deep" one another in the vein of the film *Art School Confidential,* which you probably shouldn't see. She admirably wades through the babble and actually finds things to answer.

At the end, she describes a painting that hangs on her wall at home. The painting depicts a well-dressed woman in her early forties, wearing a Talbots-style outfit and holding in front of her torso a soccer ball. The piece is entitled "Eve in the Suburbs" and, as she describes it, is making a statement on suburban culture. What she is able to (thankfully) admit is that we are Eve. The room is full of Eves who, in a few short years, will be trading their meticulously torn jeans for a pencil skirt and a pastel-colored blouse. She is saying, in essence, that having the time and resources to have a discussion as frivolous as "Christianity dialoguing with the arts" is, in itself, a huge privilege.

NOTES

1. There are lots of kids here who look like they need a good meal.
2. *Pomo* is short for "postmodern," which has come not only to describe an era, but also a "look" which includes the right kind of jeans, T-shirts, and jackets.
3. That sounds mean, I know, and it wasn't meant to be. It's just a way to describe his writing which, like Lamott's, is a sort of diary-for-the-masses. For the record, I enjoyed reading *Blue Like Jazz*.

"If Neo is right, all that we currently understand being a Christian to be has been conditioned by our being modern."

—DAN POOLE, *the fictional pastor in* A New Kind of Christian

"You know what I blame this on the breakdown of? Society!"

—MOE SZYSLAK, *bartender on* The Simpsons

MODERNISM:
THE BOOGEYMAN
COMETH

THE PROVERBIAL CAT'S out of the bag. Though I don't tune in anymore (for a number of reasons), I confess I used to watch *The Simpsons*. A lot. I probably averaged close to two episodes a day in college. The show is sometimes irreverent, usually funny, and often spot-on in its satire—like Moe's declaration on the previous page. Here's the setting: Homer's house was broken into on Christmas Eve and all the presents and decorations stolen. So Homer goes to Moe's Tavern to tell his sad story. Moe then responds indignantly with the explanation: "You know what I blame this on the breakdown of? Society!"

The joke, of course (which I am ruining by explaining), is that the general breakdown of society meaninglessly gets the blame for all our particular problems. Crime, homelessness, teenage pregnancies, stolen presents—they're all the fault of societal breakdown.

Which is sort of how the emerging church views modernism. Once upon a time the church was a brighter, fairer place. And then the Enlightenment happened, and the scourge of modernism—systematic theologies, propositions, foundationalism, certainty, creeds, monological preaching, individualism, inerrancy, logic, indoctrination, deductive reasoning—began to crack down on the church. Emerging church leaders recognize that they are advocating for "a new kind of Christian," one which will seem strange to most churchgoers. But the strangeness, they argue, is only because we have been blinded by modernism. The Christianity that we are quick to defend is only a modern version of Christianity (if it can be called authentic Christianity at all). Western Christianity has wed itself to a culture, the modern culture, which is now in decline.[1] As such, the best course of action is to trade in the modern version of Christianity for the updated postmodern model.

How bad is modernism and how pervasive its influence? Four critics make their arguments. First, McLaren:

Objectivity has great value. But like analysis, in the modern world it became a kind of narcotic to us. . . . Like *Star Trek*'s Spock, we believed that cool, emotion-free, objective logic would be our salvation.[2]

What was the goal of theology in the modern era, other than this: to describe God as a scientist describes an object—objective, detached, sanitized of subjectivity, removed from the variable of personal relationship?[3]

Compare modern Christianity's quest for the perfect belief system to medieval church architecture. Christians in the emerging culture may look back on our doctrinal structures (statements of faith, systematic theologies) as we look back on medieval cathedrals: possessing a real beauty that should be preserved, but now largely vacant, not inhabited or used much anymore, more tourist attraction than holy place.[4]

Here's Pagitt:

For the last few centuries, the Western worldview has assumed belief that leads to spiritual formation comes about in exactly the same way. People start out as empty vessels—so the model goes—that must be filled with information, which leads to knowledge, which leads to right belief. Thus knowledge is power: If we give people the information to do something, they will do it, and if we give them information they will believe.... The concept that knowledge comes through information is foundationalism—in rough terms, learning as a construction project.[5]

And Carl Raschke:

The modernist church is a managed "faith-body." . . . The postmodern church manifests the vital activity of the individual cells and their mutual "biochemistry." It is the kind of "asymmetrical horizontality" that deconstructs most paradigms of ecclesiology.[6]

And Leonard Sweet:

Postmodern spirituality is different from modern spirituality. A continental drift of the soul has taken place whereby spirituality is less creedal, less propositional, more relational, and more sensory. Logic is no longer converting anyone—only the transforming experience of the living Christ.[7]

Postmoderns are truth-seekers first, truth-makers second. Whereas modern seekers sought the knowledge of the truth, postmodern seekers want to *know* the truth in the biblical sense of that word "know"—that is, *experience* the truth.[8]

David Tomlinson catalogues a number of shifts (some of which are below) from the modern church to the postmodern church. He sees them yielding the advantage to the postmodern church. The shifts within the church include:

- from propositional expressions of faith to relational stories about faith journeys;
- from the authority of Scripture alone to a harmony between the authority of Scripture and other personal ways God mysteriously and graciously speaks to Christians;
- from a theology that prepares people for death and the afterlife to a theology of life;
- from a personal, individualistic, private faith to harmony between personal and community faith;
- from the church being a place where people take up space to the church as a mission outpost that sends people out;
- from arguing faith to the "dance of faith";
- from salvation by event to a journey of salvation;
- from motivating through fear to motivating through compassion, community, and hope; and
- from a search for dogmatic truth to a search for spiritual experience.[9]

THE MONSTER OF MODERNISM

What can be said in response to these sweeping claims about modernism and Christianity? First, the world has changed. It always does. Christians in the past were sometimes too confident in their own interpretive abilities. As much as it pains me to admit it, Charles Hodge's comparing theology to a science in which we collect and organize facts does sound antiquated (though his approach sounds worse than it is). And it is true that today's culture is less apt to say, "How could Jesus perform miracles?" and more apt to ask, "How could Jesus be the only way?" So, emerging Christians are right; the world has changed.

Second, having said that, the emerging church view of history is still naïve. Are creedal statements really the product of modern spirituality? Whenever this new spirituality supposedly started—whether the 1600s, 1700s, 1800s, or 1900s—statements of faith certainly predate modernism. What about Nicea, Constantinople, Chalcedon, and Ephesus, not too mention Trent, Augsburg, and Dort—all of which predate 1620? Does anyone really believe that creedal formulations began with modernism, as if Christians suddenly got obsessed with doctrine in the wake of the Enlightenment?

Perhaps now is an appropriate time to put in a good word for systematic theology. Are systematic theologies really the product of modern Christianity's quest for a perfect belief system? Augustine, Aquinas, and Calvin may not have been systematicians like Louis Berkhof or Wayne Grudem, but weren't they just as passionate about the right "belief system"? Weren't they writing about theology in an organized, systematic way hundreds of years before modernism? Hasn't every pastor, emergent or otherwise, preached a topical sermon or led a Bible study on a particular area of inquiry? Like, who is God? Or what about evil? Or what did Jesus accomplish? This is systematic theology—taking a question and trying to hear what all of Scripture says about it. Isn't that what McLaren has done about the kingdom or Dan Kimball about worship?

I understand that the emerging church is only addressing certain areas of inquiry that they deem are most crucial. That's their prerogative. But at some point in the conversation it would be nice if they would share their convictions on something other than community, kingdom living, and mystery. The emerging church will grow irrelevant to the very culture it is trying to reach if it can't answer with some measure of clarity, however tentatively, the most basic questions that face every human being.

Third, the emergent critique of the modern church suffers from an overpopulation of straw men. Time and again emergent authors complain that the traditional evangelical church has been overly objectified so that God is just an entity to be dissected and analyzed, with no concern for a personal relationship. They complain that believers are looked at as empty vessels waiting to be filled with information. They complain that evangelical leaders treat the church like managed faith-bodies with no concern for the vital activity of the individual cells.[10] Perhaps emergent writers were unfortunate enough to be in churches this bad—the kind that only motivated through fear, and never sent people out into mission, and never gave a theology for life, and never gave a rip about community. If so, they have my pity, because for all the weakness of the church in America, I sincerely doubt many churches are this awful.

Fourth, the emerging church greatly exaggerates the differences between modernism and postmodernism. One of the staples of emergent literature is the "from/to" lists. In addition to Tomlinson's list of thirteen shifts from modern to postmodern, Webber has his own list of fourteen shifts, Burke has a list of seven, McLaren has a list of ten, and Sweet has a list of twenty-five. (And I thought *modernism* was too linear, too neat, too tidy, and too reductionistic!) McLaren is at least candid enough to admit that people like him "too often indulge in facile dualisms."[11] Modernism was not always that bad. Postmodernism isn't always that good. And the line between the two is sometimes imaginary, or at least relatively unimportant. After all, writes Dan Kimball:

> Ancient, medieval, modern, or postmodern—emerged or emerging— when it comes down to it, we still have the same basic human needs. We all want to be accepted. We all want to know that we are loved. We all long for purpose. We also long for spiritual fulfillment and meaning. We long to know our Creator and are born with a hole in our hearts that only he can fill. These things will never change this side of heaven. This means Jesus will be the only answer to fill this eternal longing created in us, whether we're ravers, gothics, or Wiccans, twenty-year-olds or ninety-year-olds. . . . We are not facing anything new. We are not facing anything that the Holy Spirit of God moving in the emerging church cannot overcome.[12]

So if things below the surface are not that different and human need is still the same (and truth is still the same, I might add), why must Christianity "change or die"? I'm not some old fuddy-duddy pining for the good old days. I'm not opposed to new styles or new approaches, but if we are not really facing anything new on the most fundamental spiritual level, perhaps a fundamental reimagining of our Christian faith is not necessary.

WHAT'S IN A NAME?

The supposed radical difference between modern spirituality and postmodern spirituality is often nothing more than semantics. For example, many of Kimball's side-by-side comparison charts are especially guilty of hyperbolizing the differences between the modern church and the postmodern. Kimball says that preaching in the emerging church "teaches how the ancient wisdom of Scripture applies to kingdom living as a disciple of Christ" while the modern preacher "serves as a dispenser of biblical truths to help solve personal problems in modern life."[13] Those two sentences would say the same thing if not for Kimball's choice of language, employing uninspiring words like "dispenser" and "solve" for the modern church instead of cool words like "ancient wisdom" and "kingdom living." Similarly, in the modern church "the Bible is a book to help solve problems and a means to know God," and "discipleship is based on modern methodology and helps." Conversely, in the emerging church, "the Bible is a compass for direction and a means to experience God," and "discipleship is based on ancient disciplines."[14] Well, who wants problem solving and methodology when you can experience God and use ancient disciplines?

Their exaggerated use of language makes it nearly impossible to see anything good in the modern church. Who wants a CEO pastor when you can have a spiritual guide and fellow journeyer?[15] Who wants an institutional church of organized religion with hierarchical leadership?[16] The comparison charts and from/to shifts are simply unfair—the emerging church is organic instead of linear, experiential instead of spectator oriented. They have worship gatherings instead of services. Instead of systematic propositional theology, they prefer a theotopical retelling of the story.[17] What's the real difference?

Names—raw, vintage names—are crucial to the emerging church. "How do we create systems for discipleship," Kimball asks, "that do not smack of modern business or academic structures and don't feel programmed but rather embrace the mystery, awe, and wonder of God's transforming work?" The answer? New names. "Mosaic church in Los Angeles uses names like River to describe a spiritual formation retreat that 'is an immersion of your senses, emotions, body and intellect as we quest to explore our connection to God.' They have another retreat called Snow, which is a 'quest for forgiveness.' Cedar Ridge Community Church in Maryland has spiritual formation classes named Soul Findings, Journey, and Kindle."[18]

There is certainly nothing wrong with new names, but is postmodern culture so radically different from the modern church just because they have *Soul Findings*, *Journey*, and *Kindle* instead of *Discovering Membership*, *Discovering Spiritual Maturity*, *Discovering My Ministry*, and *Discovering My Life Mission*?[19]

Meanwhile, Pagitt says we must distinguish between storytelling and testimony time. "Sharing our stories is not the same thing as giving our testimonies. . . . While not sounding like 'testimonies' in the traditional sense, these stories of the way God bubbles up in others' lives serve as testaments to who God is and how God acts in our lives. Telling and hearing these stories shapes us and forms us."[20] So, let me get this straight. They aren't testimonies, just stories that serve as testaments to what God is doing in our lives. Sounds like a testimony to me.

I may be already hopelessly out of touch with the culture at my young age, but aren't some of the new names going to be obstacles to the faith more than invitations? Beside being confusing, won't many seekers find that we are trying a bit too hard when we have fusion services instead of worship and hire experience designers instead of pastors and call ourselves an "incubator for kingdom-inspired community-building, creativity, and social action"[21] instead of a church? At what point can we say that "sitting barefooted on the floor" and commenting on Ephesians as "an impromptu but extended tête-à-tête between church members and leadership" that focuses on "the intensity of interpersonal communication"[22] sounds more profound than it really is? There's nothing offensive about this tête-à-tête, but isn't it just sitting on the ground talking about the Bible?

"DIALOGUE THE WORD, TIMOTHY!"

In his letters to Timothy and Titus, Paul tirelessly commands his young disciples to teach and preach, rebuke and encourage, guard against false doctrine, and train other men to do the same (2 Tim. 2:1–2; cf. 1 Tim. 4:6, 11, 13; 5:17; Titus 1:9). Their charge is given in the most solemn terms: "In the presence of God and of Christ Jesus, who is to judge the living and the dead, and by his appearing and his kingdom: preach the word" (2 Tim. 4:1–2). Jesus came to preach (Luke 4:43); Paul went out to preach; the church was built on the foundation of apostolic preaching (Eph. 2:20); so Timothy was supposed to preach too.

These texts notwithstanding, many in the emerging church lament the central place preaching has received in Protestant worship services. Pagitt, for example, decries how preaching has become "speaching." "There was a time when I felt my ability to deliver sermons was a high calling that I sought to refine but didn't need to redefine. Those days are gone. Now I find myself regularly redefining my role and the role of preaching. . . . Preaching doesn't work—at least not in the ways we hope."[23] The problem, according to emergent leaders, isn't with the people or the preachers, but with the method of one-way communication where one clear message is spoken to passive listeners.[24]

The problem with today's preaching, in other words, is that it's modern preaching. Or so the argument goes. Robert Webber, for example, talks about two different methods of communication: discursive and communal. He argues that "discursive communication is informational. You find it in lectures, in books, and in media. The primary concern is to pass information from one person to another. This is the kind of worship one finds in churches influenced by the Enlightenment." Communal communication, the new preaching, actually is older than its discursive counterpart and "has as its concern the formation of the person and community, not just the sharing of information."[25]

According to Webber, the first Christians did not engage in discursive communication, which is a pedagogical approach to worship shaped by an Enlightenment mentality, but communal communication. "The new celebrative approach to worship, which is celebration of the victory of Christ over the powers of evil, is more typical of the worship of the early church."[26]

> We must refuse false dichotomies that force a wedge between rationality and faith, truth and experience.

Many inside and outside the emerging church share Webber's analysis. But unfortunately that analysis reinforces a host of false dichotomies—that discursive communication is only interested in information and not formation, that it is a mere lecture isolated from family and community, and that it is purely pedagogical instead of celebrative. This is not helpful. We must refuse false dichotomies that force a wedge between head and heart, rationality and faith, truth and experience.

Besides those false dichotomies, Webber offers a faulty reconstruction of history. I'm no big fan of the Enlightenment either, but it is simply wrong to attribute every hint of linear thinking, propositional preaching, or discursive communication to some modern Enlightenment corruption. Calvin preached long, theologically dense, story-less, discursive sermons. If that's a bad way to preach, fine, but it's not a product of the Enlightenment, and it's not accurate to suggest that Calvin, and others like him, intended his sermons only for information. In fact, nothing riled him more than the fancy theologians of the Sorbonne who were all speculation with no interest in transformation.

Many of those interested in postmodern worship are subtly and not so subtly denigrating the typical sermon with its exposition and subpoints by labeling it as a modern creation. But this is simply not true. Reviewing the multivolume work *The Reading and Preaching of the Scriptures in the Worship of the Christian Church,* by Hughes Oliphant Old, I picked out at random a preacher from the medieval church—thinking that maybe I would find less discursive preaching in the Middle Ages. Here's what I read about one of Bonaventure's (ca. 1217–74) Easter sermons:

> The sermon draws three points from the text. First, the text is an exclamation or proclamation of the resurrection; "Arise, O Lord" refers to rising from the dead…. The second point of the sermon, then, drawn from the second phrase in the text, "Save me," and developed by a wealth of biblical and patristic quotations, is that in the resurrection of Christ we find our perfect liberation. Three subpoints are made. (1) We are liberated from the offense of sin by the infusion of justifying grace. (2) We are liberated from the obligation of punishment through bearing the satisfaction of death. (3) We are liberated from carnal misery in the general resurrection through the collecting of reforming glory. Finally, the third point of the sermon is made. "You have overcome all my enemies." This final phrase of the text tells us of the just extermination of the power of the devil.[27]

We could trace this same kind of preaching back to the early church—the kind of preaching some deride as overly linear and mere "problem solving." Justin Martyr paints a picture of a normal worship service in the second century with rather discursive hues: "On the day called Sunday there is a meeting of all believers who live in the town or the country, and the memoirs of the apostles, or the writings of the prophets, are read for as long as time will permit. When the reader has finished, the president in a sermon urges and invites the people to base their lives on these noble things."[28]

Preaching has always played a central role, if not *the* central role, in Christian worship. This is because the importance of careful discursive exposition and instruction was not inherited from the Enlightenment but from Judaism. The Jews studied and memorized the Hebrew Scriptures, not as an idle exercise in gaining information, but as worship. The rabbis were given the task of instructing the people in the ways of the faith, teaching them the laws, comforting, admonishing, and encouraging their listeners. They were preachers. In the centuries before Christ, the Jews gave their greatest devotion to cultivating the art and science of reading and preaching the Scriptures. They understood growing in scriptural knowledge as not only essential to true piety but as glorifying to God. Old explains how this tradition of learning and preaching became part of Christian worship as well:

> This sapiential piety had its effect on the style of preaching that became popular in the centuries just before the Christian era, the time when the expository sermon came into its own. Preaching was not simply a matter of moral or theological teaching, merely inculcating the moral principles of the community, or telling again the old traditions of the community—how it came into existence and how it had maintained itself in times of trial. All this was done, to be sure, but expository preaching was also more. Preaching was the presentation of the Scriptures in which these traditions and principles had received their canonical form. Sermons therefore gave primary attention to what Scripture actually says. Expository preaching discussed the text, its grammar and vocabulary. All kinds of philological investigations were undertaken in trying to hear the Scriptures. Preachers studied the Scriptures in the original languages and cultivated a knowledge of the classical Hebrew. The results of all of this study provided material for the sermon.[29]

I am emphasizing this point about discursive preaching because I believe many emergent Christians, not to mention many evangelicals, are rejecting a kind of preaching and worship that they believe to be modern, but which is, in fact, anything but. And in so doing, they are pitting information against transformation and experiential worship against a "renewing of the mind," when the Bible never means to separate these things. The book of Proverbs is all about growing in knowledge and insight so one can live a godly life. The prophets are constantly using discourse, monologue even, to affect the wills of their hearers. Ezra and the Levites instructed the returned exiles by reading the Law and "giving them the sense of it" (Neh. 8:6–8). Israel suffered when she lacked a teaching priest (2 Chron. 15:3). And from the earliest days, the Levites were given to "teach Jacob your rules, and Israel your law" (Deut. 33:10). God's people have always been built up by the teaching of the Scriptures, and good Christian worship has always centered on clear, authoritative, expositional preaching of the Word of God.[30]

> **Pastors are supposed to be more than lost travelers with more questions than answers.**

Much of the emergent disdain for preaching is really an uneasiness about authority and control. Discussion, yes. Dialogue, yes. Group discernment, yes. Heralding? Proclamation? Not on this side of modernism. But is it really modernism we are rejecting or something weightier? The decline in preaching goes hand in hand with a lost confidence in the importance of truth claims. Preaching presupposes there is a message that must be proclaimed and believed. The very act of verbal proclamation by one man to God's people assumes that there is a word from God that can be ascertained, understood, and meaningfully communicated. This is what is being objected to in preaching, not simply the specter of modernism.

I find it disconcerting that Dorothy from the Wizard of Oz is supposed to be the new model for leadership. "Rather than being a person with all the answers, who is constantly informed of what's up and what's what and where to go, she is herself lost, a seeker, vulnerable, often bewildered," writes McLaren. "These characteristics would disqualify her from modern leadership. But they serve as her best credentials for leadership in the emerging culture."[31] In the emerging church, pastors should move from broadcaster to listener. From warrior-salesman to dancer. From problem solver to quest inspirer. From knower to seeker.[32]

No doubt, there are times when the pastor is facilitator and fellow seeker. But there are also times—every Sunday, in fact—when he must be a herald. And as he ministers among God's people, he should be able to say, by the grace of God, "Follow me as I follow Christ" (1 Cor. 11:1). It sounds humble when Pagitt says he doesn't want to be his people's pace car.[33] But aren't overseers supposed to be above reproach (Titus 1:6), able to instruct in sound doctrine and rebuke those who contradict it (1:9), and in all respects a model of good works (2:7)?

Is the best corrective to domineering CEO pastors really bewildered Dorothy leaders? How about shepherd or teacher or overseer or herald? Pastors are supposed to be more than lost travelers with more questions than answers. They are supposed to fan into flames the gift of preaching (2 Tim. 1:6), be filled with power instead of timidity (1:7), and rebuke, reprove, and exhort with complete patience and teaching (4:2).

IS EMERGENT THE NEW MODERN?

The biggest irony about the emergent church may be just this: For all their chastisement of all things modern, they are in most ways thoroughly modern. Many of the leading books display a familiar combination of social gospel liberalism, a neoorthodox view of Scripture, and a post-Enlightenment disdain for hell, the wrath of God, propositional revelation, propitiation, and anything more than a vague moralistic, warmhearted, adoctrinal Christianity.

Emergent leaders, if they are to make a lasting contribution to evangelical Christianity, need a better grasp of history in general. Let me give a few examples.

Much of Rob Bell's appeal is in his use of history to bring out the meaning of biblical texts. Bell leans heavily on popular teachers like Dwight Pryor and Ray VanderLaan for his cultural insights. I don't know Dwight Pryor, but I have heard VanderLaan speak a number of times. He is a very gifted teacher and a committed evangelical. I've really enjoyed listening to him. But his scholarship is sometimes weak and speculative. He oversimplifies differences between Greek thinking and Hebrew thinking, a habit Bell has picked up on. VanderLaan also delves deeply into the Jewish traditions behind the Bible. Many of the insights are illuminating, but many of them are misleading. Bell and VanderLaan rely heavily on the Mishna and Talmud for information about Judaism in Jesus' day. The problem is that the Mishna dates to around A.D. 200 and the Talmud a couple centuries after that. The contents of the Mishna and Talmud are not always historically reliable in the first place, and they certainly are not trustworthy documents for understanding first-century Judaism, much less the Old Testament. Scot McKnight, who thinks highly of Bell's books in general, explains:

> *Use of rabbis.* . . . Rob has an annoying habit in sermons and in books. He equates rabbinic writings, which are sources from the 3d to 9th Century AD, with Judaism of both the 1st Century (Jesus' and Paul's worlds) and the Judaism of the day of Moses. And he reinterprets things in the Bible through those rabbinic sources. At times in his uses of the rabbis it just happens that the rabbinic information is something found also for the 1st Century or ancient Israel (but rarely). He tells us fun things, scintillating and titillating things that average folks don't know, and they go, "Aha, so that's what's going on, the covenant formula is actually about sitting under the chuppah of a Jewish bride and groom. How neat to know this." . . .
>
> Here's the general rule: as we don't use contemporary conditions (globalization, etc.) to explain what the framers of the Constitution meant at that time, so we don't use the rabbis to explain Jesus and the Bible. To use the rabbis to elucidate the New Testament we need evi-

dence from the 1st Century that confirms what we find in the rabbis.[34]

Bell also makes hazardous use of parallels between the New Testament and the Roman Empire.

> The caesars claimed they were sent by the gods to renew creation. Caesar Augustus believed that as the son of a god, he was god incarnate on earth, the prince of peace who had come to restore all of creation. He inaugurated a twelve-day celebration called Advent to celebrate his birth. Sound familiar? His priests offered sacrifices and incense to rid people of their guilt. One of his popular slogans was "There is no other name under heaven by which men can be saved than that of Caesar." Another phrase they used often was "Caesar is Lord." Throughout the Roman Empire, the caesars called on the people to worship them as the divine saviors of humankind, and a city that acknowledged Caesar as Lord was called an *ekklesia*.[35]

While it is certainly true that the Caesars were worshiped as gods, there are a number of problems with Bell's retelling of the first century. First, it is unlikely that Augustus actually believed he was god incarnate. The Caesars received worship and allowed adoration and even commanded veneration, but this does not mean any Caesar, especially Augustus, actually thought he was divine. Augustus received the worship of the people as if he were a god, but he also insisted that "first citizen" was the highest title he needed.[36] In both instances he was being politically shrewd more than sincere.

Second, Bell's description of the advent is not very careful. Bell's citation for the paragraph above is the book *Christ and the Caesars* written over fifty years ago by the German New Testament scholar and ancient coin expert Ethelbert Stauffer. Stauffer describes a twelve-day advent celebration. But I can't find where he says Augustus called the celebration advent. The word *adventus* was used by Virgil, which is where many of the laudatory terms for Augustus come from. But the term was simply the Latin word for *coming*. Virgil believed a new day, a golden age, had arrived with the coming of Augustus, a belief that Augustus was happy to celebrate. But whether it was called "advent" is unclear, and it wasn't to commemorate Augustus' birth, but more generally his new reign.[37] In addition, it should be remembered that the Christians didn't celebrate Advent until the fourth century, so it is hardly a case of the church copying Augustus.

Third, *ekklesia* is simply the Greek word for assembly. It was used in the political sphere to be sure, but I'm not sure why Bell thinks it was used of cities.

Fourth, I've seen the line about "no other name but Caesar" quoted on emergent sites all over the Internet (sometimes as a saying, sometimes as an inscription on a coin), and I've heard Rob Bell say it before, but I don't think it is true. I am perfectly willing to be corrected in light of solid documented evidence, but as far as I can tell the saying is a historical urban legend that is being repeated based on a misreading of Stauffer's book. Here's what Stauffer says in summarizing two coins in honor of Augustus:

> The symbolic meaning is clear: a new day is dawning for the world. The divine saviour-king, born in the historical hour ordained by the stars, has come to power on land and sea, and inaugurates the cosmic era of salvation. Salvation is to be found in none other save Augustus, and there is no other name given to me in which they can be saved. This is the climax of the Advent proclamation of the Roman empire.[38]

Notice, Stauffer does *not* suggest this was a saying of the day or the inscription on a coin (that's a lot to fit on a coin!). He merely summarizes the historical milieu by using the biblical language of Acts 4:12 to make his point that the Romans saw Augustus as the savior of the world.[39]

Fifth, Bell needs to be careful that his historical parallels don't undermine

Christian faith. I'm not convinced that all his parallels are legitimate, and if they are, they need to be documented. But if they all can be documented and the connection well proven (which I seriously doubt), I hope Bell will help us see how Christianity was not simply a repackaging of pagan myths about Mithra and the Caesars. There's a young man I know who walked away from Christianity because he saw Mithra-Jesus parallels (not from Bell) and decided the whole Christ thing was a cheap imitation. Most scholars think the Paganism-Christianity parallels are way overblown, but if they are not, we need to show our people why we believe the Jesus stuff is true when all the other stuff is not.

> Emergent leaders need ... to avoid dashing off slipshod summaries of church history.

Doug Pagitt is also guilty of some historical parallelomania. Like Bell, Pagitt needs to do more to support his speculations. If he is going to suggest that Pelagius came to his understanding of human ability because it fit with the Druids, and Augustine came to his position of human inability because it fit with Roman spirituality,[40] he needs to do some more work to demonstrate this is so, especially when (1) Pelagius studied Greek theology, not Druid runes; (2) the controversy broke out in Rome and later in Palestine, not in the British Isles; and (3) the writings from Pelagius and Augustine show both arguing mainly over Scripture texts.

Simply put, emergent leaders need some restraint so as to avoid dashing off slipshod summaries of church history, like the one on John Calvin in McLaren's *Generous Orthodoxy*.[41] Calvin did not become a pastor at age eighteen. He received a benefice—a minor office in the church working for the Bishop—at age twelve and broke off studying for the priesthood and began studying law at age eighteen. Calvin did not work on the *Institutes* between the ages of nineteen and twenty-five (most scholars believe he wasn't even converted until he was in his twenties). He worked on it while in Basel, January through August of 1535, writing six chapters for the 1536 edition of the Institutes that would swell to eighty chapters by 1559. And more importantly, Calvin did not write the *Institutes* to fill the "dangerous vacuum" left after the rejection of Catholicism with "a lean and pure intellectual system." Calvin never saw himself as instituting an intellectual system or even a systematic theology.

He wrote the *Institutes* for two reasons: (1) as a defense before the king of France that the Protestant church was the legitimate church and should be treated fairly, and (2) as an elementary instructional tool for new or struggling Christians. Calvin labored for his own Frenchmen, "for I saw that many were hungering and thirsting after Christ and yet that only very few had even the slightest knowledge of him."[42] If some in the emergent church don't like Calvin or Reformed theology, fair enough. But they should know what they are rejecting and avoid ill-informed historical reconstructions. The emergent church simply needs to do its historical homework.

More important than all this scholarly sloppiness, I wish emergent leaders could see that what they critique is much older than they think and what they affirm is rarely as new as they imagine. The emergent church may not be identical with the theological modernism of the late nineteenth and early twentieth centuries, but many of the similarities are striking. As Mark Driscoll has pointed out, it's telling that Doug Pagitt hears his own views in the obscure modernist theologian Henry Churchill King. Pagitt quotes King approvingly, citing his 1899 work, where he argues: "The days of the great theological system are doubtless past; not because the great truths do not abide, but simply because the task is differently conceived."[43]

For Pagitt to admit that his theological method is not new is a huge step forward in the conversation. So much of the impetus for change in the emerging church is carried along by a desire to cast off our modernist shackles and meet the challenges of our new postmodern world. And so much of this impetus is ultramodern; it is not post-anything.

The preference for ethics over doctrine, the reservations about God's wrath and judgment, the perceived need to retranslate the Christian faith for a new time, the devaluing of propositional truths, the chastisement of firm doctrinal boundaries, the understanding of missions as social compassion and not conversion—these are all impulses of the modern world. So are the broad tolerance of general religious sentiment that is lacking in specificity and definition, the unwillingness to assert the Bible's complete truthfulness, the downplaying of original sin, and the direct appeals to bettering the world apart from the call to repent and be born again.

As emergent leaders stalk the boogeyman of modernism in conservative evangelicalism, it needs to be pointed out that he lurks within their own house too, not as a creature hidden under the bed here or in a corner there, but as their own shadow, standing next to them, in the dark perhaps, but always there. There is nothing new under the sun, just the same shadows in different places across the centuries.

NOTES

1. Eddie Gibbs and Ryan K. Bolger, *Emerging Churches* (Grand Rapids: Baker, 2005), 29.
2. Brian D. McLaren and Tony Campolo, *Adventures in Missing the Point* (Grand Rapids: Zondervan, 2003), 260. Similarly, "The kind of people who would come to faith along the path I was trying to clear for them would probably not end up just like the people waiting for them in church. They would be like a bunch of wild-eyed artists and excitable children and rugby players walking into a roomful of buttoned-down accountants and engineers" (Brian D. McLaren, *A New Kind of Christian* [San Francisco: Jossey-Bass, 2003], xvi).
3. Ibid., 262.
4. Brian D. McLaren, "Emerging Values," *Leadership* (Summer 2003), 35.
5. Doug Pagitt and the Solomon's Porch Community, *Reimagining Spiritual Formation* (Grand Rapids: Zondervan, 2004), 114–15.
6. Carl Raschke, *The Next Reformation* (Grand Rapids: Baker, 2004), 156.
7. Leonard Sweet, *SoulTsunami* (Grand Rapids: Zondervan, 1999), 199.
8. Ibid., 380.
9. Dave Tomlinson, *The Post-Evangelical* (Grand Rapids: Zondervan, 2003), 42–43.
10. One of the ironies is that while the emerging church decries information and the gaining of mere biblical knowledge as sufficient, or even necessary, for spiritual formation, there is a loud cry to gain knowledge of the culture and its postmodern antecedents. It's terribly modern to acquire knowledge about the Bible, but what you don't know about postmodernism can be deadly. "In the postmodern age, what you don't know, or what you know wrong, can hurt you. It can also kill you" (Sweet, *SoulTsunami*, 146).
11. McLaren and Campolo, *Adventures in Missing the Point*, 280.
12. Dan Kimball, *The Emerging Church* (Grand Rapids: Zondervan, 2003).
13. Ibid., 175.

14. Ibid., 215.

15. Ibid., 230.

16. Ibid., 140–41.

17. Ibid., 180.

18. Ibid., 217.

19. Rick Warren, *Purpose Driven Church* (Grand Rapids: Zondervan, 1995), 130.

20. Pagitt, *Reimagining Spiritual Formation*, 56–57.

21. This is the name of the community Dieter Zander, formerly of Willow Creek, helped found in San Francisco.

22. Description is taken from Raschke, *The Next Reformation*, 176.

23. Doug Pagitt, *Preaching Re-Imagined* (Grand Rapids: Zondervan, 2005), 10, 18.

24. Ibid., 20ff.

25. Robert E. Webber, *The Worship Phenomenon: A Dynamic New Awakening in Worship Is Reviving the Body of Christ* (Nashville: Abott Martin, 1994), 74.

26. Ibid., 145.

27. Hughes Oliphant Old, *The Reading and Preaching of the Scriptures in the Worship of the Church,* vol. 3 (Grand Rapids: Eerdmans, 1999), 359.

28. Quoted in Nick Needham's chapter "Worship through the Ages," in *Give Praise to God,* Philip Graham Ryken, Derek W. H. Thomas, and J. Ligon Duncan III, eds., (Philipsburg, N.J.: P&R Publishing, 2003), 376.

29. Old, *Reading and Preaching the Scriptures*, vol. 1, 93.

30. Cf. Harold M. Best, *Unceasing Worship* (Downers Grove, Ill.: InterVarsity, 2003), 158: "If anybody understands multiple meanings within the same thing, it is God. Nonetheless, I firmly believe that the best preaching, as poetic and elegant as it can become, cannot afford to drift too far into meaning many things at once. As important to the human soul as the Psalms and the poetic utterances of the prophets are, the preaching that issues out of them should lead back into the firmness and direct applicability of propositional truth." Best is an organist and composer and former dean of the Conservatory of Music at Wheaton College.

31. McLaren and Campolo, *Adventures in Missing the Point*, 158ff.

32. Ibid., 160ff.

33. Pagitt, *Preaching Re-Imagined*, 79.

34. Jesus Creed, "Rob Bell and His Sex God 2," http://www.jesuscreed.org/?p=2146#comment-57001 (accessed on March 13, 2007). Cf. *Velvet Elvis*, 125. Witherington is another scholar, sympathetic with Bell's broader ministry, who nevertheless cautions him against his indiscriminate use of Jewish sources. McKnight also mentions Bell's sometimes undiscerning use of etymologies. Along these lines, every pastor should read D. A. Carson's *Exegetical Fallacies*, 2nd ed. (Grand Rapids: Baker, 1996), especially the chapter "Word-Study Fallacies."35. Bell, *Velvet Elvis*, 162.

36. For a compelling narrative account of Octavian's rise to power and his subsequent rule as Caesar Augustus, see Tom Holland, *Rubicon: The Last Years of the Roman Republic* (New York: Doubleday, 2003), 338–78.

37. Ethelbert Stauffer, *Christ and the Caesars* (London: SCM, 1952), 83.

38. Ibid., 88.

39. Elsewhere Stauffer echoes 1 Corinthians 7:30 when he writes of Augustus, "He knew how to possess everything as though he possessed nothing" (ibid., 98).

40. Pagitt, *Listening to the Beliefs*, 128–29.

41. The following examples come from McLaren, *Generous Orthodoxy*, 210ff.
42. This line comes from the opening paragraph of the 1536 Institutes, as quoted in T. H. L. Parker, *John Calvin: A Biography* (Philadelphia: Westminster, 1975), 36.
43. Pagitt, *Listening to the Beliefs*, 121–22.

"I'm a living cliché just like the rest of these guys. I'm the guy who keeps dropping out and changing his major just because he's afraid he really sucks at everything."

—**BARDO,** *Art School Confidential*

CHAPTER 8

WHERE EVERYBODY KNOWS YOUR NAME: DIALOGUING FOR THE SAKE OF DIALOGUE

THE BOOK IS CALLED *How (Not) to Speak of God* by Peter Rollins. Similar to *A Heretic's Guide to Eternity* and *A Generous Orthodoxy,* it has the requisite fetchingly rebellious title. And it also has what has become the emergent stamp of success—the Brian McLaren endorsement where he says he's crazy about the book. Just nuts about it. It's changed his life.

The book is coming with Kevin and me to *Champps*—for the record, *Champps* is a sports bar, if you're okay with that, and a restaurant to my mother and many of her friends. We're going to watch the Chicago Bears on Monday Night Football (and if I had sold more copies of my first book, I could afford to order the official drink of the emergent church, a pint of Guinness).

As we've said earlier, Rollins is the founder of the Ikon community in Northern Ireland, a group that describes itself as "iconic, apocalyptic, heretical, emerging and failing." He also has a Ph.D. in postmodern thought, which means he can reasonably invoke the names of Derrida and Foucault and get away with it. At times, I feel as if the emergent church is like that friend who goes off to college as an eighteen-year-old, and for the first year or so when he comes home feels like he has to quote Nietzsche just to impress you with his newfound intellect.

The book is a simple paperback, devoid of any author photo; however, sensing an opportunity almost lost, the publisher has included a Pete Rollins bookmark in every copy. Rollins looks the part—just good-looking enough to keep you looking, but disheveled enough to let you know that he's about more than keeping you looking at him. In fact, he kind of looks like a younger, skinnier Jeff Daniels (think *The Squid and the Whale* rather than *Dumb and Dumber.*)

FEARFUL ORTHODOXY AND QUARTERBACK RATINGS

This book is currently taking the emerging community by storm, ripping its way through blog-world at an alarming rate. It is thoughtfully written, from what I can ascertain so far, in kind of a Brian McLaren meets Erwin McManus marriage of philosophical jargon and words like *river*, *journey*, and *flawed*. It is also McLarenian in that one of its arguments is that orthodoxy is more about ethics, or "praxis," than Scripture or the cross. This makes me uneasy, as does the fact that Bears quarterback Rex Grossman has thrown ten interceptions and only two touchdowns in the last three games. His quarterback rating last week was 1.35. If Pete Rollins ever writes a book explaining the quarterback rating and how it is figured, the first pint is on me.

The book is relatively short and is laid out in two parts—roughly stated, the first part is what Rollins thinks about things, and the second part features examples of "experiences" that have taken place at Ikon. Not surprisingly, knowing myself, I turn toward the end to the chapter entitled "Queer." I must be a sucker for controversy. This should be interesting.

The chapter describes a recent Ikon gathering at a local pub, where the "congregation" (wrong word, he'd say, but the best I can do) entered to find a guy on a makeshift stage, stripped to the waist. The guy was being circled by a girl with a paintbrush painting things like "queer," "homo," "fag," etc., on the guy's chest.[1] It is very intentionally shocking at some level, but it keeps me turning the page. Around the guy were placed rocks that had been carefully wrapped in bubble wrap—the message being that we need to stop throwing insensitivity rocks at people who may look and act differently than we do. Or that we at least need to soften the rocks by padding the rough edges.

It seems kind of analogous to Donald Miller's now-famous-in-Christian-circles description in *Blue Like Jazz*, where he holed up in a confessional but instead of listening to confessions, apologized to his guests for the ills perpetrated by Christians over the centuries. The bare-chested performance art is similar, but not as effective. I wonder, momentarily, how such a lesson would be received here at *Champps*.

FOOTBALL, THE TRUTH, AND DIVERSITY

On screen Kevin and I watch 80,000 fans in a corporate monolith called the Edward Jones Dome screaming that the Rams will score with first and goal inside the five-yard line. Some of them have their face painted, and few, I'm guessing, are aware that there may be a "New Reformation" afoot.

There's no escaping the fact that there is absolute truth in football. Football is about defending lines, and in a culture of ultrasensitivity and rampant deconstructionism, the game has changed very little in the one-hundred-plus years it has been around. At the end of every play, and at the end of every game, players know where they stand in the grand scheme of things. I loved the simplicity of the game when I played, and I still do.

The Rams try to run off-tackle with Steven Jackson, right into the teeth of the Bears defense. If the Bears defense were the emergent discussion, Brian Urlacher would be its Brian McLaren—the head honcho. The hammer.

Truth be told, a football team is a lot like what the emergent church says it is. It is diverse. Football is really the only place where I've seen "diversity" (black and white together) work in a way that never seems forced, heavy-handed, or stilted. There is community on a football team. For better or worse, these are the guys you ride the bus with, eat meals with, shower with, and laugh with. At the risk of sounding like the guy with the voice on NFL Films, they are relationships forged in hard times—wind sprints, injuries, lame coaches, and everything else that comes with the wild ride that is football.

There are ethics in football—and the overriding ethic is that the better you are, the more you play. If you stink, you sit. The same goes for most other sports as well. And much like the emergent church, you spend a lot of time talking, at pubs, and sometimes sharing your faith. Substitute Guinness for Miller Lite or black coffee, and you get the idea.

HAVING THE PERFECT YEAR

It's December, which means it's holiday letter time. I hate holiday letter time. You know the time of year—it's the time when successful Christian couples send you the glossy photo of themselves in the yuppie uniform of the year surrounded by a passel of lovely children. This year it's khaki pants and white T-shirts. The blonde housewife looks a little tired but nevertheless hot in a conservative Christian meets *Desperate Housewives* sort of way. And there's the husband, who has put on a little paunch since he sat on the Young Republicans committee in college and was head of the class in his business school.

The letter tells you what you already know, which is, of course, that things are going Really Well. These letters follow a well-known pattern. There is the anecdote about the vacation, and how they came back feeling really refreshed. And then the paragraph about Hubby's promotion, and how he has been working really hard in between leading the praise team at church and sitting on such and such committee. Mom is working really hard home-schooling—maybe even harder than Dad! (But she has retained her sense of humor!) She's also having fun selling _____ (go ahead, fill in the blank: Creative Memories, Pampered Chef, facial creams, or beaded jewelry) on the side and making a little bit of extra money. Yay! The kids are excelling in sports and school. And then the conscience kicks in—and results in the paragraph about how we were praying about doing a short-term missions trip or adopting internationally, and then—Shazaam—God blessed us with another pregnancy! Yay again!

I'm glad I got a letter like this today, because it does remind me of why the emergent movement, for all of its theological disasters (or un/disasters) has some legitimate beefs. Because if church culture is about having a perfect year like this, so that we can produce such letters, then yes, it all is a big sham, and we need authenticity (or at least contrived authenticity) desperately.

Luckily, I don't regularly interact with many Christians like this. Something I've learned in the five-plus years I've spent at my church is that everybody struggles, and for the most part people are pretty honest about it.

= = = =

Speaking of struggles, I am struggling to work through the Rollins book now and am finding that I am only retaining and understanding about 30 percent of the material, thanks in large part to lots of garden-variety philosophical jargon coupled with lots of new words. If one of Rollins's un/spoken goals was to get me to believe that he is wildly intelligent, he has really succeeded.

There is a discernible pattern developing in the reading of Rollins's liturgies, which occupy the second half of the book. In each of them, the congregation enters the bar—and while reading, I mentally substitute my own favorite dingy, run-down bar, "The Peanut Barrel" in East Lansing, in the place of the one he describes—and is met by ambient house music over which the DJ occasionally lays down voice tracks. There is always something to look at in the center of the room—sometimes a projected image of something provocative, and other times it is sackcloth and ashes on a table, or champagne and cake.

After a time, a storyteller approaches the stage carrying "what looks like a Bible" and typically reads a story that resembles a biblical parable, yet with the ending changed significantly. For example, a man with sight is "healed" but as a result becomes blind. Usually the liturgies are set up such that the listener will be forced to think more about social justice, or life without God. Or a crucifixion without a resurrection to follow. There is no good news presented, and indeed, it seems that there is no news at all. Which, again, is completely intentional. I'm not at all saying that Rollins omitted these things because he goofed; they are omitted intentionally.

The liturgies typically wrap with a sort of tactile, audience participation segment in which people do things like walking outside to burn images of God in a trash barrel, or tying pieces of sackcloth and ash around their wrists as a reminder of what they've heard. And in every liturgy they are sent home with a trinket, or an artifact, to remind them of what they have experienced and to "aid in their reflection during the week." Once, this was a CD emblazoned with a Meister Eckhart quote that played nothing but forty-five minutes of silence. Deep.

I am struck by the fact that what is billed as a sort of unchecked creativity has produced ten liturgies that are remarkably similar in look, feel, and purpose. This is not a critique so much as an observation that Ikon may be more like its more traditional counterparts than it would like to think. At the beginning of the tenth liturgy we are reminded by Rollins that Ikon "has no substantial doctrinal centre . . . just as a doughnut has no interior, but is made up entirely of an exterior."

I am reminded of what goes on in seeker-friendly megaplexes all across the country on Sunday morning—slickly produced music, followed by multimedia clip, followed by drama, followed by ambiguously thought-provoking/inspirational message with a minimum of Scripture at its center.

= = = =

The "Living" section of the Saturday, January 27, 2007, edition of the *Atlanta Journal Constitution* features a long interview with Brian McLaren, promoting his upcoming visit to Columbia Theological Seminary in Decatur, Georgia. The conference, entitled "Conversations in Theology, Practice, and Hope," comes with a $275 price tag and features emergent heavyweights

McLaren, Tony Jones, Diana Butler Bass, Doug Pagitt, and Karen Ward and is aimed at helping mainline congregations become part of the emergent church movement. Of the speakers listed, only Pagitt and Ward are actually pastors.

My mother-in-law gave me the article because she knows I am working on this book, and because she "has friends" who are exploring the emergent movement as well. "My friends like the *Noomas* (Rob Bell's short films)," she tells me.

"I like the *Noomas* too," I reply, feeling bad momentarily for going after *Velvet Elvis* (and the Michigan cottage, for that matter) in the first chapter I wrote for this book, chapter 2. I mean, how bad can it all be if my mother-in-law and her friends are into it? I have to feel like if this somehow started as a rebellion movement, or an "underground" thing, those days, for now, are over. If my mother-in-law's suburban crowd, not to mention the *Atlanta Journal Constitution,* is on board, then it is as mainstream as mainstream can be. I start, for a minute, to feel like the bad guy.

In addition to the usual biographical features on McLaren's life, the piece lays out a sort of primer on the emerging (or emergent[2]) church.

According to the piece, "the movement's innovations go beyond worship and extends to theology. McLaren isn't preoccupied with hell—who's in and who's out." It seems to me to be the proverbial Wide Gate, and for a movement that has generated so much controversy, is completely un/controversial. As an addendum, the paper lists nine characteristics of emerging churches:

1. Identify with the life of Jesus.
2. Transform the secular realm.
3. Live highly communal lives.
4. Welcome the stranger.
5. Serve with generosity.
6. Participate as producers.
7. Create as created beings.

8. Lead as a body.

9. Take part in spiritual activities.

Out of curiosity and for the sake of comparison, I looked up the guiding principles of the Unitarian Universalist Association on the UUA Web site:

We, the member congregations of the Unitarian Universalist Association, covenant to affirm and promote

1. The inherent worth and dignity of every person;

2. Justice, equity and compassion in human relations;

3. Acceptance of one another and encouragement to spiritual growth in our congregations;

4. A free and responsible search for truth and meaning;

5. The right of conscience and the use of the democratic process within our congregations and in society at large;

6. The goal of world community with peace, liberty and justice for all;

7. Respect for the interdependent web of all existence of which we are a part.

Both lists, for the record, are full of good and noble things; however, there is nothing said in either list of guiding principles about Jesus' death and resurrection and the need of both for our salvation. There is lots of ambiguity, like "take part in spiritual activities" and "identify with the life of Jesus." Then the thought came to me, *If you stopped a random handful of Americans on the street, they would all aspire to identifying with the life of Jesus in much the same way they would hope to identify with the life of Martin Luther King or Muhammad Ali.* The tough part is that "taking part in spiritual activities" won't help a person in the afterlife, regardless of whether or not McLaren is ready to dialogue on that topic. Hell is tricky because, though I may not be preoccupied with it now, when it is time to be "in or out" it may be too late to engage the topic.

McLaren's non-stance on homosexuality, in the same article, is just as ambiguous:

> Frankly, many of us don't know what we should think about homosexuality. We've heard all sides, but no position has yet won our confidence so that we can say "it seems good to the Holy Spirit and us." . . .
>
> Perhaps we need a five-year moratorium on making pronouncements. In the meantime, we'll practice prayerful Christian dialogue, listening respectfully, disagreeing agreeably. When decisions need to be made, they'll be admittedly provisional. We'll keep our ears attuned to scholars in biblical studies, theology, ethics, psychology, genetics, sociology, and related fields. Then in five years, if we have clarity, we'll speak; if not, we'll set another five years for ongoing reflection. After all, many important issues in church history took centuries to figure out.[3]

I find it hard to believe that McLaren has trouble figuring out what to believe on an issue that seems, to my admittedly un-seminary-trained eye, to be so cut and dried in Scripture. As cut and dried as adultery, theft, murder, covetousness, and a litany of other sins that even emergents can agree upon, with a minimum of dialogue. I also have to believe that we can lovingly take stands on these issues. I have a homosexual friend[4] that I'm certain knows my faith, and also knows how I feel about his lifestyle, but that doesn't stop us from having lunch, talking about our careers, and generally getting along. I'm thankful that just because I'm a Christian he doesn't lump me in with the "bad-comb-over, polyester suit, Southern-accent" crowd that has probably made him feel terrible at some point in his life. But for me to pretend that I'm "taking a few years to determine my position" on his lifestyle would perhaps be the most awkward, patronizing thing I could possibly do.

Sometimes, offering a clear proposition, not a muddy, indefinite "dialogue," is the loving thing to do.

Notes

1. Peter Rollins, *How (Not) to Talk of God* (Brewster, Mass.: Paraclete, 2006), 134.
2. I know, there's a difference . . . and for the sake of simplicity I understand it to be that if we compare it to the political continuum, "emergent" would be on the far left, with "emerging" somewhere to the right of that. I've also heard it described that "emergent" is ready to throw out such theological ballast as the existence of hell and the authority of the Scriptures, while "emerging" may just be doing some things differently to reach a different group of people.
3. "Brian McLaren on the Homosexual Question," in "Out of Ur," a *Leadership Journal* blog, http://blog.christianitytoday.com/outofur/archives/2006/01/ brian_mclaren_o.html
4. I know, I know, the "I have a gay friend" thing is the classic bigot's defense, but what can you do? I'll probably get ripped for this paragraph either way.

In the end, I didn't pick Christianity. I picked Jesus instead, because Jesus seemed cool and treated people kindly.

— **BARRY TAYLOR** *in* Emerging Churches

CHAPTER 9

JESUS: BRINGER OF PEACE, BEARER OF WRATH

EMERGENT CHRISTIANS love Jesus. It's clear they want to be Jesus-followers and teach others the way of Jesus. It's also clear that for most emergent Christians the message of the kingdom is the central message, the "lost message," even the "secret message" of Jesus. The word *kingdom* is, after all, found in the Gospels over one hundred times and forms the heart of Jesus' teaching in the Synoptics. And emergent Christians are right. Jesus came to announce and usher in the kingdom of God. This is plain from even a cursory reading of the Gospels.

"THY KINGDOM COME"

For those in the emerging church, Jesus' message of the kingdom is a manifesto about God's plan for humanity here and now. It is the secret and subversive announcement that God is working out His plan for peace, justice, and compassion on the earth. The kingdom message is a summons to participate with God in His dream for humanity, His revolution of love and reconciliation. It is an invitation to join the party of God and be a part of His worldwide mission to heal and be healed. It is a call to join the network of God that breaks down the walls of racism, nationalism, and ecological harm. The kingdom of God is like a dance of love, vitality, harmony, and celebration.[1]

Joining the kingdom is not a move in status (i.e., from unsaved to saved), but a move in practice.[2] Jesus' message was not about affirming the right doctrines, but about following His teachings and treating others rightly.[3] Christianity is essentially a messianic way of living.[4] It's about hoping for what God hopes for, about not turning God's dream for the world into a nightmare. "The kingdom of God, then, is a revolutionary, counter-cultural movement— proclaiming a ceaseless rebellion against the tyrannical trinity of money, sex, and power."[5] In short, as members of the kingdom we follow Jesus as "the best possible way for a person to live."[6]

The problem with this view of the kingdom is not what emergent leaders affirm about the kingdom, but what they reject or marginalize in order to affirm what they do. The emergent church emphasizes a way of life and following Jesus' example, no doubt because they feel those twin aspects of the kingdom have been buried beneath altar calls and saving souls. Fair enough, as long as they don't overreact and make the kingdom little more than a plan for world peace.

In his classic work *A Theology of the New Testament*, George Eldon Ladd takes seven dense chapters to explain the kingdom of God in the Gospels. It cannot be reduced to a single concept, argues Ladd, but at its root the kingdom refers to the reign and rule of God. This reign is both present and future; it has come and is coming; it is already inaugurated and not yet consummated.[7]

Moreover, the God of the kingdom is not just the God of ethical intentions. He is the seeking God, the inviting God, the fatherly God, and also the judging God.[8] Ladd summarizes:

Our central thesis is that the Kingdom of God is the redemptive reign of God dynamically active to establish his rule among human beings, and that this Kingdom, which will appear as an apocalyptic act at the end of the age, has already come into human history in the person and mission of Jesus to overcome evil, to deliver people from its power, and to bring them into the blessings of God's reign.[9]

It would take another chapter to unpack this statement and defend it, but I believe Ladd's careful biblical work still stands. Many emergent Christians would probably agree with Ladd's statement. But while I see a lot in their works about Jesus coming to overcome evil, I see little about Jesus coming to deliver us from the power of evil in our own lives by His death and resurrection, little about how we must believe in Jesus in order to experience the kingdom blessings, and little about the kingdom beyond this present age. Although McLaren in a few places acknowledges that the old question about getting saved still matters, this clearly is not the most pertinent question for the emergent church. The question is not "How do I get to heaven after death" but "What kind of life does God want? What does life in the kingdom look like?"[10] Salvation isn't something we get but something we experience and spread as a part of God's mission.[11]

For emergent Christians the good news is that God is doing a new work right here, right now on planet earth:

> I am discovering (to my wonder, joy, and amazement) that I have mistakenly placed the emphasis of the good news on the eternal. In the Gospels, Jesus wasn't talking about something distant when he proclaimed the good news. It was something for NOW. People could become a part of the Kingdom of God . . . not a heavenly dwelling but the place where God is King. The place where God turns everything upside down. The place where the light shines and people can be known for who they are and loved.[12]

The stuff of our evangelistic tracts—"God's grace, God's forgiveness . . . the free gift of salvation"—is, at best, only "a footnote to a gospel that is much richer, grander, and more alive, a gospel that calls you to become a disciple and to disciple others, in authentic community, for the good of the world."[13] The meat of the gospel has to do with justice, compassion, and transformation.[14]

But where is the good news in this? Our cursed world needs more than a plan for refurbished morals. It needs a Savior because it is so full of sinners. I just cannot understand how the gospel as a call to become a disciple for the good of the world is richer, grander, and more alive than a gospel that announces God's grace, forgiveness, and the free gift of salvation. We're told by emergent leaders that we should not be asking people, are you ready to meet God? Instead, we each should be asking, what kind of person do I want to become in the next fifty years, and what kind of world do I want to create?[15] This message is all call and command and no news of God's redemptive work on our behalf. This makes me wonder, does the emergent church really believe in original sin? The need for mercy? What about the reality of eternity? Occasionally emergent authors write about the hope of eternity,[16] but then they strangely go out of their way to explain that eternal life doesn't actually mean life after death.[17] I understand the emergent concern about living rightly in this life. That was a concern of Jesus. But why are heaven and hell as eternal destinations so routinely marginalized in emergent books? If heaven and hell are real and endure forever, as Jesus believed them to be, they ought to shape everything we do during our short time on earth.

The emergent church is right to remind evangelicals that the kingdom of God is not all pie in the sky and the great by and by. But, as C. S. Lewis quipped, "Either there is 'pie in the sky' or there is not. If there is not, then Christianity is false, for this doctrine is woven into its whole fabric. If there is, then this truth, like any other, must be faced, whether it is useful at political meetings or no."[18] In addition to kingdom living, "getting saved," as we say, might have mattered to Jesus too. He told the disciples that if they followed Him they would inherit eternal life in the age to come (Mark 10:30). He told them not to fear him who can kill the body, but rather fear Him "who can destroy both soul and body in hell" (Matt. 10:28). He told stories about those in paradise enjoying the pleasures of God and those in hell enduring great torment (Luke 16:19–31).

For Jesus, eternal life is eternal because it is life unending after death, not simply because it "interacts with the eternal dimension of the Spirit."[19] Eternal life is the opposite of perishing and facing condemnation; it is life without end (John 3:16–18). "I am the resurrection and the life. Whoever believes in me, though he die, yet shall he live, and everyone who lives and believes in me shall never die. Do you believe this?" (John 11:25–26) asked Jesus. Surely this Easter message is a bit more than a footnote to the gospel. The emergent emphasis of justice and compassion would be more of a helpful corrective if it went hand in hand with a firm, unashamed belief, made central and upfront, in the reality of everlasting punishment and everlasting reward, the resurrection of all men either to life or judgment, and the necessity of faith in Jesus Christ.

> Emergent leaders are hoping for heaven on earth before Jesus returns to earth to bring the new heaven and new earth.

What the emergent manifesto suffers from is an imbalance of too much "already" and not enough "not yet." The fancy term is "over-realized eschatology." That is, emergent leaders are hoping for heaven on earth before Jesus returns to earth to bring the new heaven and new earth. Emergent leaders dare us to imagine a world without poverty and war and injustice. That's good. We need to be stirred to have faith in the God of the impossible. But we should not expect something God has not promised, especially when He has promised the opposite. Jesus said the poor would always be with us (John 12:8) and wars and rumors of war would continue to the very end (Matt. 24:6). This doesn't mean we are pro-poverty warmongers. But it does mean that wars won't go away just because we follow the secret message of Jesus.[20]

We need a little more New Testament–inspired realism. People are not basically good. Diverting money away from weaponry to fight the causes of conflict like "injustice, lack of compassion, racism, corruption, lack of free and ethical press, and poverty—and the fear, hatred, greed, ignorance, and lust that fuel them" may or may not be good political strategy.[21] But it certainly won't rid the world of violence and war. First of all, because "the heart is deceitful above all things, and desperately sick; who can understand it?" (Jer. 17:9). And second, because the New Testament (see especially Jesus' parables and the book of Revelation) shows us a picture of righteousness and wickedness growing together in conflict right until the very end.

What is absent from the emergent understanding of the kingdom is the words of Jesus to Nicodemus, "Truly, truly, I say to you, unless one is born again he cannot see the kingdom of God" (John 3:3). What's missing is a call to conversion. "Repent, for the kingdom of heaven is at hand" were the first words preached by John the Baptist and Jesus (Matt. 3:2; 4:17), informing us that the kingdom is for the penitent. And the first words of the Sermon on the Mount are "Blessed are the poor in spirit, for theirs in the kingdom of heaven," alerting us that the Sermon on the Mount can only be lived out in complete reliance on Jesus Christ.[22] The kingdom manifesto is not a blueprint for ordering the world. It is the way of holiness for those who have repented of their sins, been regenerated, and put their faith in Jesus Christ.

There's a reason the bulk of every Gospel deals with the last week of Jesus' life. Because they're Gospels! Absolutely, the gospel has ethical implications. Believing the gospel means learning to obey all that Jesus commands (Matt. 28:19–20). It is right and good for social action to be a partner of evangelism.[23] But the gospel is not the summons to live a life that betters the world. The gospel is a message about Jesus' life, death, and resurrection. As I've heard John Piper say, we are meant to read the Gospels backwards. That's why Matthew announces in chapter 1, "you shall call his name Jesus, for he will save his people from their sins" (v. 21). "On the basis of who he was and what he accomplished, Jesus made his demands. The demands cannot be separated from his person and work. The obedience he demands is the fruit of his *redeeming work* and the display of his *personal glory*."[24]

EMERGENT POLITICS AND THE LIBERATING LEFT

Without the personal glory of Christ and His redeeming work front and center in the gospel, the kingdom of God often ends up sounding largely political. I'm sure there are some on the political right who resonate with the emerging church, but it is undeniable that left-wing politics is a common thread running throughout the emergent literature. From Donald Miller's rants against Republicans to the McLaren/Campolo list of social action concerns, the movement is clearly more comfortable left of center. This is not really surprising. Political conservatives enjoyed their heyday under Clinton, and in 2008, with a presidential election pending, the liberals are having their turn under Bush. It's always harder to be in power than out of it.

But Christians on both sides must be careful that the message of Jesus isn't over-identified with politics. Isn't this why the Religious Right is being chastised (sometimes fairly, sometimes unfairly)? American Christianity has at times sounded a lot like the platform of the GOP. Emergent leaders need to be careful they do not make the same mistake in the opposite direction. Emergent Christians shouldn't position themselves as the neutral middle ground when their concerns read like talking points of the Democratic National Committee: racism, environmental degradation, militarism, corporate greed, poverty, Third World debt, overpopulation, consumerism, AIDS, and imperialism.

My concern is not that emergent Christians might be Democrats, any more than I am concerned that Southern Baptists might be Republicans. My concern is with an imbalanced list of political "kingdom" concerns. God may not be a Republican or a Democrat, but from reading the emergent literature, it sure seems like He votes Democrat. No doubt emergent leaders would argue that they are trying to correct an imbalance themselves, but one imbalance does not deserve another. "Two issues seem to be at the top of the list for many of my

Christian friends," writes McLaren, "ending abortion (by making it illegal?) and doing something about homosexuals (by outlawing them? Jailing them? Shaming them? Asking them to leave the premises?)."[25] With subtlety like this, it's not hard to see that McLaren's true concerns lie elsewhere. No one can be equally passionate about all issues, but I wish McLaren would do more than hurl sarcasm at prolifers and gay marriage opponents. Shouldn't we care for the poor *and* the unborn? Shouldn't we care about justice *and* righteousness? After all, "religion that is pure and undefiled before God, the Father, is this: to visit orphans and widows in their affliction, *and* to keep oneself unstained from the world" (James 1:27, emphasis added).

More generally, Christians on the right and left must remember that while Jesus' message certainly had political implications (most notably, He was Lord and Caesar was not), Jesus never started a political party, nor do we any have record of Him crusading against social and political ills. It's true that the gospel has social implications. But the social gospel is something else entirely. Rauschenbusch and his followers often equated social action with the gospel so that the kingdom of God was no longer concerned with individual salvation and future life, but with the elimination of intolerance, corruption, injustice, and militarism.[26] This message is hardly a secret or lost one since the mainline Protestant establishment has been saying it for a hundred years.[27] The problem is not in working toward the elimination of injustice, though the specific activities lumped under "justice" are often debatable. The problem is in thinking that this is the main business of the church as church. But when the church's business is mainly political and its unifying creeds are political instead of doctrinal, the church and state overlap until the church becomes redundant. Which is why the Religious Right has been getting such a beating of late, and why people are leaving the politically liberal mainline churches in droves, and why the emerging church will become little more than a venue for left-leaning politics if they continue to view historic Christian doctrine and faith as ancillary to the gospel.

The emergent church, like Protestant liberalism before it, is quite certain about God's politics yet equally uncertain about God's theology. I'm just the opposite. I don't claim to have the divine word on minimum wage increases, activist judges, or global warming. Don't get me wrong—I have opinions on these subjects and hope these opinions are well informed and perhaps even right. But I am much more certain about God's view on the atonement than I am about His view on CEO salaries.[28] On the right and the left, we would all do well to heed Hart's advice as he summarizes the 1969 guidelines from the Lutheran Church, Missouri Synod (LCMS):

> On rare occasions the church's influence may be "direct and inten-tional" when some social issues present themselves "about which the Scriptures speak so explicitly and clearly" that the institutional church is bound to speak. But because this kind of influence "*always* carries the risk of politicizing the church," it should be done infrequently and "only on the basis of clear and unambiguous teaching of Scripture, where the church's *most fundamental* concerns are at stake. . . . It asserted that the LCMS should "remain alert to the hazard of issuing superficial moral judgments or urging particular forms of action in complex secular mat-ters for which there is no clear Word of God."[29]

This makes refreshingly good sense to me. Too often well-meaning Republicans and Democrats have been quick to politicize the gospel, unneces-sarily alienating their brothers and sisters, and quick to pronounce divinely sanctioned judgments on things they don't understand. I guess as a gospel minister I tend to focus on, well, the gospel—the life, death, and resurrection of Jesus. I am dogmatic, yet humble (I hope), about orthodoxy, while I am open-minded, yet opinionated, about politics. That is to say, the difference between emerging churches and what I am aiming for in my church is the dif-ference between unity based on social issues and unity based on theological issues. Orthodoxy means right doctrine that overflows in right living, which can be variously applied in the political sphere. For emerging churches, however, it seems that orthodoxy means right living immediately applied in the political sphere without attention to doctrine.

There are, however, more serious concerns with the emergent view of Jesus than just an overly realized, sometimes overly politicized kingdom message. Many emergent authors are very close to discarding, and some already have, historic understandings of the atonement, the existence of eternal punishment, and the uniqueness of Jesus Christ in salvation.

MAN OF SORROWS

Why did Jesus die? There is no one answer to that question. Jesus died for many reasons. Or to put it another way, the death of Jesus accomplished many things. In yet another book of fifties, John Piper lists fifty reasons why Christ suffered and died.[30] Every reason is supported by explicit texts from the Bible. Piper shows that Jesus died to show His own love for us (Eph. 5:2, 25; Gal. 2:20), to destroy the hostility between races (Eph. 2:14–16), and to create a people passionate for good works (Titus 2:14). Jesus also died to rescue us from final judgment (Heb. 9:28), provide the basis for our justification (Rom. 3:24, 28; 5:9), and complete the obedience that becomes our righteousness (Phil. 2:8; 3:9; Romans 5:19; 2 Cor. 5:21).

None of the fifty reasons should be ignored, especially the first one: Christ suffered and died to absorb the wrath of God. Piper cites three texts:

Galatians 3:13: Christ redeemed us from the curse of the law by becoming a curse for us—for it is written, "Cursed is everyone who is hanged on a tree."

Romans 3:25: God put forward [Christ] as a propitiation by his blood, to be received by faith. This was to show God's righteousness, because in his divine forbearance he had passed over former sins.

1 John 4:10: In this is love, not that we have loved God but that he loved us and sent his Son to be the propitiation for our sins.

The word *propitiation* means Christ's death appeased God's just wrath. It means that Jesus died in our place and took the divinely meted out punishment we deserved. This is called penal substitution—penal because Christ's death paid our penalty, and substitution because Christ died in our place. This view of the atonement is not the only way to explain Christ's suffering and death, but without this view Christ's death cannot be explained correctly nor in its full glory. Christ was wounded for our transgressions and crushed for our iniquities (Isa. 53:5). That is the heartbeat of the gospel.

It is not the heartbeat of the emergent gospel.[31] Rather, the cross is a moral example, "showing God's loving heart, which wants forgiveness, not revenge, for everyone. . . . The cross calls humanity to stop trying to make God's kingdom happen through coercion and force, which are always self-defeating in the end, and instead, to welcome it through self-sacrifice and vulnerability."[32] This line of reasoning wouldn't be so bad, if McLaren didn't also voice—I don't see any indication that this isn't his voice coming through in the story—this verdict on substitutionary atonement: "That just sounds like one more injustice in the cosmic equation. It sounds like divine child abuse. You know?"[33] Steve Chalke and Allan Mann, in what McLaren calls a "provocative and helpful" book,[34] go even further down this sad road, describing penal substitution as "a form of cosmic child abuse," which, they write, contradicts the statement "God is love" and "makes a mockery of Jesus' own teaching to love your enemies and to refuse to repay evil with evil."[35]

Likening the cross to "cosmic child abuse" is a decidedly ungenerous way of describing penal substitution and a condescending way to talk of the atonement. I can only hope that others in the emergent church do not feel the same way about the suffering of Jesus as Chalke does and, it seems, McLaren does. In light of the tests above, Carson's warning is appropriate: "I have to say, as kindly but as forcefully as I can, that to my mind, if words mean anything, both McLaren and Chalke have largely abandoned the gospel."[36] How else can you describe things when two men describe atonement for our sins as cosmic child abuse?

The apostle Peter had no problem seeing the cross as a model for our suffering *and* as a payment for sin (1 Peter 2:21–24). I wish the emergent church wouldn't either. The assertion that the cross is simply where Jesus absorbed our pain,[37] when the New Testament says Jesus was made to be sin for us, is biblically incomplete.

Along with jettisoning penal substitution, many leaders in the emergent church are undermining other crucial aspects of biblical soteriology. For example, Chalke flatly rejects original sin, claiming "Jesus believed in original goodness."[38] Similarly, Tomlinson finds total depravity "biblically questionable, extreme, and profoundly unhelpful."[39] Instead of being dead in our sins and trespasses, we "can choose how to 'actualize' ourselves to become more fully human by making choices about our relationships to each other and God. We can choose to grow spiritually, morally, and intellectually. The *imago Dei* is not a fixed 'nature' but a capacity to 'be' God-like."[40] So the atonement did not accomplish anything on our behalf. God's attitude toward us didn't change. Jesus simply enacted and represented the forgiveness that was already in the heart of God.[41]

It's no wonder, then, that the suffering and death of Christ in much emergent writing becomes evidence of how valuable we are to God. Jesus didn't condemn and judge His disciples. They needed to be encouraged to achieve their true potential. Their question was not, do I believe in God?, as much as does God believe in me?[42] The main problem in the universe, according to many emergent writers, seems to be human suffering and brokenness. Make no mistake, suffering and brokenness are a result of the fall, but the main problem that needs to be dealt with is human sin and rebellion. Where sin is the main problem we need a crucified Substitute. Where pain and brokenness are the main problems, we need to learn to love ourselves.[43] God is no longer a holy God angry with sin, who, in His great mercy, sent His Son to die on our behalf so that divine justice might be satisfied. God becomes a vulnerable lover who opens Himself up to hurt and rejection in order to be with us because we are worth dying for.[44]

I have no doubt that this message will find a receptive audience, but it is not the message the apostles proclaimed and for which they died. Christians don't get killed for telling people that God believes in them and suffers like them and can heal their brokenness. They get killed for calling sinners to repentance and proclaiming faith in the crucified Son of God as the only means by which we who were enemies might be reconciled to God (Rom. 5:10).

TO HELL WITH HELL?

Though many in my denomination would not accept the teaching, I belong to a Reformed confessional tradition that clearly teaches the doctrine of eternal punishment.[45] The Canons of Dort speak of God's decision to "condemn and eternally punished" the reprobates for "their unbelief" and "all their other sins." For God is a "just judge and avenger."[46] The Belgic Confession confesses that "the evil ones will be convicted by the witness of their own consciences, and shall be made immortal—but only to be tormented in the everlasting fire prepared for the devil and his angels."[47] Even the irenic Heidelberg Catechism affirms that God "is terribly angry about the sin we are born with as well as the sins we personally commit. As a just judge he punishes them now and in eternity."[48]

There's actually nothing terribly Reformed about this doctrine of eternal punishment. Christians of all stripes have believed in the wrath and justice of God for most of Christian history. It's only been in the last couple of centuries that the doctrine of divine retribution has come under serious attack.

Protestant liberalism was one of the first to question God's wrath, fearing that it made God look like a heartless, capricious tyrant. This squeamishness about the hard edges of Christianity is what prompted H. Richard Niebuhr to describe theological liberalism as "a God without wrath who brought men

WHY WE'RE NOT EMERGENT

without sin into a kingdom without judgment through the ministrations of a Christ without a cross."[49]

But the avoidance of hell is not just a "liberal" problem. Evangelicals in recent decades have soft-peddled the doctrine as well, opting instead for a therapeutic God who encourages our self-esteem. Likewise, some missiologists argue that the missionary enterprise should no longer be seen as a venture to save people from hell, but only as an effort to bring God's kingdom of justice and shalom to all people.

Isn't there a place for passionate, blood-earnest warning . . . to implore people on Christ's behalf?

More recently, emergent church leaders have practiced a studied agnosticism about hell and God's wrath, deliberately avoiding the topic in sermons or writing, because, they say, it's not our business who is there—if anyone is there at all.[50] Divine wrath, when it is mentioned, often is caricaturized as befitting a sociopath. Thus McClaren writes, *"God loves you and has a wonderful plan for your life, and if you don't love God back and cooperate with God's plans in exactly the prescribed way, God will torture you with unimaginable abuse, forever—that sort of thing."*[51] McLaren recognizes that hell language is in the Bible, but hell is just one imagery among many to describe the negative consequences of rejecting God's way.[52]

This understanding of hell, common in the emergent church, raises two questions. First, do these negative consequences of rejecting God's way last forever? It sure seems as if the answer for McLaren is no. When Jesus spoke of coming judgment on "injustice and hypocrisy" (what about unrighteousness and unbelief?), he was, according to McLaren, simply following in the footsteps of the Old Testament prophets.[53] Yet Jesus speaks of "an hour . . . coming when all who are in the tombs will hear his voice and come out, those who have done good to the resurrection of life, and those who have done evil to the resurrection of judgment" (John 5:28–29). And Messiah Jesus warns of eternal fire (Matt. 25:41). He tells of a man who died and went to Hades, where he was "in torment" and "in anguish in this flame" (Luke 16:23–24).[54] The other question that must be answered is whether hell is simply the natural result of going our own way. It's easier to think of hell as nothing more than the consequences of bad choices. But the New Testament does not allow us to take God's activity out of the equation. John Piper, citing Matthew 10:28, Luke 19:27, and Matthew 25:41, 46 explains.

> Hell is not simply the natural consequences of rejecting God. Some people say this in order to reject the thought that God sends people there. They say that people send themselves there. That is true. People make choices that lead to hell. But it is not the whole truth. Jesus says these choices are really deserving of hell. "Whoever says, 'You fool!' will be liable to [that is, guilty of, or deserving of] the hell of fire" (Matt. 5:22). That is why he calls hell "punishment" (Matt. 25:46). It is not a mere self-imposed natural consequence (like cigarette smoking leading to lung cancer); it is the penalty of God's wrath (like a judge sentencing a criminal to hard labor).[55]

If preachers in the past sometimes suffered from an unhealthy fascination with hell, today's ministers, including not a few emergent leaders, are guilty of an undue ambivalence on the subject. David Hansen writes, "There is an important place in the ministry for honest questioning over doctrinal issues. But I'm not proud of my tossing and turning over hell. Some pastors wear their agnosticism about hell as a badge of honor. I've tried it. I've acted as if struggling to believe our Lord's words were a virtue. But I always found that when I become proud of my doubts, they suddenly become the sin of unbelief."[56]

Granted, there is no place for giddiness concerning God's wrath, but isn't there a place for passionate, blood-earnest warning? Isn't it biblical to move past agnosticism about hell and implore people on Christ's behalf: Be reconciled to God (2 Cor. 5:20)? Could it be that our evangelism languishes, our preaching lacks authority, and our congregations lose focus because we don't have the doctrine of hell to set our face like a flint toward Jerusalem?

We need the doctrine of eternal punishment. Time and time again in the New Testament we find that understanding divine justice is essential to our sanctification. Believing in God's judgment actually helps us look more like Jesus. In short, we need the doctrine of the wrath of God.

First, *we need God's wrath to keep us honest about evangelism*. Paul reasoned with Felix about righteousness, self-control, and the coming judgment (Acts 24:25). We need to do the same. Without the doctrine of hell, we are prone to get involved in all sorts of important God-honoring things, but neglect the one thing that matters for all eternity, urging sinners to be reconciled to God.

Second, *we need God's wrath in order to forgive our enemies*. The reason we can forego repaying evil for evil is because we trust the Lord's promise to repay the wicked. Paul's logic is sound. "Do not take revenge, my friends, but leave room for God's wrath, for it is written: 'It is mine to avenge; I will repay,' says the Lord" (Rom. 12:19 NIV). The only way to look past our deepest hurts and betrayals is to rest assured that every sin against us has been paid for on the cross and/or will be punished in hell. We don't have to seek vigilante justice, because God will be our just judge.

Third, *we need God's wrath in order to risk our lives for Jesus' sake*. The radical devotion necessary to suffer for the Word of God and the testimony of Jesus comes, in part, from the assurance we have that God will vindicate us in the end. That's why the martyrs under the throne cry out, "How long, Sovereign Lord, holy and true, until you judge the inhabitants of the earth and avenge our blood?" (Rev. 6:10 NIV). They paid the ultimate price for their faith, but their blood-stained cries will be answered one day. Their innocence will be established when God finally judges their persecutors.

Fourth, *we need God's wrath in order to live holy lives*. Paul warns us that God cannot be mocked. We will reap what we sow. We are spurred on to live a life of purity and good deeds by the promised reward for obedience and the promised curse for disobedience. If we live to please the flesh, we will reap destruction from God. But if we live to please the Spirit, we will reap eternal life (Gal. 6:6–7). Sometimes ministers balk at the thought of motivating people with the threat of eternal punishment. But wasn't this Jesus' approach when He said, "Do not be afraid of those who kill the body but cannot kill the soul. Rather, be afraid of the One who can destroy both soul and body in hell" (Matt. 10:28 NIV)? Sometimes we need to literally scare the hell out of people.

Fifth, *we need God's wrath in order to understand what mercy means.* Divine mercy without divine wrath is meaningless. Only when we know that we were objects of wrath (Eph. 2:3), stood condemned already (John 3:18), and would have faced hell as God's enemies were it not for undeserved mercy (Rom. 5:10) can we sing from the heart, "Amazing grace, how sweet the sound that saved a wretch like me!"

Sixth, *we need God's wrath in order to grasp how wonderful heaven will be.* Jonathan Edwards is famous (or infamous) for his sermon "Sinners in the Hands of an Angry God." It's still read in American literature classes, usually as a caricature of the puritanical spirit of colonial New England. But few people realize that Edwards also preached sermons like "Heaven Is a World of Love." Unlike most of us, Edwards saw in vivid colors the terror of hell and the beauty of heaven. We can't get a striking picture of one without the other. That's why the depiction of the heavenly New Jerusalem also contains a warning to the cowardly, unbelieving, vile, immoral, idolaters, and liars whose place is in "the fiery lake of burning sulfur" (Rev. 21:8 NIV). It's unlikely we will long for our final salvation if we don't know what we are saved from.

Seventh, *we need the wrath of God in order to be motivated to care for our impoverished brothers and sisters.* We all know the saying that Christians are so heavenly minded they are of no earthly good. The idea is that if all we think about are heaven and hell we'll ignore ministries of compassion and social justice. But what better impetus for social justice than Jesus' sober warning that if we fail to care for the least of our brothers we will go away to eternal punishment (Matt. 25:31–46)? The wrath of God is a motivator for us to show compassion to others, because without love, John says, we have no eternal life, and if we don't share our material possessions with those in need, we have no love (1 John 3:17).

Eighth, *we need God's wrath in order to be ready for the Lord's return*. We must keep the lamps full, the wicks trimmed, the houses clean, the vineyard tended, the workers busy, and the talents invested lest we find ourselves unprepared for the day of reckoning. Only when we fully believe in the coming wrath of God and tremble at the thought of eternal punishment will we stay awake, keep alert, and be prepared for Jesus to come again and judge the living and the dead.

IN WHAT WAY IS JESUS THE ONLY WAY?

This book isn't big enough for me to launch into a detailed discussion about pluralism, inclusivism, and exclusivism, and I probably wouldn't change anyone's mind in a few pages anyway. But let me at least state my position: I believe the Bible teaches—and historic evangelicalism affirms—that salvation comes but one way: through hearing the gospel of Jesus' death and resurrection and putting conscious faith in the person and work of Jesus Christ. I believe this is taught in passages like John 14:6, Acts 4:12, and Romans 10:5–17. I believe eternal life is only for those who believe that Jesus is the Son of God sent by the Father (John 5:24; 6:27, 40, 47, 54).

I also believe that Scripture puts humanity, at its most fundamental level, into two opposing categories: sheep and goats (Matt. 25:31–46), wheat and weeds (Matt. 13:36–43), believers and unbelievers (1 Cor. 14:22), the righteous and the wicked (Mal. 3:18), those marked with the name of the Lamb and those marked with the name of the Beast (Rev. 13:11–14:5). As hard as it can be to admit it, for we all have friends and family who do not worship Jesus, the Bible frequently teaches that some belong to God and some do not. There's an inside and an outside to the New Jerusalem (Rev. 21:14–15).

Emergent leaders know their Bibles well enough to know that Jesus said, "I am the way, and the truth, and the life. No one comes to the Father except through me" (John 14:6). No emergent leader I've read would be so bold as to say, "Well, that's just rubbish. Jesus was wrong." But what they mean by "the way" is often very different.

Jesus was not making claims about one religion being better than all other religions. That completely misses the point, the depth, and the truth. Rather, he was telling those who were following him that his way is the way to the depth of reality. This kind of life Jesus was living, perfectly and completely in connection and cooperation with God, is the best possible way for a person to live. It is how things are. . . . Perhaps a better question than who's right, is who's living rightly?[57]

So Jesus is the only way not in that He provides sole access to God the Father such that if we do not know Jesus we do not know God. Rather, Jesus is the only way in that He shows the only way to truly live. What makes Christianity unique, Chalke argues, is the call to love those who mistreat us and oppress us.[58]

In other emergent writers, it's unclear exactly how unique Christianity really is. "Look, my understanding of the gospel tells me that religion is always a mixed bag, whether it's Judaism, Christianity, Islam, or Buddhism," McLaren explains. "Some of it reflects people's sincere attempts to find the truth, and some of it represents people's attempts to evade the truth through hypocrisy. . . . And some of it represents our own ego, our own pride, as we try to suppress the truth and look holy while we do it. . . . But isn't that the point of the gospel—that we're all a mess, whatever our religion, in need of God's grace."[59]

Elsewhere McLaren affirms making disciples, after lots of dialogue and humility and understanding and willing acceptance, but even then there is a caveat. "I don't believe making disciples must equal making adherents to the Christian religion. It may be advisable in many (not all!) circumstances to help people become followers of Jesus *and* remain with their Buddhist, Hindu, or Jewish contexts."[60] I hope I am wrong, but I can find no indication in McLaren's writings that belief in Jesus as the Christ and the unique Son of God is necessary for entrance into heaven or the kingdom. On the contrary, I read lots of passages where he admonishes those who "prefer the rigid boundaries and impermeable walls of their narrow domains and constricted turf" and lots of passages that say, implicitly, or in this case explicitly, "the kingdom of God is open to all, except those who want to ruin it by dividing it against itself."[61] I can't help but wonder, is the death of Jesus necessary for anything? Is faith in Jesus, not merely participation with Him in kingdom living, essential in any way? Is anything unique about Jesus besides His dynamite teaching? And if there is something unique about the person and work of Jesus, does it matter if anyone knows it or believes it?

McLaren argues that pronouncements about heaven and hell do not fit with his missional calling: "Blessed in this life [is] to be a blessing to everyone on earth."[62] McLaren is often critical of Christians for ignoring the totality of Abraham's call. He calls it bad monotheism and not missional for us to take the first part Abraham's call ("I will bless you") and the not the second ("all nations will be blessed through you").[63] But in what way are the nations blessed through Abraham? Paul argues, "And the Scripture, foreseeing that God would justify the Gentiles by faith, preached the gospel beforehand to Abraham, saying, 'In you shall all the nations be blessed.' So then, those who are *of faith* are blessed along with Abraham, the man of faith" (Gal. 3:8–9 emphasis added). It's fine that McLaren doesn't want to play God and sentence people to hell, but if he is truly interested in imparting the Abrahamic blessing, his missional calling should include calling people to faith in Jesus Christ and warning them that they are under a curse apart from this faith (Gal. 3:10–14).

Once a Jewish man named Sam told McLaren he was turned off to Christianity because he heard a preacher on TV say that if Hitler had prayed a little prayer he would be in heaven. Then Sam explained that his son, a volunteer in the Israeli army, one night came across a Palestinian. The other soldiers with him began giving the Palestinian a rough time, but Sam's son objected—to the point where he pulled a gun on his own soldiers. Sam's son was put in jail, but eventually vindicated for doing the right thing.

Sam asked Brian, "Would God send my boy to hell because he never said the magic words, but He would send Hitler to heaven?"

McLaren didn't answer his question. Instead he said, "Sam, I think your son acted a lot like Jesus would have acted. Jesus cared for outsiders, just as your son did, and Jesus gave up His life to protect us all, just as your son risked his life for that guy. So I think your son was following Jesus' example, and I can see why you're so proud of him. Really, I think God feels about Jesus a lot like you feel about your son. And I know God must be proud of your son too."[64]

Granted, McLaren was put in a bit of a pickle, as all of us are when someone "dares" us to condemn someone to hell. But as Michael Horton points out, not only does McLaren present us with the false choice between justification by saying a sinner's prayer or justification by loving one's neighbor, but he effectively told the man that good people go to heaven. At least he gave the impression that Sam's son is okay before God.

Too often emergent leaders force us to choose between salvation by following Jesus' example or salvation that doesn't care about good works. But this is another false dilemma. By God's common grace people often show the work of the law written on their hearts (Rom. 2:15), but Paul makes clear that we don't always do what the law requires, such that good works can never justify us in God's sight (Rom. 3:20). Therefore, Abraham is our example, not because he tried to make the world a better place,[65] but because "Abraham believed God, and it was counted to him as righteousness" (Rom. 4:3; Gen. 15:6).

McLaren and others in the emergent church are right to want a gospel available for all. Where they misstep is in neglecting to mention, and sometimes outright denying, that the gospel is (1) first and foremost a message about what Jesus accomplished, and (2) it is for those who repent of their sins and call on Jesus Christ as Lord. Does the emergent Jesus demand that all nations worship Him as their God and Savior or merely that everyone live like He did? McLaren argues that "Jesus didn't get crucified for being exclusive; he was hated and crucified for the reverse—for opening the windows of grace and the doors of heaven to the tax collectors and prostitutes, the half-breeds and ultimately even the Gentiles."[66] But is this really so—Jesus was crucified for opening the doors of heaven too wide? Obviously, Jesus was chided for fraternizing with sinners and tax collectors, but why did the Jews crucify Him? They killed Jesus for His outrageous Godlike claims—that He was the Son of God and the King of Israel (Matt. 26:63–66; 27:39–43).

Jesus consistently upset Jewish scruples about Torah, but it was His self-identification that drove them to murder. "This was why the Jews were seeking all the more to kill him, because not only was he breaking the Sabbath, but he was even calling God his own Father, making himself equal with God" (John 5:18). I'm sure emergent Christians are sincere in their love for Jesus, but what kind of love is it that makes so little of His glory as the long-awaited Messiah and the Son of the living God (Matt. 16:16), the Alpha and Omega (Rev. 1:8), the righteous Judge (2 Tim. 4:8), the conquering King who rules the nations with a rod of iron (Rev. 2:26–27), the great I am (John 8:58), and the Lamb who was slain to take away the sin of the world (John 1:29)? Chesterton is right. "Those who charged the Christians with burning down Rome with firebrands were slanderers; but they were at least far nearer to the nature of Christianity than those among the moderns who tell us that the Christians were a sort of ethical society, being martyred in a languid fashion for telling men they had a duty to their neighbors, and only mildly disliked because they were meek and mild."[67] The early church was important because it was intolerable, and it was intolerable because it was intolerant. Not socially intolerant or coldhearted or obnoxiously abrasive, but intolerant of any salvation but the cross, any God but theirs, and any Lord but Christ.

NOTES

1. These metaphors and descriptions are taken from Brian D. McLaren, *The Secret Message of Jesus* (Nashville: W Publishing Group, 2006), 138–48. McLaren makes these suggestions because kingdom language "is outdated and distant," evoking "patriarchy, chauvinism, imperialism, domination, and a regime without freedom" (139). For similar comments from Walter Rauschenbusch, the leader of the Social Gospel at the beginning of the twentieth century, see Russell D. Moore, *The Kingdom of Christ* (Wheaton, Ill.: Crossway, 2004), 184.

2. McLaren, *Secret Message*, 111.

3. Brian D. McLaren, *The Last Word and the Word after That* (San Francisco: Jossey-Bass, 2005), 121.

4. Brian D. McLaren, *The Story We Find Ourselves In* (San Francisco: Jossey-Bass, 2003), 125.

5. McLaren, *Secret Message*, 134.

6. Rob Bell, *Velvet Elvis* (Grand Rapids: Zondervan, 2005), 21.

7. George Eldon Ladd, *A Theology of the New Testament*, rev. ed. (Grand Rapids: Eerdmans, 1993), 68ff.

8. Ibid., 79–88.

9. Ibid., 89–90.

10. McLaren, *Secret Message*, 118.

11. Brian D. McLaren, *A New Kind of Christian: A Tale of Two Friends on a Spiritual Journey* (San Francisco: Jossey-Bass, 2001), 132.

12. E-mail message quoted in Spencer Burke with Colleen Pepper, *Making Sense of Church: Eavesdropping on Emerging Conversations about God, Community, and Culture* (Grand Rapids: Zondervan, 2003), 148.

13. Brian McLaren in *The Church in Emerging Culture*, Leonard Sweet, gen. ed. (Grand Rapids: Zondervan, 2003), 215.

14. According to Bell, the gospel is good news for the world because it means we start living like Jesus, which makes life better for everyone (*Velvet Elvis*, 166). Not only does this gut the gospel of its center, Jesus' saving death on the cross, but it is also grossly simplistic. The truth is that when people start following Jesus it doesn't mean good news for everyone. If Paul's ministry is any indication, half the people will love us and half the people will hate us for believing in Jesus. Didn't Jesus say He came not to bring peace, but a sword, and that families would be divided on account of Him? (Matt. 10:34–39; cf. Luke 2:34–35).

15. McLaren, *The Last Word*, 171.

16. McLaren writes, "A central element, then, of Jesus' message—and of his life—is this radical confidence that death is not the end, that this life is not all there is, and that there will be a real resurrection" (*Secret Message*, 189).

17. Ibid., 36.

18. C. S. Lewis, as quoted in Moore, *The Kingdom of Christ*, 52.

19. McLaren, *The Last Word*, 151.

20. Cf. McLaren, "If people believe that wars are necessary and justified, then wars will continue to happen. If people believe in redemptive violence, then violence will proliferate. But if they believe the secret message of Jesus, they will believe that there are creative alternatives to war and violence, and by the grace of God, fewer and fewer wars and less and less violence may happen as a result. And someday, by the grace of God, perhaps war will go the way of slavery and colonialism—so that we can say that the kingdom of God has more fully come" (*Secret Message*, 160).

21. Ibid.

22. Lloyd-Jones explained in a sermon fifty years ago, "For whom is the Sermon on the Mount intended? To whom does it apply? What is really the purpose of this Sermon; what is its relevance? . . .The principles, it was said, were there laid down as to how life should be lived by men, and all we have to do is apply the Sermon on the Mount. We can thereby produce the kingdom of God on earth, war will be banished and all our troubles will be ended. That is the typical social gospel view." He concluded that "these ['Blessed are'] statements mean that no man can live the Sermon on the Mount in and of himself, and unaided" (*Studies in the Sermon on the Mount* [Grand Rapids: Eerdmans, 1976], 13–14).

23. See John R. W. Stott, *Christian Mission in the Modern World* (Downers Grove, Ill.: Intervarsity Press, 1975), 27. Stott's take on mission is all the things we expect from him: charitable, balanced, and wise. Stott affirms the necessity of social action but doesn't hesitate to say that the church's first priority should be evangelizing the millions who don't know Christ (15–17, 19, 23, 35).

24. John Piper, *What Jesus Demands from the World* (Wheaton: Crossway, 2006), 23; italics in original.

25. Brian D. McLaren and Tony Campolo, *Adventures in Missing the Point* (Grand Rapids: Zondervan, 2003), 122.

26. Cf. Darryl Hart, *A Secular Faith: Why Christianity Favors the Separation of Church and State* (Chicago: Ivan R. Dee, 2006), 103.

27. For example, the Federal Council of Churches, precursor to the National Council of Churches (NCC), issued this statement in 1939 just after World War II broke out: "We call upon the churches now to seek peace, not for safety's sake or for profit's sake but for Christ's sake and a kindlier world. We could not, and would not, be immune from the world's problems and pain. By generous gift and practical service let us know the fellowship of His suffering in war-torn lands. With willingness to sacrifice let us join with others in preparing the outlines of a just peace, or an economic life undisfigured by poverty and greed, and of a world order in which common needs and service of all nations may find a home" (*Secular Faith*, 191). Similarly, three decades later, the NCC-backed Consultation on Church Union (COCU) declared its "struggle against racism, poverty, environmental blight, war, and other problems of the family of man" (ibid., 196–97).

28. McLaren compares the announcement of the kingdom of God to a television news interview with a prophet who announces: "Now it's time! It's time to decommission weapons programs and reconcile with enemies! It's time for CEOs to slash their mammoth salaries and give generous raises to all their lowest-paid employees!" (*Secret Message*, 24).

29. Hart, *A Secular Faith*, 233–34.

30. John Piper, *The Passion of Jesus Christ* (Wheaton, Ill.: Crossway, 2004).

31. Cf. D. A. Carson, *Becoming Conversant with the Emerging Church* (Grand Rapids: Zondervan, 2005), 157–87.

32. McLaren, *The Story We Find Ourselves In*, 105–6.

33. Ibid., 102.

34. McLaren, *Secret Message*, 226.

35. Steve Chalke and Allan Mann, *The Lost Message of Jesus* (Grand Rapids: Zondervan, 2003), 182–83.

36. Carson, *Becoming Conversant*, 186.

37. Chalke and Mann, *The Lost Message*, 181.

38. Ibid., 67.

39. Dave Tomlinson, *The Post-Evangelical* (Grand Rapids: Zondervan, 2003), 126.
40. Ibid., 125. Commenting on this passage, Pagitt argues that "many post-evangelicals find connection with an Eastern-Hebraic understanding that implies that God can be found in people." This understanding may be Eastern, but it is not Hebraic. The Old Testament posits a radical Creator-creature distinction. "For my thoughts are not your thoughts, neither are your ways my ways, declares the Lord. For as the heavens are higher than the earth, so are my ways higher than your ways and my thoughts than your thoughts" (Isa. 55:8–9).
41. Ibid., 101.
42. Chalke and Mann, *The Lost Message*, 98–99. Cf. Bell, *Velvet Elvis*, "I have been told that I need to believe in Jesus. Which is a good thing. But what I am learning is that Jesus believes in me. I have been told that I need to have faith in God. Which is a good thing. But what I am learning is that God has faith in me" (134).
43. Cf. Donald Miller, *Blue Like Jazz* (Nashville: Nelson, 2003), 231.
44. Cf. Rob Bell, *Sex God* (Grand Rapids: Zondervan, 2007), 98, 112ff.
45. Much of this section is based on an article I developed for *Church Herald*, the official magazine of the Reformed Church of America. It will be published in an upcoming issue of the magazine.
46. *Ecumenical Creeds and Reformed Confessions* (Grand Rapids: Faith Alive Christian Resources, 1988), CD, I.15.
47. Ibid., BC 37.
48. Ibid., HC 10.
49. H. Richard Niebuhr, *The Kingdom of God in America* (New York: Harper and Row, 1959), 193.
50. McLaren, *New Kind of Christian*, 124ff. See also Bell, *Velvet Elvis*, 146, who writes about heaven and hell, yet describes both places as "full of forgiven people."
51. McLaren, *The Last Word*, xii. Emphasis in original.
52. Ibid., 80–81.
53. McLaren, *Secret Message*, 23.
54. This is not even to mention other New Testament warnings of judgment (e.g., Acts 17:31; Heb. 9:27) and coming retribution (the entire book of Revelation).
55. John Piper, *What Jesus Demands of the World* (Wheaton, Ill.: Crossway, 2006), 93.
56. David Hansen, *Art of Pastoring* (Downers Grove, Ill.: InterVarsity, 1994), 78.
57. Bell, *Velvet Elvis*, 21.
58. Chalke and Mann, *Lost Message*, 121.
59. McLaren, *New Kind of Christian,* 66.
60. McLaren, *Generous Orthodoxy*, 293.
61. McLaren, *Secret Message*, 169–70.
62. McLaren, *Generous Orthodoxy*, 122–23.
63. Ibid., 120–21.
64. McLaren in *The Church in Emerging Culture*, 220.
65. McLaren, *The Story We Find Ourselves In*, 67.
66. McLaren, *New Kind of Christian*, 127.
67. G. K. Chesterton, *The Everlasting Man* (1925; repr., San Francisco: Ignatius Press, 1993), 182.

From here on out, I am only interested in what is real. Real people, real feelings, that's it, that's all I'm interested in.

—RUSSELL HAMMOND, *guitarist,* Almost Famous[1]

CHAPTER 10

REAL TOPEKA PEOPLE:
IN SEARCH
OF
COMMUNITY

RACHAEL COOK'S business card says that she will be my "Experience Designer" for my visit to Westwinds, an "Ancient/Future" community church in Jackson, Michigan. According to the back of the business card, Westwinds is "engaging people toward full life development in Jesus." They have a weekend experience called "Fusion," which I will be experiencing on a Saturday night with a friend.

This is probably a good time to interject again, or possibly for the first time, that I don't have a problem with a more "experimental" worship structure. I'm not necessarily an advocate of straight-up Psalm singing followed by an hour of verse-by-verse exposition. Taking the words "associate pastor" or "director of small group ministries" and replacing them with words like "Experience Designer" strikes me as a little silly, but nothing I'm willing to die on the hill— or in this case on the message board—for.

On the Westwinds Web site, visitors can use something called "Human Transcendence Technology," which is, as far as I can understand it, based on their description, "a web based experiential prayer module." I am prompted, on this page, to pick an "ethos," with my choices being "urban, sun and water."

I choose urban because I live in the city, but for the record I have nothing against sun and water either. Another page pops up, on which I am encouraged to use the "Prayground Mixer" to cue up some tinny, ambient tunes to aid in my prayer experience. After clicking through all of the choices—eight in all—I settle on something that can only be described as "the Casio keyboard you got for Christmas in the eighth grade meets the Vienna Boy's Choir." I'm then encouraged to use a ball device to rotate a cube that is filled with lots of pictures—some angels, a hand in the air, some Christ iconography. Via links at the top I can "change ethos" and chat or blog about the experience. In the interest of full disclosure I try the "sun" ethos for a little while too.

= = = =

According to a brochure entitled "A Theology of Space," everything at Westwinds is intentional, right down to the suite of offices, which has been renamed "Designer Studios." What were once called Sunday school classrooms are now called "Life Development Studios." Oddly, the "lobby" is still called the "lobby," a place "of life exchange and story sharing where people can make those initial connections of 'doing life together.'" There is also coffee.

I have briefed myself on some of Westwinds' history via a series of CDs by Dr. Ron Martoia, Westwinds' former pastor, who is now a "transformational architect"; his passion is helping "people, and the organisms they serve, design and then journey through the experience of deep revolutionary change."[2]

Dr. Martoia, like many of his emergent contemporaries, is now full-time in the revolutionary-change consulting business. He is also heading up a new, experimental learning community in Jackson called "Vortex," which "hosts immersive learning experiences as well as weekly yoga classes." On his CD, subtitled *Relationship with God Once My Beliefs Blow Up,* Martoia asserts that

God invites us into a relationship that happens "independent of having all of the doctrinal systems worked out." He blames, at different times, modernism, proof-texting, the "concordance approach," and modern discipleship programs for people's supposed lack of spiritual growth. He proposes a "story submersion spiritual formation"—Bible as a storyteller instead of Bible full of rules and propositions to "ingest." He says that the rules in the text "don't apply to us anyway." Says they are "completely irrelevant to us." It seems to my untrained ear, no disrespect intended, to be the garden-variety emergent argument.

Another one of Martoia's major critiques is that our churches try to "mimic" the New Testament church, which to me sounds like not such a bad idea. But upon reflection and dialogue with people, he thinks this is an unreasonable model. Not "workable," he says. Also not surprising is Martoia's revelation that he comes out of a conservative Bible church, as do many of his emergent contemporaries. What sorts of things, biblically, do we need to let go by the wayside, he asks? Is it possible that we live in another very, very pivotal time period in history,[3] he asks again?

Oddly, though, what I also gather from Martoia's CDs, as well as Westwinds and its materials, is that it has clung to many vestiges of a more "traditional" church experience. He still speaks of people becoming saved, being baptized, and becoming "members" of the congregation. The youth group does traditional youth group stuff—summer camps, winter camps, ski trips, Cedar Point amusement park, etc. They don't make the teenagers finger-paint about their feelings, which I'm sure is a big relief for them, at some level.

"Doubts occur when there are immature or pre-digested understandings that are no longer satisfying," according to Martoia. At this point he stops and says that "there are a couple of kids up here that keep talking, and I feel like I'm competing with them." He then cites a *Time* magazine article that raises doubts about the biblical canon being more about faith than politics. About new gospels, and found documents that should or should not have been a part of the Scriptures. He invites the congregation to doubt with him.

= = = =

A quick read through the *Grand Rapids Press* Religion section (February 10, 2007) is telling. There is a breathily written article entitled "Church 'more spiritual than religious,'" in which the author describes the "10:03" service at "The Journey," a new Grand Rapids downtown church located—you guessed it—in a renovated factory building right next to a coffee shop. The church, started by Bill Freeman, a former television news reporter and radio talk-show host, will feature "songs heard on mainstream radio" such as U2's "Still Haven't Found What I'm Looking For," which may be the most over-ridden pony in the entire emergent movement.

"The sermons are going to be based on the Bible, but they will also use other sacred sources such as the Quran or something Ghandi or the Dalai Lama said," explains Freeman in the piece, written as though it is seeing the antiestablishment church-in-jeans model explained for the first time. "So it's Bible plus."

Freeman added that he will encourage a "sermon-as-discussion" format, and goes on to say that he will try to make the space look "kind of 'night clubby' like a comedy club." He also intends, for the record, on wearing jeans and a sport coat.

The section is framed by a feature on Rob Bell, who is launching a second title through Zondervan Publishing called *Sex God.* The article, titled "All You Need Is Love," explains that Bell's first book, *Velvet Elvis,* sold a tidy 200,000 copies, and that Bell is about to embark on another tour to promote *Sex God.* According to the Web site SexGodTour.com, Bell will hit several college towns to sign the book and show his short films.

Adjacent to the Bell story is a piece on Calvin College, and how it will be hosting a "talk on faith on an international scale." According to the piece, nearly 330 students, primarily from Christian colleges, convened last week at Calvin for its second annual Faith & International Development Conference. The three-day discussion explored what role Christians can play in "peace building and reconciliation, global health, environmental care, and economic justice." The article doesn't mention that what it may have cost to house and feed nearly 330 well-heeled Christian college students could have made for a nice love gift to Africa or some other such starving locale. But dialogue is king these days, as it seems that the church that isn't dialoguing about The Poor is indeed no church at all.

Meanwhile, a small ad in the lower right corner of page D3 advertises "Traditional Worship" at New Community Church. The ad, which possesses nothing in the way of creativity, advertises "beautiful hymns of the church with John VanderMeer at the organ" and "preaching from the Bible," as though this is a new and novel concept.

$$= = = =$$

This week I had two friends send me an article entitled "Five Streams of the Emergent Church" by Scot McKnight. McKnight, to use a political metaphor, would probably be described, and describe himself, as a "moderate" emergent. And my friends, knowing about this project, have written, explaining—and I'm paraphrasing—"What McKnight writes about doesn't sound so bad. What's the big deal?"

It strikes me that when I see the emergent movement described by Scot McKnight, I like it a lot better than when I see it hashed out by Brian McLaren or Tony Jones. McKnight, rightly, critiques the emergent "you're in or out" evangelical critique.

> This emerging ambivalence about who is in and who is out creates a serious problem for evangelism. The emerging movement is not known for it, but I wish it were. Unless you proclaim the Good News of Jesus Christ, there is no good news at all—and if there is no Good News, then there is no Christianity, emerging or evangelical.

He goes on to acknowledge that the overarching political motivation for emergent comes from the left (he even uses the terms "latte-drinking" and "hippie-wannabe"), but encourages them to maintain their social-justice heart without veering into social gospel territory. It may be too late, but the message is good. McKnight even lays out his own positions on homosexuality and abortion, which is more than I have seen from anyone in the movement. And he does so in a very unassuming way, so as not to say, "I'm the guy who is defined by the fact that I think homosexuality is sin."

McKnight also does an admirable job of attempting to define "missional"—a word that has found its way into many emergent cohort non-mission statements, as well as the movement's focus on orthopraxy (right living). He suggests that emergents aren't throwing their theological babies out with the bathwater; rather, they have just shifted a focus to right living. Again, nobody is going to argue with a "live like Jesus might have" mantra.

Finally, McKnight addresses worship[4] and the idea of "prophetic rhetoric" being one of the streams flowing into the "emergent lake." But instead of anything prophetic, he just addresses the emergent tendency to hyperbolize, or, to put it simply, say things for shock value. He puts out as an example the usual "I don't think Jesus would like Christians" line that has been used, now, thousands of times to describe evangelicals in what could be called a very broad stroke.

= = = =

"Ain't gonna let nobody turn me 'round, turn me 'round, turn me 'round."

"Ain't gonna let injustice, turn me 'round, turn me 'round, turn me 'round."

A quick look around the room at Mars Hill Bible Church, at the five thousand or so other middle-class, suburban white people, and I really wonder what injustice it is they're singing about. Not finding their size at the Gap?

All kidding aside, I'm surprised to see that the clientele at Rob Bell's church is so, well, normal. And I can honestly say that watching thousands of tall, white Dutch folk—baby boomers, yuppies, college and high school kids—belting out a Civil Rights–era spiritual is just about the weirdest thing I have ever seen. My black buddy L.J. would blow his stack if he saw this. I'm glad he's not here.

As you've probably heard, the church meets in an old mall and is one of the fastest growing churches in the history of churches. The setup is a sort of theatre in the round, with a square dais in the center of the room, around which are lots of chairs, and on top of which is a staggeringly good-looking praise team, singing "Turn Me 'Round" like they are about to march through the streets of Birmingham. "Gonna keep on walking, keep on talking, marching on to freedom land."

Numbers continually flash on the four big screens above the dais. The numbers, I'm told by my wife, correspond to a number on her wristband (10640), and a number on my son's wristband (the same number). He was deposited in "Toddler Cove" earlier with Ian, Kevin's son. Toddler Cove, down the mall hallway from "Baby Bay," was crawling with toddlers and their parents. It was a weird sort of Chuck E Cheese-meets-Willow Creek-meets 1984 kind of experience. I wondered for a second if I would ever see Tristan again.

After the singing ends, the place rips up in applause when Rob ascends to the stage. He will not be giving the message this morning, but takes care of some announcements and gives a five-minute promotion for one of his buddy's books, which is newly released. "In true Mars Hill fashion, let's create a riot at Schuler's Books on the night of his signing." I nudge Kevin and tell him that I expect a similar pulpit promo for the release of my next book. Bell then quickly lays out a plan to stop child homelessness in Grand Rapids, help the "under-resourced" in Grand Rapids, and help the "under-resourced" in Burundi.

I had trouble sleeping last night, because I learned that my in-laws would be in attendance at Mars Hill this morning as well. I was both worried that Mom was coming to check up on me, and also worried about my ability to be objective about what I would see. Would I be able to enjoy and acknowledge the good things, and Bell's good intent to reach more people for Christ? I spent half the night rereading *Velvet Elvis,* specifically, Bell's view of God's faith in man. On pages 133–34 of *Velvet,* he tells the story of Peter rushing out of the boat to meet Jesus walking on the water. Peter began to sink, and Jesus rebuked him for his lack of faith.

Who does Peter lose faith in? Not Jesus; he is doing fine. Peter loses faith in himself. Peter loses faith that he can do what the Rabbi is doing. If the rabbi calls you to be his disciple, then he believes that you can actually be like him. . . . What I'm learning is that Jesus believes in me. . . . God has faith in me.

So the point of all of this, according to *Velvet Elvis,* is that God came to earth, to die, to help us realize the great potential inside us. It's no wonder that this is popular. It's the spiritual equivalent of Rocky ascending the steps of the Philadelphia Art Museum and then digging deep to knock out Apollo Creed. Even more troubling is Bell's view of the atonement, on page 146, where he teaches that Jesus died for everyone, which reconciles everyone to God. Thus, people must simply choose whether or not they want to live in that "reality."

So this reality, this forgiveness, this reconciliation, is true for everybody. . . . This reality isn't something we make true about ourselves by doing something. It is already true. Our choice is to live in this new reality or cling to a reality of our own making.

There is nothing mentioned of those who reject God, and their fate, as laid out in Scripture. No wonder I had trouble sleeping.

= = = =

After Rob finishes, he turns the stage over to another young, shaven-headed guy in jeans and a long-sleeve white T named Brad Gray. Brad, we learn, is a student at a nearby seminary, and after a few moments it is clear that he, like Bell, is a very gifted and winsome public speaker. I am reminded just how talented these guys are as communicators. Indeed, if they weren't pastoring churches, they would no doubt be leaders in other fields. Bell encourages Gray to not be nervous as he speaks, saying, "Just pretend this is a big living room, and if there's something you think you shouldn't say, say it anyway!" More clapping and laughter.

I won't attempt to reconstruct the sermon here, nor will I critique it, as this is far from my area of expertise. Suffice it to say that it is heavy on "story." Gray tells the story of a five-week tour of the Holy Land, during which his wife became pregnant. "It was a surprise," he says. "I slipped one past the goalie!" More laughter. He then launches into a long review of where the child may have been conceived, settling on Jerusalem. "The baby is going to come out speaking Hebrew!" he says. The crowd is eating it up. My wife, on the other hand, is locking up. We are struggling to get pregnant, and I can see her whole countenance turn icy. To steal Brad's metaphor, we pulled the goalie over three years ago, put all our best players on the ice, and still haven't scored a goal. I slip an arm around her shoulder and catch her eye for a minute, giving her the universal nod for "this will be over soon; it'll be okay." I draw a picture of "Hello Kitty" on my notebook and show it to her, trying anything to get a laugh. This could be a long afternoon.

As this is a sermon on "pain," I know already where Gray is going with it. He's going to talk about losing the pregnancy to a miscarriage, and how hard that was. His main point is a diatribe against the human tendency to use the phrase "How are you?" as a conversation opener. "This doesn't help," he says, when people are going through hard things. He describes another trip he took to Africa this summer, in which all the kids in the slums ran up to him and said, "How are you?" It was their way of saying, "Hey, there's a white American."

Gray ties all of this into the story from Mark 9, in which Jesus meets a father whose son is possessed by a demon. Before healing the boy, he says, Jesus entered into a relationship with the father, a model of how we need to help people in their pain.

"If people haven't dealt with their own pain, they can't help you deal with your pain," he says. "The people who helped me the most were the people who entered into our pain with us." Pain. Pain. Pain. "In our community, it is unacceptable to journey alone . . . . We've got to journey together. We will not become whole without one another and without God."

I glance over at my wife again, quite sure that Gray is unaware of the pain he is causing her. "This feels like the last day of church camp," she writes on my notebook. The day where we are supposed to walk forward to throw our pine cone in the fire, or nail our particular sin to the cross.

He has, though, succeeded in bringing the audience from joke mode to crying mode in a very short time. After he wraps there is more music, and the chance for people to come forward and be prayed for. Hundreds stream down and cry at the foot of the square dais. This Jesus-as-therapist message, clearly, is meeting a need and touching a chord.

At the end of the talk we stream out into the lobby for a short break before Rob Bell's fifteenth *Nooma* is premiered. The place, again, is more "normal" than I expected. There are no prayer labyrinths; nobody is painting. I run into a couple of people I know in the lobby, greeting them both with "How are you?" Old habits die hard.

BEING CULTURALLY RELEVANT
AND GOSPEL FOCUSED: AN INTERVIEW

Dale Van Dyke, pastor of Harvest Orthodox Presbyterian Church in suburban Grand Rapids, looks not unlike Rick Moranis, circa *Honey, I Shrunk the Kids*. He is in my living room today, in jeans and a casual shirt, to discuss his take on the emergent movement. It was a talk he gave, nearly a year ago at my church, that provided the majority of the motivation for this book.

To say that Van Dyke's methods, with youth at least, are unorthodox would be an understatement. He leads a weekly Wednesday night class in which twenty-five high school students voluntarily read chapters from *Bible Doctrines*, by Wayne Grudem, and answer a series of questions. If they haven't finished the chapter they aren't allowed to attend. This is quite a departure from the usual "try to be hip enough to get the cool kids to show up and everyone else will follow" model of youth ministry that has provided much of the spark for the emergent movement.

"The kids know that most of the other stuff is fluff," he says. "They want truth, and they want to feel like what they're doing is important."

I ask Van Dyke about the emergent assertion that guys like him, with churches like his, are out of touch and culturally irrelevant.

"It sort of makes me laugh," he says. "People haven't changed in terms of the reality of the conscience, and the reality of sin, guilt, and fear. Everything that's been 'the issue' since Adam is still 'the issue.' I don't have a problem with asking, 'Are we communicating well?' But I still believe that the preached word is still God's primary means of communicating with culture. It's a man set on fire. Give this fifty years and it will be something that you study in your religious history books, but the debris will be all over the place in terms of people who have just absolutely walked away from the church."

Van Dyke also addresses the breathless excitement with which some in the emergent movement view what they're doing. The idea that they are ushering in the next great reformation. He is the first to admit that he feels equally passionate and frustrated, which is evident from his comments.

"Leonard Sweet drives me straight up the wall," he says. "It's pure historical ignorance . . . or arrogance. It's as though the church for the last two thousand years hasn't had a clue what they're doing, and now, thanks to guys like Leonard Sweet, we can start doing church.

"I read *SoulTsunami,* where he says, 'God has hit the reset button on the world.' What does that mean? Is that so profound?"

"I want to protect my heart, though," he says. "I don't want to be arrogant, and I don't want to be angry."

We agree, for the next hour, to steer clear of latte jokes, Guinness jokes, and any references to sofas and scones.

"I have no problem with the 'Paul in Athens' model of people doing church a little bit differently to communicate the gospel," he says. "But you always need to go back to teaching the gospel, preaching the Word of God, and a vibrant ministry of mercy inside and out. If you're doing that, do it in your living room. I don't have a problem with that."

"All these churches now, they're building coffee shops," he says. "I love coffee shops! But if you're depending on a coffee shop to bring people in, you've lost it." And all of the marketing quirks that drove us nuts about the church-growth movement will soon begin to drive us nuts about this one. It's still marketing, but to a different demographic. "The main thing is no longer the main thing.

"But people will go to hell over this," he says. "You just don't get up in front of ten thousand people on Sunday and play around with the Word of God.

Van Dyke, also from Grand Rapids, became concerned when he read Bell's *Velvet Elvis* and published his own short rebuttal entitled *Jumping Off the Mark: A Response to Rob Bell's* Velvet Elvis.[5]

"When I first heard about Rob in Grand Rapids I was excited that there was another young, dynamic evangelical guy in town," he says. "He was dispensational and Baptist, but still evangelical and a solid guy. We had a family leave to go to Mars Hill, and I was concerned with this idea that Scripture sets the 'direction' but not the 'boundaries.' But then I read *Velvet Elvis*, and red flags went up all over the place."

At this point my wife asks Dale about the *Noomas*, Rob Bell's short film series.

"They're incredibly well done, and they seem to be making a point," he says. "At best it's moralism. At best it's a moral lesson, but there's no gospel.

"I think the fundamental issue is the gospel—the good news about what Christ objectively believed, what He objectively is, and what He objectively accomplished for sinners, which is received by right faith alone. It becomes moralism almost immediately when it leaves that base. For Rob it's 'why argue about dogma? Let's just live the Jesus way.'"

Which is tough to argue with, on the surface.

"Jesus lived the way He lived to fulfill the law for us," Van Dyke says. "Christ is the end of the law, and if you've missed that you've missed the point. We've got to get back to the objective reality of what Christ accomplished. Moralism flat out doesn't work. It either creates Pharisees or it makes you despair. That's the beauty of preaching the gospel . . . they hear Jesus. 'My sheep hear My voice.' Without that, I have no power to change anybody. Without that it's just Rob Bell.

"You look at liberalism and it's the same thing—'let's just stop arguing about doctrine and follow Jesus.' The Sermon on the Mount is not a moral game plan for how to live a better life. It's supposed to decimate you, and in it Jesus makes the most unbelievable claims about Himself that you have to deal with. Either He's God or He's not. Jesus refuses to let you put Him in a moral teacher role."

But that picture is a Jesus we can control. He can be easily fit into our lives in that we can take what we want to take and discard the rest.

"At the end of the day it doesn't help you die well," he says. "Just follow Jesus . . . I don't think I've done well enough. I can't think about Africa and The Poor every minute of every day.

"It's all based on the idea that we can bring heaven to earth. The utopian dream. 'We've got to fight oppression, we've got to end poverty, and we've got to create a heaven on earth, because that's what Jesus wants us to do.'"

I don't understand how that's saleable. Even living in our neighborhood, which certainly isn't bad, but is decidedly lower-income blue-collar, there are people here that will be born, live, and die basically in poverty. And it's, of course, much worse in Africa. Though we help, we can't delude ourselves into thinking that we're going to change everyone's financial picture and then share the gospel with them. Again, the real point seems to me to be about helping people die well.

"Look at the history of the church," he says. "When has the church done the most civil good? When the gospel is at the core. There's nothing like the Word of God."

NOTES

1. Rocker Hammond and teen reporter William Miller are walking together in Topeka, Kansas, trying to "find something real," when a VW bus containing the "real Topeka people" drives behind them and finally pulls up beside them.
2. This according to his bio at www.velocityculture.com
3. As if anyone here is going to say, "You know, there's nothing special at all about our time period in history. Nothing revolutionary, nothing noteworthy, no big changes happening." I would argue that nearly all time periods in history can be argued for as pivotal, and perhaps at the same time argued for as not terribly noteworthy at all in terms of man and his motivations.
4. McKnight uses the words "smells and bells" to describe sense-oriented emergent worship gatherings. He doesn't come down one way or another on this, except to say, in essence, "Hey, we're creative; what do you expect?"
5. Available at Harvest Orthodox Presbyterian Church in Grand Rapids; the Web address is www.harvestopc.org. This is an excellent resource, which I wish I could reprint in its entirety.

Not having a gimmick is my gimmick.

—STEVE DUNNE, Singles

CHAPTER 11

WHY I DON'T WANT A COOL PASTOR

I ACTUALLY KIND OF like Tony Jones, the thirty-eight-year-old leader in the emergent movement, who works part-time for an outfit called Emergent Village . . . when he isn't writing books and speaking. I am taking his class, for one afternoon, at Olivet Nazarene University (ONU), which is part of a one-week intensive course on "Postmodernism and Youth Ministry" for youth pastor types.

The audience is an interesting mix of Jones fans, who have come to Kankakee, Illinois, to hear their favorite blogger, and earnest Midwestern[1] youth pastors who are either taking the class as part of a master's degree program or are simply looking for new ways to connect with their students. They are all white males, with the exception of one girl, and none of them—myself included—knows what to do when Tony encourages us to "lie on the floor, walk around, dance, or type e-mails" while he is praying and speaking. One guy with sideburns and a cup of coffee attached to his palm gets up and awkwardly goes to sit in the windowsill in an effort to appease Jones. This makes me chuckle inside. Tony Jones doesn't look as "emergent-y" as I might have expected, if what I might have expected might have been frosted tips, hipster glasses, and torn Levis. He has a good deal of charisma, once he gets going, and I counted one reference to *Saturday Night Live*, one reference to *Desperate Housewives*, the obligatory *Matrix* shout-out, two references to *24,* and several references to Moby during the first hour of the class.

In fact it is Moby, he says, who is something of a poster child for postmodernism. He then flashes a picture of the gaunt hipster/vegan/musician wearing a 50s-era space helmet. The room is silent.

"Moby is a Christian," he adds, after explaining the origins of electronica/trance music to an audience who, it's safe to say, didn't before know the origins of electronica/trance music.

The ONU crowd is, again, unsure how to react. This is a conservative campus—one where, at least in 1994 when I spent a semester here as a freshman, students weren't allowed to drink, dance, or wear screen-printed T-shirts. They have either come a long way since 1994, to allow a card-carrying, Guinness-quaffing emergent in the door, or they're just blissfully unaware.

"Some of you, if you read my blog, may be surprised that I don't have horns and a tail," he says, of his critics. "But my heretical nature comes out in more subtle ways."

This is another example of a sort of forced "shockingness" I've come to expect from some in emergent circles. Throw out a word like "heretic" and see how people react.

Jones looks like a friend of mine, Tim Kubiak, who played quarterback for my arena football team last season, another reason why I'm predisposed to liking him. He is also a police chaplain, a volunteer baseball umpire, and a genuinely winsome guy. For more than a minute I feel like if I wasn't writing a book titled *Why We're Not Emergent*, Tony and I could probably be fast friends, trading pop culture references and talking about Minnesota sports long into the night. I actually hope we still get to do that, because at some level, though our beliefs differ widely, this is all "just business."

He has assigned the group what I would call a "usual" lineup of preemergent-talk readings—John Caputo, Phyllis Tickle, etc. The class is already complaining that Caputo is too dense, and Jones encourages them to think philosophically about their ministries. To move out of a "praxis" mind-set, and into a "theory" mind-set, as this is a university setting and universities deal with theory. He encourages us, when introducing ourselves, to think of a question that we would "like to have more deeply questioned" this week, because, as he says, we "will not be trying to find answers."

And he even apologizes for the next statement before he makes it, admitting the fact that what he is about to say could come off as a little cliché:

"Truth is not a destination," he says. "Truth is actually a journey."

THE QUEST FOR REASONABLE FAITH

Jones says that we're here not to determine absolute truth, but we're in a quest for a "reasonable faith." Reasonable according to whom, and whether what is reasonable for me will be reasonable for Moby, Jones, Africa, Bono, or anyone else, he doesn't say. And whether that same faith will be reasonable for me at age fifty, he doesn't say either.

"I find most theology really boring. I want to do my own theology," Jones said in an interview with Scot McKnight that took place a few weeks after the class. "I don't want to be an acolyte for somebody else's theology. I'm interested in reading French sociology, postmodern deconstruction, things like that. And then have a theology that bubbles out of that."[2]

McKnight also asks Jones if he is, in fact, emergent, and, "What is it about Brian McLaren? What's the allure?"

"Emergent isn't a new name brand of Christianity," Jones says. "It's a way of thinking . . . but people are asking me all the time if they're emergent. If you're asking that question, you're already emergent."

"On the allure of Brian McLaren," he continues. "I was at a conservative, pietist school in Illinois a few weeks ago teaching [he is referring, here, to Olivet Nazarene], and the dean of ministry and theology wanted to take me out to dinner. So we went out to the Red Lobster [laughter here, from the crowd who are all, also, too hip for Red Lobster]. This guy said, 'When I read Brian McLaren I feel angry at the end.' He's angry that all of his undergrads are reading Brian McLaren. He feels like Brian is pulling people out of the church and giving them nowhere to go. I think the allure of Brian is his playfulness in the way he writes. He'll make a very strong claim and then say in parentheses, 'I know I'm just being provocative here.' He hits you over the head with a velvet hammer, so that you don't know how subversive it actually is.'"

= = = =

I'm back in class, where Jones quotes Umberto Eco[3] when he says that (and I'm paraphrasing) "postmodernism is not a silencing of the past . . . . Rather, it reaches into the past and drags it, kicking and screaming, into the future, but always with a hint of irony." It is this irony, Jones says, that allows the movement to achieve genuine humility. Humility, to Jones, means admitting that "we could very well be wrong about all of this."

Call me old-fashioned, but it doesn't fill me with hope and warm feelings to hear my pastor (or my overpriced conference speaker) suggest that he may be, and probably is, wrong about all of this, as per Jones's postmodern definition of humility. Or as per the first two chapters of Brian McLaren's *A Generous Orthodoxy*, I want to believe, and do believe, that people can know things and still be humble.

= = = =

I returned from the talk, followed by a few days at the Senior Bowl in Mobile, Alabama, to find this entry on Jones's blog, in which he amusingly bemoans the fact that he had to spend an evening living incarnationally (my words) and engaging a diverse culture that included 50,000 Minnesotans gathered for a monster truck event:

In order for Tanner to earn a "Group Activity" badge for Cub Scouts, we joined his den at MonsterJam a week ago. Yes, that's the "sport" where monster trucks race each other around in circles and run over smaller cars. I had a few surreal moments therein:

—The Metrodome was nearly full—probably 50,000 people—leading me to seriously reconsider my contention that Minnesotans are generally more intelligent than the rest of the American population. (No, the election of Jesse Ventura had not caused me to reconsider this.)

—As Lee Greenwood's "I'm Proud to Be an American" was playing at massive decibel levels, an enormous American flag was carried into the middle of the stadium by about two dozen people. Tanner (6), fresh off of a week of public education, said, "Dad, are they singing about Martin Luther King, cuz he wanted freedom?" "Not exactly," I told him.

—About halfway in to the evening, I realized that every event was rigged so that Grave Digger would win. A quick Wikipedia check later that night explains that "Digger," was purchased from driver Dennis Anderson by Clear Channel Communications in 1998. Of course it was.

—The emcee, a rotund man who ran around the track and cajoled us through our earplugs into cheering, had obviously failed to watch the ESPN report on the 25th anniversary of "The Wave." The Wave is over, dude. It's passé. No one does it anymore.

—The thought occurred to me that I'm very likely the only Red-Letter Christian who's ever been to MonsterJam.[4]

Jones's entry does beg the question: Why is it "living incarnationally" to drink Chai and listen to sitar music at a coffee shop, but not living incarnationally to eat cheese fries and watch big trucks crush things? Isn't this a "culture" that deserves to be engaged and indeed—if this language isn't too passé—to be "saved" just like the rest of us? And are we so naïve as to think that if Bob Dylan or Moby suddenly wanted us to believe that putting on black turtlenecks and watching monster truck rallies was the path to super-terrific-mystical-enlightenment, that we all wouldn't be snapping up Grave Digger turtlenecks like there was no tomorrow?

"Engaging the culture," according to my philosopher friend Dave's wife, is always a matter of "what culture?"

Jones's friends, or at least the ones who respond to his blog entries, did what they were supposed to do and mourned with him over the fact that he had to do the monster truck thing. They made more jokes at the expense of people who do the "wave" and buy American. For such an open-minded and people-affirming group of bloggers, it struck me as a little mean-spirited.

= = = =

Cory Hartman is not a cool pastor. He is a tall white guy with a crew cut, and has had the crew cut since I lived across the hall from him in college. Guys with Cory's build are often described as "lanky." His room was always quiet, and it was that room where I would go to unload about relationships, how much I hated school, how I couldn't sleep, etc. Cory and his roommate kept an immaculately clean room, and they were, regardless of the hour, always sitting quietly at their desks, studying.

He is taking me on a driving tour of Passaic, New Jersey, which is where he lives and pastors a small church. If you're reading this book, you've probably never been to Passaic. It is made up predominantly of Puerto Rican immigrants, Indian immigrants, and African-Americans, and walking through the downtown area, you get the distinct feeling of being in another country. Cory drives me through the housing project where he almost got mugged delivering pizzas. He idles in front of the doorway to one of the buildings and begins telling me the long story (Cory is a long-talker; think "senate filibuster") of delivering pizzas there one night. I am getting nervous and would like him to move the tour along, so as to avoid another story.

If Cory wasn't so busy "living missionally," he would probably have time to read all of the books on missional living, which would tell him to intentionally get a house in an urban area, get some kind of job that would allow him to rub shoulders with "regular people," and then "do life" with them. My feeling, though, is that Cory is living missionally by default. He took the job delivering pizzas because he was, at the time, The Poor.

"I have a cousin who never smoked until he started going to an emergent church," he says, half joking, when I ask him his impressions of the movement. "My impression is that for some, the movement is bigger than Guinness or U2 or smoking in church," he says. "But for a lot of people it's still just about those peripheral things. It's become a safe harbor for people who have either been wounded or think they've been wounded by mainstream evangelical churches."

He admits that aside from a smattering of articles and a couple of Brian McLaren books, he hasn't interacted much with the movement. He has the friend who has bought the coffee shop and named it "Ecclesia." But he is also open to the idea that we are experiencing a cultural shift, one that could impact the way that people "do" church. "But I still see the continued necessity," he says, "of the pastor/flock relationship. And I think there is a place for borders and creeds.

"If I could use a musical analogy, I like McLaren's 'old stuff,' " he says. "I've read a book called *The Church on the Other Side* and *A New Kind of Christian*. But if you expand your time horizons all the way back to the apostles, that kind of Christian—the Neo kind—isn't new.

"I'm concerned about the lack of historical perspective among emergents," he says. "That those who are claiming to be doing something radical may just look like another fad in twenty years. And I'm concerned about a fad that takes people away from the church and doesn't really lead them anywhere. The loss of that "fence" between truth and falsehood is worrisome.

"My other main concern is they seem to have adopted the American demographic marketing model. I may be wrong, but I'm afraid that a movement that claims to care about justice, community, and inclusivity seems to just be tailor-made for white, suburban, affluent professionals in their twenties and thirties. That concerns me from a self-delusion standpoint."

= = = =

Cory and I are trying to find a church in another New Jersey town (Whippany?) where we'll buy tickets to go and see perhaps the least emergent thing ever invented: a football coach (in this case Rutgers head coach Greg Schiano) giving an evangelical talk on Good Friday.

Cory is filling me in on all the things I'll need to do to become a Christian Literary Force.

"You need to have *Why We're Not Emergent* action figures," he says, as a starting point. "And then inspirational wall hangings, wristbands, and preferably a prequel." I laugh, but a marketing initiative of that magnitude, while rendering me a complete sellout, would really help in paying the mortgage.

"Maybe just the action figures?" I ask, rhetorically.

= = = =

First Baptist Church in Passaic, Hartman's church, is nothing special. It features a huge, beautiful, falling-apart red brick building that was built in 1891 and then renovated after World War II by a handful of the current members. I'm being led in a tour of the building by Jack, Cory's four-year-old son. He is lobbying for a trip up to the attic, but I can only imagine what an attic in a building like this must look like, and try to steer him away from it. Jack shows me his Sunday school room where generations of kids have learned the gospel, the basement, and then the section of the sanctuary where the organist plays a huge, old pipe organ.

The congregation at First Baptist is old school. Literally. As people begin to file in for the service, it strikes me that Cory, his wife, Kelly, son Jack, and daughter Orphie and I may be the only people under age seventy in the room. Cory explains that there is no place in the emergent discussion for people in his congregation.

"The word *emergent* means different things, depending on who defines it," he says. "If Scot McKnight is defining it, then I might go as far as to say that I am, but if it's just a reflection of 'what the kids are into these days,' then definitely not."

Clearly, it's been a long time since Cory's congregation thought about what the kids are into. These folks would get very little out of a discussion of spiritual metaphor in *The Matrix*, or an evening playing Sufjan Stevens records and talking about the unfairness of federal minimum wage laws.

"The bottom line," he continues, "is that birds of a feather flock together. People go where they like it."

"People go where they like it" isn't going to sell books, *mi amigo*. I think this but don't say it. Cory is making last-minute preparations for the service, and it becomes clear to me that while most of his parishioners are decades older, they all really love my friend. This makes me proud.

= = = =

I count a grand total of nine people in the pews behind me. I am seated in the second row, as close as I've ever sat in a church service, and am seated with Cory's family. I have been awake for a long time. I never sleep well on the road and spent the previous day hoofing it around New York's Manhattan through a downpour.

It occurs to me that churches like these manage to be "sensory" without being sensory. We sing old hymns including "He Was Wounded for Our Transgressions" and "What Wondrous Love Is This" behind the huge, beautiful wall of sound generated by the pipe organ. The sermon is entitled "The Passion According to John."

After preaching through the story of Christ's last supper with His apostles,

Cory steps out from behind the podium and serves the sacraments to each member of the congregation. I always get a little bit choked up at Maundy Thursday services, and this one is no exception. Seeing my friend serve his flock, and seeing them respond to him, makes me think about my church and how much I miss it, but how cool it is to be worshiping with new brothers and sisters in Christ who are old enough to be my grandparents in Christ.

After the sacraments, and after Cory finishes reading about Christ's death and resurrection, we sing "Up from the Grave He Arose." It is dim inside the sanctuary, and the lights from Gregory Avenue stream through a beautiful stained glass rendering of Christ. Behind me, a seventy-seven-year-old woman belts out the words to the hymn as if her very life depends on it. I tear up a little bit.

I find the woman after the service, and she grabs me by the upper arms, like grandmothers often do. "I'm so glad you're here," she says. I tell her how much I enjoyed her singing, and she tells me that God has put a song in her heart. She has outlived everyone in her family, and explains to me that this church, now, is her family. She has lived her whole life in Passaic, in an era before study-abroad experiences and overseas missions opportunities for middle-schoolers made the world a much smaller and more transient place. Before groupies would trek to Grand Rapids to be close to Rob Bell and, in fairness, to Minneapolis to be close to John Piper.

She used to run around this church as a little girl, she says. I imagine her running through the basement to Sunday school classes, and then getting married here in her late teens, before finally burying her husband here just a few years ago.

It occurs to me, coming to the end of this text, that we've no doubt left out a great deal. There were books that went unread, blogs that we couldn't get to, and conferences we didn't attend. Those who aren't inclined to the emergent/emerging thing will probably support most of what we've written, and those who call themselves emergent will find a million reasons to find fault with it. The idea that people read much of anything and have their minds changed by it is less and less realistic to me. People, usually, just dig in.

And then, soon, these books become nothing more than a sort of cold, intellectual pawn-pushing, in an effort to craft the most perfect argument that can then be vehemently defended for the sake of the argument itself. Responses and rebuttals will be written. Rinse. Repeat. And like D. A. Carson in an earlier chapter, I'm realizing that I'm tired of it.

Are all emergents purveyors of the kind of "hollow and deceptive philosophy" Paul preaches against in 2 Timothy? Probably not. I'm sure there are good churches that look emergent, just like there are bad churches that have the appearance of orthodoxy. But watching Cory preach tonight gives me the same sense of peace I get when I watch Kevin preach. It comes from knowing that when he is old and gray he will be faithfully preaching the Word of God, just as he is now, regardless of where the culture may be, and whether we're having church in a beautiful old building, a coffee shop, a concrete bunker with plastic chairs in the suburbs—or someone's basement, in secret, because we may live in a culture that no longer lets us worship out loud. He will be calling the "balls and strikes" of Christ's death and resurrection as the only way to eternal life.

As the evening wraps up, there is an old couple at the front of the church working together to fold up a communion tablecloth. I stand at the back and watch them for a moment, trying really hard not to look like I'm watching them for a moment. They goof on each other in a good-natured way. They have probably survived layoffs, sick children, cancer, and many other things as a part of this body, but, clearly, they are enjoying each other's presence now.

I take out my cell phone and call my wife, to tell her that I love her, and that I saw an old couple that reminds me of the kind of old couple I want to be in about fifty years. And to tell her that I'm really glad that we have a pastor who, instead of being "with it," is committed to being with God.

NOTES
1. There are more Indianapolis Colts and Chicago Bears sweatshirts in the room than indie-rock T shirts and coffee mugs.

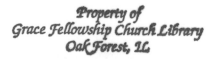

2. http://kingdomnexus.squarespace.com/keeping-jesus-revolutionary/
3. Eco is the author of, among other things, *Foucalt's Pendulum*, and he is often invoked by people young and old (mostly young) when they are trying to appear smarter than they actually are, because most people just flat out don't get his stuff. Count me in as one of those people. For the record, I do think Tony Jones is smart.
4. "Various Surrealities at Monster Jam," January 29, 2007, Tony Jones blog at http://theoblogy.blogspot.com/2007_01_01_archive.html

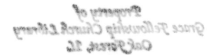

He who has an ear, let him hear what the Spirit says to the churches. To the one who conquers I will grant to eat of the tree of life, which is in the paradise of God.

—REVELATION 2:7

LISTENING
TO ALL THE
CHURCHES OF
REVELATION

IF WE HAD TO DISTILL our advice for the emerging church into one sentence, it would be this: Listen to all the churches in Revelation. Emergent leaders need to celebrate all the strengths and shun the weaknesses of the seven churches in Revelation 2–3—and admit that Jesus' prescription for health is more than community, authenticity, and inclusion.

Many people do not realize that the book of Revelation, besides being an apocalypse and a prophecy, was also a letter—a letter addressed to seven real churches in Asia Minor. The number seven suggests that the churches were more than real churches; they were also representative churches, symbolic of the church universal. In other words, the problems in these seven churches are the root problems in all churches. Their strengths are our strengths and their weaknesses are our weaknesses.

Unlike the rest of Revelation, the letters to the seven churches are easy to preach. The content is immediately relevant, the application is on the surface, and the structure is obvious. There are eight parts that appear in almost every letter: (1) instructions to write to the angel of the church in such and such a place; (2) a statement about Jesus that matches the problem in the church. This section begins with "These are the words of . . . " and then it describes Jesus; (3) a section of commendation, often beginning with "I know your deeds"; (4) an accusation section—"But I have this against you"; (5) a call to change and repentance—"Do this"; (6) a statement of what the Lord will do, either as an encouragement to press on or as a warning of judgment; (7) a promise to "him who overcomes"; and (8) an invitation—"He who has an ear, let him hear what the Spirit says to the churches."

EAVESDROPPING ON ASIA MINOR

The seven letters conform to a definite pattern, but the churches themselves are all different. They struggle with different sins and shine in different areas.

Ephesus was your loveless, fundamentalist church. They were orthodox, moral, and hardworking. But they didn't love the lost or even one another. Instead, they were doctrinally sound navel-gazers. To them and to us, Jesus says, "Love."

Smyrna was your persecuted church, similar to suffering believers living in countries in today's 10/40 window. These Christians were afflicted, slandered, and impoverished. But they were spiritually rich. They were vibrant, but fearful. To them and to us, Jesus says, "Be faithful."

Pergamum was your ungrounded, youth-movement church. They were faithful, passionate witnesses. But they had compromised with the world and accommodated to their sexually immoral and idolatrous culture. They were witnessing, but undiscerning. To them and to us, Jesus says, "Discern."

Thyatira was your warmhearted, liberal church. They were strong in love, faith, service, and perseverance. But they undervalued doctrinal fidelity and moral purity. They were loving, but over-tolerant. To them and to us, Jesus says, "Think."

Sardis was your flashy and successful, but shallow, megachurch, or your Bible-belt church chock-full of nominal Christians. They had a great reputation. But in reality they were spiritually dead. They were the church of the white washed tombs. To them and to us, Jesus says, "Wake up."

Philadelphia was your small, storefront, urban ghetto church. They felt weak and unimpressive. But they had kept the Word of God and not denied His name. They were a struggling, strong church. To them and to us, Jesus says, "Press on."

Finally, Laodicea was your ritzy, influential church out in the rich part of town. They thought they had it all together. But they were as spiritually poor as they were materially rich. The church was filled with affluence and apathy. To them and to us, Jesus says, "Be earnest."

Surely, there is something for everyone to love and hate about these churches. We can all see our besetting sins mirrored here, even if we can see the sins of our neighbor churches more easily. And while it is certainly legitimate to see individual churches as more relevant to our particular settings, we must pay attention to what Jesus says to all seven churches.

And that's my beef with the emerging church. Doctrinally minded evangelical Christians like me would get more out of emergent critiques if they recognized that there are just as many undiscerning, overtolerant Pergamums and Thyatiras in North America and the United Kingdom as there are loveless Ephesuses. I pick these three churches not because they are most important but because they best represent what is right with the emerging church (a good eye for Ephesus problems) and what is wrong (a blind eye to Pergamum-Thyatira problems). Emerging and non-emerging Christians need to listen to all three churches.

GETTING IT RIGHT—AND WRONG

Those of Us in Ephesus (Revelation 2:1–7)

The Christians at Ephesus were hard workers and full of patient endurance.

They were faithful, indefatigable, and doctrinally sound. They did not tolerate wicked men. They tested the false apostles and spied out false teaching. A few years after Revelation was written, the church father Ignatius wrote to Ephesus and again praised them because he heard the report that no heresy or sect or false teaching could even gain an audience in the Ephesian church—they were taught so well.

The church at Ephesus was also ethically sound. Its members hated the practice of the Nicolaitans—the anything-goes crowd of the day. The Nicolaitans were the ones who said, "You're free in Christ. Live like you're free and get rid of these rules. Go with the flow. Accommodate the culture. Jesus was the great sexual liberator. God's grace is wide and inclusive. Live as you like." The Ephesians were not drawn away by such notions. In fact, Jesus commended them for two virtues scarcely mentioned in the emerging church: intolerance (of false teaching) and hatred (of immorality). For all the talk in emerging circles about the supremely inclusive kingdom of God, it should not escape our notice that Ephesus was not praised for their inclusion, but for their exclusion.[1]

Jesus might say to an Ephesus church today, "You are very faithful people. You declare the truth in an age of error. You can spot false teaching and wrong living and do not follow it. You are hardworking, truth-defending, immorality-hating Christians. I commend you for that." If Revelation 2:1–7 is any model, Jesus wouldn't chastise contemporary Ephesus churches for being fastidious about doctrine and morals. Those are genuinely good things. The problem is, as the emerging church is right to point out, those are not the only things.

The church at Ephesus was your exemplary fundamentalist, evangelical church with a good Protestant work ethic and a close eye on theological orthodoxy. This was good, but these aren't the only things that matter in a church. Ephesus had one big, cancerous problem. They didn't love.

At one time, there was great love in this church (Eph. 1:15–16), but it had been lost. At first glance it seems that their love *for God* had grown cold, but in the Old Testament whenever God's people are said to forsake their love for

God they are pictured as adulterous and idolatrous (see Jer. 2 and Hos. 4 for example), which doesn't fit Ephesus. No, it wasn't the loving feeling they had lost. They had stopped doing something that they used to do (which is why Jesus tells them to do the works they did at first). Their fault wasn't with the first great commandment, but with the second. They loved God, but they did not love their neighbors as themselves.

They stopped loving one another in the church. They had keen minds and busy hands, but shriveled hearts. They were a classic case of 1 Corinthians 13—"If I have prophetic powers, and understand all mysteries and all knowledge, and if I have all faith, so as to remove mountains, but have not love, I am nothing" (v. 2). The church at Ephesus was strong in some areas, but without practical, tangible love for one another, they were in danger of becoming worthless as a church. The people cared about being right, but they no longer cared about one another. My guess is their precise, careful eye for theological and moral error had become a precise, careful eye for finding fault in one another.

This is the great danger for doctrinally sound churches. They can be quick to judge and slow to forgive. They analyze everything and everyone. They are so used to fighting against the world that when they get bored with that they turn and fight among themselves. They always need to be against something, always purifying something, always looking for error or inconsistency. This is why many denominations that split end up splitting again. Fighting gets in their blood.

I realized a number of years ago that it didn't matter if I was against all the things I should be against, if I wasn't *for* anything. That's the Lord's point to Ephesus. "You hate what I hate. That's good. But you do not love what I love." I can tell in my own spirit when I am arguing a point to be right and when I am arguing a point out of love. Hopefully, this book is the latter. There is a big difference between the two. Do I want to be right because "I know this is right, moron, and why can't you see it?" Or am I arguing my point because "I love you and I know this will be good for you and honor Christ"?

Ephesus' lovelessness manifested itself in another kind of sin, not just a lack of life-giving fellowship but a lack of life-giving witness. The followers of Christ were so busy battling and protecting and defending that they had turned inward to self-protection and suspicion. They were navel-gazers, with no vision or purpose outside themselves. They were great at keeping the world out of the church, but they were terrible at taking the church out into the world.

Consequently, Jesus, He who walks among the lampstands, threatened to take away their lampstand that was failing to give light—even though they were to be the light of the world. Jesus calls all followers to "let your light shine before others, so that they may see your good works and give glory to your Father who is in heaven" (Matt. 5:16).

The light at Ephesus had grown dim. They had good deeds, but not in love for one another. They defended the light, but they were not shining it into the dark places of the world. They were not bearing witness to Jesus Christ in their love or in their testimony. And as a result, Jesus says, "I will come and take away your light if it does not shine." And, sadly, He did. There is no church at Ephesus. This is not the reason every church closes its doors. But certainly it has been true many times and continues to be true that churches which refuse to live and shine and bear witness in the world will die. Let this be a warning to all Ephesus churches: Give the gospel away or lose it.

It is sad but true. Theologically astute churches and theologically minded pastors sometimes die of dead orthodoxy. Some grow sterile and cold, petrified as the frozen chosen, not compromising with the world, but not engaging it either. We may think right, live right, and do right, but if we do it off in a corner, shining our lights at one another to probe our brother's sins instead of pointing our lights out into the world, we will, as a church, grow dim, and eventually our light will be extinguished.

Those of Us in Pergamum (Revelation 2:12–17)

I daresay that most emergent Christians either came from Ephesus churches or perceive Ephesus churches to be the overwhelming problem in the Christian West. The emerging church sees loveless, lightless, listless churches everywhere and rebukes them. Where such churches exist, their rebuke is justified (though not the emergent remedies). But it also seems clear to me that emerging leaders are blind to the failings of Pergamum and Thyatira churches.

The church at Pergamum had one main strength. Its people were faithful in witness. It was not popular to be a Christian in Pergamum. (Satan dwelt there, after all.) And yet, believers there did not renounce the name of Jesus. They were strongest in the very areas where Ephesus was weakest. The Ephesians didn't love anymore. They turned their lights inward on one another instead of out in the world. But those at Pergamum held together. They were loyal and did not turn on one another when they faced persecution. They were bold in their witness to an enemy culture. They would tell you about Jesus and stand up for Him, even if it cost them their lives.

But they were undiscerning, which is why Jesus introduced Himself as He who wielded "the sharp two-edged sword." The Christians at Pergamum didn't have a keen eye for orthodoxy and moral uprightness like those at Ephesus. They held to the teaching of the Nicolaitans. In short, they had been deceived.

Ephesus was under-engaged with the culture; Pergamum over-identified with the culture. The Christians in Pergamum bore witness to Jesus, but they had compromised in what it meant to follow Him. Undiscerning tolerance was Pergamum's crippling defect. Their indifference to religious and moral deviancy was not a sign of their great relevance to the culture, or their great broad-mindedness, or a great testimony to their ability to focus on God's love; it was a blight on their otherwise passionate, faithful witness.

We don't know how Pergamum was deceived and why they tolerated the Nicolaitans. Perhaps they were untaught, ignorant on some key aspects of discipleship. Maybe Pergamum was filled with the kind of Christians that are

WHY WE'RE NOT EMERGENT

always against rules: "Christianity isn't about dos and don'ts. It's about a relationship." (As if the relationship were not guarded and preserved by rules. Try telling your wife after you've had an affair, "Come on. I thought our marriage was about the relationship, not all these dos and don'ts.")

Pergamum reminds us of what can happen to young people who aren't taught well or to youth movements that lack grounding in the Scriptures. People get converted, sometimes dramatically, and they live vibrant, courageous, evangelistic Christian lives, but they are also confused, undiscerning, and antinomian, thinking the gospel and grace make moral law unnecessary.

Maybe the Christians at Pergamum were saying, "Hey, look, the important thing is that we all love Jesus. Don't get hung up on secondary matters." Maybe they were in dialogue with the Nicolaitans, attending lots of warm fuzzy meetings where they tried to understand one another and gain an appreciation for their differing perspectives. Most likely, the cultural pressure was simply too strong. Idolatry and sexual immorality were so rampant that they became like high places for the church at Pergamum. They didn't see the danger and the wickedness of what the false teachers were promoting, and so they became overly accommodating.

Those of Us in Thyatira (Revelation 2:18–29)

The believers in Ephesus were praised for their good deeds and strong work ethic; those in Thyatira were commended just as highly. They possessed the deeds that the Ephesians had and the love that the Ephesians lacked. Thyatira was a vibrant church. Its people loved, served, believed, and endured.

This was probably the kind of church you walked into and immediately felt like you belonged. "Great to meet you. Let me introduce you to my friends. Here, I'll show you how you can get plugged in, use your gifts, do ministry. We're so glad you're here." It was that kind of church—friendly, caring, full of service to one another and probably to the community. This church loved. That's the good part.

But there was a bad part too. Their love was blindly affirming. The big problem at Thyatira was tolerance. They tolerated false teaching and immoral behavior, two things He who has eyes as piercing as fire and feet as pure as burnished bronze is fiercely intolerant of (2:20). Jesus says, "You're loving, which is great, but your tolerance is not love. It's unfaithfulness."

I imagine Thyatira as a church with lots of community programs, a concern for social justice issues, a desire to be inclusive. But somewhere along the line warmheartedness overtook clear-mindedness.

Most Christians and most churches go liberal for one of two reasons. Either they are disillusioned conservatives who have seen nothing but legalistic, angry fundamentalism, or they are passionate social activists who, in their desire to love everyone, end up rejecting nothing. Thyatira's problem was the opposite of Ephesus. I fear that emerging Christians are in danger of repeating Thyatira's error: they love what Jesus loves but do not hate what Jesus hates.

A VISION FOR THE WHOLE CHURCH

Emergent church leaders need a vision for the church that encompasses all the letters of Revelation. They need to see and talk about the problems of over-tolerance and under-definition as well as the problems of lovelessness and listlessness. There are undoubtedly many Ephesus churches, as emergent leaders are quick to point out, but these same leaders underestimate the problems of Pergamum and Thyatira. As a result, they end up rebuking not just the faults of Ephesus churches, but their strengths as well, tearing down what Jesus commends in order to strengthen what Jesus condemns.

Emergent Christians, to use the language of Revelation, have many good deeds. They want to be relevant. They want to reach out. They want to be authentic. They want to include the marginalized. They want to make kingdom disciples. They want community and life transformation. Jesus likes all this about them. But He would, I believe, also have some things against them, some criticisms to speak through other brothers and sisters. Criticisms that shouldn't be sidestepped because their movement is only a "conversation," or because they only speak for themselves, or because they admit, "We don't have it all figured out." Emergent Christians need to catch Jesus' broader vision for the church—His vision for a church that is intolerant of error, maintains moral boundaries, promotes doctrinal integrity, stands strong in times of trial, remains vibrant in times of prosperity, believes in certain judgment and certain reward, even as it engages the culture, reaches out, loves, and serves. We need a church that reflects the Master's vision—one that is deeply theological, deeply ethical, deeply compassionate, and deeply doxological.

THE KING ON THE THRONE

In the end, it all comes back to God. We become what we worship. If God is relational, inviting, and mysterious overwhelmingly more than He is omnipotent, just, and knowable, then the gospel becomes a message overwhelmingly about community, inclusion, and journey. But if God is overwhelmingly holy, righteous, and graciously sovereign, then the gospel becomes a message about sin, justification, and undeserved mercy. To borrow from Jonathan Edwards, what we need to recover is a vision of God in all His "diverse excellencies."[2]

Aslan the lion, the Christ figure in the *Chronicles of Narnia,* is grandly multidimensional. He's loving, but he's not safe. He's good and terrible at the same time. Susan and Lucy want to bury their heads in his mane and feel his breath. But they also go "trembly" at the sight of him. In one place, Lewis describes Aslan's paw touching the Pevensie children, saying, "And though it was velveted, it was very heavy."

Jesus is like that—in some ways, soft and velveted, but also heavy and sharp.

I don't doubt that emergent Christians agree that God is a God of diverse excellencies. But I don't, as of yet, see a mature picture of these excellencies in emergent books. Take Donald Miller, for example. At the end of *Blue Like Jazz,* Miller gives his reasons for embracing Jesus.

All great characters in stories are the ones who give their lives to something bigger than themselves. And in all of the stories I don't find anyone more noble than Jesus. He gave His life for me, in obedience to His Father. I truly love Him for it. . . . I think the difference in my life came when I realized, after reading those Gospels, that Jesus didn't just love me out of principle; He didn't just love me because it was the right thing to do. Rather, there was something inside me that caused Him to love me.

That last sentence is flat-out wrong and a denial of original sin, total depravity, and God's free grace in election. This next part is just insufficient:

I think I realized that if I walked up to His campfire, He would ask me to sit down, and He would ask me my story. He would take time to listen to my ramblings or my anger until I could calm down, and then He would look me directly in the eye, and He would speak to me; He would tell me the truth, and I would sense in His voice and in the lines on His face that He liked me. He would rebuke me, too, and would tell me that I have prejudices against very religious people and that I need to deal with that; He would tell me that there are poor people in the world and I need to feed them and that somehow this will make me more happy. I think He would tell me what my gifts are and why I have them, and He would give me ideas on how to use them. I think He would explain to me why my father left, and He would point out very clearly all the ways God has taken care of me through the years, all the stuff God protected me from.[3]

There are true statements here. Jesus does like us. Praise the Lord for that. He does speak truth, and cares about our hurts, and is patient with our ramblings. But the Jesus in this paragraph is little more than a therapist. He listens to our problems, sets us straight, helps us use our gifts, and explains our dysfunctions. But let us not forget: Jesus is more than a coping mechanism. We may desire sweet fellowship with a kind, caring Jesus, but if He is to help us in any real way, He must be more than a sensitive good listener—He must be strong, exalted, and mighty.

Compare Donald Miller's description of Jesus with Jonathan Edwards's vision. Edwards had times of great emotion and fellowship with God. He wept and marveled at Christ, but it was a fuller, deeper, richer, more complete Christ he marveled at. He wrote:

> Once . . . in 1737 . . . I had a view, that for me was extraordinary, of the glory of the Son of God, as Mediator between God and man, and his wonderful, great, full, pure and sweet grace and love, and meek and gentle condescension. . . . The person of Christ appeared ineffably excellent, with an excellency great enough to swallow up all thought and conception . . . which kept me the greater part of the time in a flood of tears, weeping aloud. I felt an ardency of soul to be, what I know not otherwise how to express, emptied and annihilated; to lie in the dust, and to be full of Christ alone; to love him with a holy and pure love; to trust in him; to live upon him; to serve and follow him; and to be perfectly sanctified and made pure, with a divine and heavenly purity.[4]

A therapist-Christ does not evoke an ardency of soul that wishes to be annihilated, emptied of self and filled with Christ and made pure with a divine and heavenly purity. We need a Christ from above. For only when we see Christ as one like a Son of Man, with eyes of flame, a voice like many waters, a mouth like a sword, and a face like the sun will be able to overcome life's trials and temptations and confess with the apostle John that we are companions "in the suffering and kingdom and patient endurance that are ours in Jesus" (Rev. 1:9 NIV). We need to know Jesus not just as the dreamer-poet ushering in His kingdom of shalom and acceptance. We need to know Him as the glorified Son of

Man of Revelation 1. We need to know Him in all His diverse excellencies.

If there is one thing I have tried to do as pastor, it is to lift up apparent opposites that don't need to be opposite. I pray fervently that my church not be a lopsided church that excels in one kind of virtue at the expense of other virtues. Obviously, we won't be able to do all things equally well as a church, but my hope is that we could be marked by grace and truth, logical precision and warmhearted passion, careful thinking and compassionate feeling, strong theology and tender love, Christian liberty and spiritual discipline, congregational care and committed outreach, diversity without doctrinal infidelity, ambition without arrogance, and contentment without complacency.

I believe this is God's vision for the church. And I don't believe anyone in the emerging church is saying anything like this—perhaps in a sentence here or there but not in any balanced way. I fear emergent leaders are creating a host of false dichotomies that will produce lopsided churches, even as they respond to lopsided churches in the opposite directions.

THE LION AND THE LAMB

Our churches must be rich in diverse excellencies because such is the character of God. He is sovereign, powerful, omniscient, and holy. And He is merciful, patient, wise, and loving. If we are a church with lopsided virtues, we will not reflect the character of God, who is perfect in all His multifaceted ways.

And neither will we reflect Jesus. We need to know Jesus Christ as both Lion and Lamb. The lionlike Jesus in Matthew 23 who said, "Woe to you, teachers of the law and Pharisees, you hypocrites! You travel over land and sea to win a single convert, and when he becomes one, you make him twice as much a son of hell as you are," is the same Christ as the lamblike Jesus in Matthew 25 who said, "I tell you the truth, whatever you did for one of the least of these brothers of mine, you did for me." And the lamblike Jesus in Matthew 27 who cried out, "My God, my God, why have you forsaken me?" is the same Lord as the lionlike Jesus in Matthew 28 who declared, "All authority in heaven and on earth has been given to me."

We need to worship lionlike, lamblike Jesus and glory in all His attributes.

KNOWING GOD

It is no coincidence that the problems of the seven churches in Revelation 2 and 3 are followed by a majestic vision of Him who sits on the throne in (ch. 4) and the Lamb who was slain (ch. 5). The magnificent picture of the sovereign, holy God of the universe sitting on the throne and the Lamb at His right hand follows seven very practical, specific letters. Indeed, the vision of God in chapters 4 and 5 is the answer to the problems posed in chapters 2 and 3.

Each of the churches is called to overcome. But how do you do that? The answer is found in chapters 4 and 5. You get a breathtaking glimpse of God and the Lamb. You take your eyes off your earthly situation and gaze into heaven and see what true reality looks like. No matter the church's problem, what is most needful is to see God in His glory. Lost your first love? Being persecuted? Impure? Bad theology? Spiritually dry? Full of weakness? Apathetic? You need to know God better.

David Wells is right: "God now rests too inconsequentially upon the church . . . . His Christ, if he is seen at all, is impoverished, thin, pale, and scarcely capable of inspiring awe, and his riches are entirely searchable. . . . It is God that the church needs most—God in his grace and truth, God in his awesome and holy presence."[5]

One of the things that keeps me grounded as a pastor is to ask myself, "Will this help me and my people die well?" Promoting radical uncertainty does not help people die well. Calling people to live the life of Jesus while minimizing the death of Jesus as the substitutionary sacrifice who turned away our Father's wrath does not help people die well. Calling us to simply experience the wild, unexplainable journey of faith doesn't help much when it comes time to reach our eternal destination.

What puts a rock under our feet and hope in our hearts is the certain knowledge that God is holy, righteous, loving, all-knowing, all-powerful, eternal, independent, sovereign, and merciful; that He created the world good only to have Adam plunge the human race into sin and bondage to ever-increasing wickedness; that God purposed in eternity past to save those whom He would call and that in the fullness of time He sent His Son, Jesus Christ, to live the life we couldn't and die the death we deserved; that Jesus will come again to judge the living and the dead, justly condemning the unbelieving to eternal punishment and granting the followers of Jesus to live forever in never-ending, always increasing enjoyment of God.

Resting in all of this helps us do what all the mysterious paradoxes and postmodern uncertainties never could—it helps us die well. Call it linear, dogmatic, or hopelessly otherworldly, but it's what Christians have held onto for millennia as their only comfort in life and in death. And by God's grace such an articulation of the Christian message will emerge and reemerge, unapologetically and unhesitatingly, as front and center in all our churches. It is, after all, as Jude put it so long ago, "our common salvation" and "the faith that was once for all delivered to the saints."

Notes

1. In *Generous Orthodoxy* (Grand Rapids: Zondervan, 2004), Brian McLaren writes: "*Compromise* (like tolerance) is a dirty word for many Christians. It suggests a lowering of standards. But it is a beautiful word (like tolerance) if you are trying to live in community with others, with Scripture, reason, tradition, and experience in dynamic tension. In this light, compromise and tolerance suggest keeping a high (uncompromised!) standard of unity and high level of respect for your brothers and sisters who disagree with you" (235). I am not arguing that *tolerance* is a dirty word that is never befitting Christians, only that McLaren and other emergent leaders can scarcely imagine why intolerance would ever be justified. In so doing, they are more generous than Jesus.
2. "The Excellency of Christ," *The Sermons of Jonathan Edwards*, Wilson H. Kimnach, Kenneth P. Minkema, and Douglas A. Sweeney, eds. (New Haven, Conn.: Yale Univ. Press, 1999), 161–196.
3. Donald Miller, *Blue Like Jazz* (Nashville: Nelson, 203), 238,
4. *The Works of Jonathan Edwards, Volume I* (Edinburgh, Scotland: Banner of Truth Trust, 1995 [1834]), xlvii.
5. David Wells, *God in the Wasteland* (Grand Rapids: Eerdmans, 1994), 225.

ACKNOWLEDGMENTS

MANY AUTHORS would agree that this is the best part of writing a book. The only hard part is trying to remember all the people who deserve acknowledgment.

Thanks, first off, are due to my dear wife, Trisha. She is all the things husbands always write about in the acknowledgment section and more: a wonderful support, a great mother, a vibrant Christian, a strong woman. I love you. Ian, Jacob, and Elizabeth, thank you for keeping Daddy young.

My parents, Lee and Sheri DeYoung, have been models of hard work and quiet faithfulness for all my years. Thank you for loving me without giving me a big head. Thanks for teaching me to tithe and telling me John Calvin was a "good guy" when I wasn't so sure. Thanks for making me go to church twice every Sunday.

My parents-in-law, Roy and Barbara Bebee, have been a great encouragement to me. I never thought I'd be such good friends with my wife's parents. Thanks for your support. You can be my PR agents anytime.

Dave DeWit and the whole gang at Moody have been terrific—responsible, responsive, professional, heartfelt, supportive. I'm grateful to David Wells for writing the foreword, for writing his books, and for teaching me at Gordon-Conwell in Massachusetts. New Geneva Seminary in Colorado Springs has been a great home away from home on my study leaves. Thanks, guys.

I've been blessed by the friendships of a number of faithful, friendly, and gospel-centered pastors, Dale Van Dyke, Doug Phillips, and Ron Sanford, to name a few. The staff at University Reformed Church is great. I'm glad to be with you all—Ben, Katie, Kristina, Jon, Vanessa, Dave, Kevin, Becky, Jenny, and Lisa. Thanks to my siblings—Peter, Kristen, and Karissa—for your interest in the book and me. Ditto to the Fight Club—Dietzy, Carter, McKnight, Eastie, Joey, Will, Mikey, and Brink.

Ted and Kristin Kluck are everything friends should be—serious and funny, intelligent and silly, ready with applause and ready with sarcasm. I never thought we'd be such good friends when I arrived. Now I can't imagine being here without your friendship. Tristan, you're cool too. Thanks for the wave every Sunday.

There are too many wonderful people at University Reformed Church to thank, but if you are reading this you're probably one of them. I love being your pastor. Thanks for bearing with me.

= = = =

I would be remiss if I started my acknowledgments anywhere else but with my wife, Kristin. She has been kind, loving, patient, and sacrificial throughout my writing career—acting as editor, encourager, accountant, and a welcome distraction. Kristin has always loved the Scriptures and pursued truth. I love her for this, among many other things. We had fun doing this together, didn't we, Lovey? "It's gonna be real. It's gonna be fun. Who's coming with me?" (Thanks also to Cameron Crowe for writing *Jerry Maguire*).

A special thank you to Wayne Grudem for writing *Bible Doctrine*. This dry, systematic, and propositional text helped us work through some hard things in our life, and helped us to better understand the Bible.

Thanks as well to Kevin DeYoung, my coauthor, for pastoring our church with courage, passion, and a talent that I have rarely seen. Kevin is a great author, and an even greater friend. You too, Trisha, Ian, and Jacob. To our friends—specifically David and Amie, Evan and Jenny, Johnny and Bethany, and Bruce and Jan—whose words encouraged me when I was tempted to dwell on the fact that we would be ripped to pieces on message boards all across the country upon publication of this book. Thanks for your support.

To the crew at Moody Press—Dave DeWit, Tracey Shannon, and the many others who worked hard on this project—thank you for taking a chance on this.

I want to thank the churches I've attended throughout my life, starting in childhood, where the Bible has been preached and the gospel valued—Grace United Methodist in Hartford City, Upland Community (formerly Upland EMC), Westminster Presbyterian in Muncie, and finally University Reformed Church in East Lansing. I've had lots of fun within your walls, and appreciate the way you've loved both me and my family.

Finally, I would like to thank my parents, Ted and Karen Kluck, for raising me in a home where the gospel was preached clearly and upheld. Dad, you had the courage to go against the grain when you trusted God with your life in high school, which couldn't have been easy, and our family has reaped the benefit. Your marriage is an example of Christ's love for the church.